James Robertson

Father of Tennessee

BY

BILL BAYS

ABOUT THE BOOK

This is the story of America's first western frontier, when brave men and women crossed the Blue Ridge and Allegheny Mountains to find better lives for themselves and their families.
James Robertson led the first group of settlers over the mountains and founded the first white settlement in what would later become East Tennessee. But they were not alone. Centuries earlier, the Cherokees came from the north, conquered the local tribes, and settled there.

In the year before the Declaration of Independence on July 4, 1776, British Indian agents began inciting the Cherokees, Shawnees, and other western tribes. The frontiersmen mobilized their militias and eventually defeated the Cherokees. Afterward, James Robertson was appointed an Indian agent to keep the peace.

In 1779, Robertson entered into an agreement with Richard Henderson and John Donelson to settle the area around the French Lick, which would later become Nashville. After their arrival in 1780, Indian attacks soon commenced. Using large-scale attacks and small ambushes, the protracted war against the settlers lasted for fifteen years. Richard Henderson fled, and John Donelson was killed. James Robertson determination and steadfast leadership was the glue that kept the infant settlement together.

George Washington appreciated Robertson leadership and appointed him brigadier general of the Western Militia. Andrew Jackson military training began as a private serving in General Robertson militia. Jackson learned well and years later replaced Robertson after his retirement. Boone, Clarke, Sevier, Shelby, Blount, and Bledsoe were other leaders who trusted James Robertson. James Robertson long military and civic career began before the American Revolution and ended after the Battle of Talladega during the War of 1812. He was a brave, intelligent and patriotic leader who believed in Manifest Destiny and founded Nashville, the nation westernmost settlement of that era.

Gotham Books

30 N Gould St.
Ste. 20820, Sheridan, WY 82801
https://gothambooksinc.com/

Phone: 1 (307) 464-7800

© 2024 *Bill Bays*. All rights reserved.

No part of this book may be reproduced, stored in a retrieval system, or transmitted by any means without the written permission of the author.

Published by Gotham Books (March 26, 2024)

ISBN: 979-8-88775-924-1 (H)
ISBN: 979-8-88775-605-9 (P)
ISBN: 979-8-88775-606-6 (E)

Because of the dynamic nature of the Internet, any web addresses or links contained in this book may have changed since publication and may no longer be valid.

The views expressed in this work are solely those of the author and do not necessarily reflect the views of the publisher, and the publisher hereby disclaims any responsibility for them.

CONTENTS

Introduction vii
Chapter 1: The Journey 1
Chapter 2: Establishing A Settlement 7
Chapter 3: Dangerous Neighbors 11
Chapter 4: Nancy Ward-Pocahontas Of The West 16
Chapter 5: Creating A Frontier Community 19
Chapter 6: The Massacre 26
Chapter 7: Cherokee Billy 34
Chapter 8: Prelude To War 38
Chapter 9: The Battle Of Point Pleasant 43
Chapter 10: The Transylvania Purchase 50
Chapter 11: Events Leading To War 58
Chapter 12: The Declaration Of Independence 63
Chapter 13: Cherokees Attack 69
Chapter 14: Russell's Rangers Fight The Raven 74
Chapter 15: Colonel Christian's Campaign 77
Chapter 16: Assassination Of Chief Cornstalk 81
Chapter 17: War On The Western Frontier 84
Chapter 18: Peacekeeping 94
Chapter 19: The French Lick 98
Chapter 20: Making Plans 102
Chapter 21: The Journey 105
Chapter 22: Manifest Destiny 109
Chapter 23: The Voyage 111
Chapter 24: A New Government 123

Chapter 25: Terror And Bloodshed 126
Chapter 26: Other Conflicts 130
Chapter 27: Encouraging News... 134
Chapter 28: The Battle Of Freeland's Station 141
Chapter 29: Battle Of The Bluff... 144
Chapter 30: Robertson's Speech 149
Chapter 31: The Treaty Of Paris 153
Chapter 32: New Civil Authority 157
Chapter 33: The Lost State Of Franklin 160
Chapter 34: Legislator And Diplomat 165
Chapter 35: Transitions 169
Chapter 36: Grief Amid Change 171
Chapter 37: The Coldwater Expedition 175
Chapter 38: The Arrival Of A Future President.....................184
Chapter 39: Brown's River Voyage 189
Chapter 40: Bloodshed And Diplomacy 194
Chapter 41: The United States Of America...............................199
Chapter 42: President Washington 203
Chapter 43: Meanwhile On The Frontier 207
Chapter 44: Southwest Territory 210
Chapter 45: Northwest Territory 214
Chapter 46: A Son Saves His Father 218
Chapter 47: All-Out War On The Frontier 225
Chapter 48: The Battle Of Fallen Timbers 231
Chapter 49: The Nickajack Expedition 235
Chapter 50: The Aftermath 241
Chapter 51: Statehood... 244

v

Chapter 52: Call To Serve Again 248

Chapter 53: Aaron Burr And Andrew Jackson 253

Chapter 54: Other Events 259

Chapter 55: Robertson Serves In The War Of 1812 266

Chapter 56: Honor And Re-Internment 272

Bibliography 275

Index 283

About The Author 292

INTRODUCTION

The American Revolution presented formidable challenges for men and women throughout the thirteen colonies. During that time of crisis, various individuals had the mettle to triumph over adversity and overcome obstacles that caused many to withdraw in despair. Ordinary people learned to do extraordinary deeds when faced with seemingly insurmountable obstacles and extreme danger. From a modern perspective, the Patriots' collective accomplishments and sheer toughness seem distant and unreal in comparison to our own comfortable existence.

James Robertson was an ordinary man who joined the Patriot rebellion against British tyranny. Like all the rest who stood up against the world's most powerful nation, he knew that the outcome was uncertain. Being killed on the battlefield or hanged for treason weighed heavily as consequences for anyone who dared to join the Revolution.

Uncommon accomplishments are rarely a solitary affair. Many of James Robertson's successes resulted from his collaboration with others. Most of his contemporaries who helped him accomplish so much during his lifetime have been forgotten over time. Others who are still famous today include: George Washington, Andrew Jackson, Daniel Boone and George Rogers Clark.

The life story of James Robertson includes associations with the aforementioned heroes of American history, as well as lesser-known figures whose accomplishments were associated with his. For example, John Sevier and William Blount worked closely with Robertson in creating the Southwest Territory that later became the State of Tennessee.

Robertson's extraordinary service began in 1769 when he established the first white settlement in what is now the State of

Tennessee. His long career ended with his death in 1814 while serving at his post during the War of 1812. During his exceptional lifetime, Robertson was a pioneer, Indian fighter, Indian Agent, treaty negotiator, frontier surgeon, founder of Nashville, diplomat, legislator, judge, justice of the peace, farmer, businessman and Brigadier General in the United States Army.

In an era of tremendous turmoil and warfare, James Robertson distinguished himself as a peace-loving man who continually worked to bridge the racial and cultural divide between whites and Indians. In doing so, he earned the respect and gratitude of government officials and Indians on both sides of that divide who sought his help in negotiating equitable treaties. Presidents from Washington to Madison were grateful for Robertson's help in negotiating treaties with various Indian tribes as he led the Nation's westward expansion.

Because of his service to the State of Tennessee, Governor Willie Blount proclaimed that James Robertson was the "Father of Tennessee". Andrew Jackson, who later became President of the United States, echoed that sentiment. In his book, <u>Winning of the West</u> published in 1889, future President Theodore Roosevelt reconfirmed Robertson's status as the "Father of Tennessee". In 1934, author Thomas Edwin Matthews published Robertson's biography, General James Robertson, Father of Tennessee.

James Robertson's unofficial honorary title of "Father of Tennessee" was first bestowed upon him shortly after his death and was sustained throughout the nineteenth and twentieth centuries by the aforementioned authors. Because memories fade over time, an easy-to-read twenty-first century Robertson biography will give today's reader a clear understanding of this truly extraordinary man's contributions to the State of Tennessee and the Nation.

Chapter 1

THE JOURNEY

In the summer of 1769, five men on horseback snaked steadily up a winding game trail in the Appalachian Mountains. A pack horse loaded with supplies followed each rider. As the men climbed, they dismounted occasionally to traverse obstacles such as fallen trees or large rocks. All were experienced hunters and trackers, yet each had his own reasons for crossing the forbidding mountain range. Although the imposing mountain chain had been a natural barrier to westward expansion of the colonies, they were willing to risk their lives to enter the territory beyond.

The leader of the group, Daniel Boone, loved the beauty and solitude of the wilderness. He had already explored the vast territory over the mountains, where he found an abundance of deer, elk, buffalo, panther, beaver, otter, and mink. He knew he could earn more in less than a year by selling their pelts than he could by farming for several years back home in North Carolina.

Boone expected that they would encounter Indians who lived in the territory beyond. From experience he understood that they could either be friendly and helpful—or deadly foes. Some thought nothing of killing a white interloper and removing his scalp as a trophy to bring back home to display in a ceremonial scalp dance. Boone comprehended better than anyone the need for constant vigilance and keen observation. The slightest gesture or facial expression might betray an Indian's true intentions.

Directly behind Daniel rode his brother Squire. Like Daniel, he had a tall, sinewy frame and was clad in buckskin. Although he would become less famous than Daniel, Squire was his equal when it came to woodcraft and personal bravery.

The third rider was Michael Stoner, a friend of the Boones and an equally skilled woodsman. Like the others, Stoner was clad in a fringed buckskin hunting shirt, buckskin breeches, and moccasins made of buffalo hide. Behind Stoner rode one other experienced over-mountain man, whose name has been lost over time.

This forgotten explorer was followed by a twenty-eight-year-old newcomer named James Robertson. Robertson differed from the others because he had the least experience hunting and exploring; and unlike the others, it was his first expedition over the mountains.

Robertson was the second oldest of ten siblings and had a limited formal education. His worldly experience mainly consisted of working on his father's farm and attending the local Presbyterian Church on Sundays. He was a newlywed and had married his wife, Charlotte Reeves, a year earlier. By chance, he had become acquainted with his neighbor, Daniel Boone. Over time, he had listened with rapt attention as Boone shared yarns about the vast game herds; Indians, and the rich soil just waiting to be tilled by those who would be bold enough to settle the land that was there for the taking on the other side of the mountains. Eventually, Robertson decided to accompany Boone and the others to find out firsthand if the area was indeed suitable for settlement.

Robertson's father had recently died, and the family farm would soon be sold in order to settle his estate. With a wife and baby to support, James needed to find a way to make a living.

North Carolina did not offer many prospects. In 1769, its backcountry was not an ideal place to settle with a family. Rebellion against the crown was smoldering in the form of the Regulator Movement. Inland settlers resented the actions of the colonial government, which favored residents of the more prosperous coastal towns over those who lived in the remote western areas. Some of the locals had begun harassing officials by burning residences and offices in open rebellion against the crown's authority that allowed corrupt sheriffs, clerks, and other county officials to charge exorbitant fees while pocketing some of the proceeds.

In that environment, Robertson decided it was time to move on. While many believed Boone's stories of the western territory were exaggerated and too good to be true, Robertson felt that he had little to lose. Even if Boone's tales were only partially true, they offered hope for a better life. He shared his thoughts with his family and friends, who all agreed that he should accompany Boone on his next trip. If the prospects seemed promising on the western side of the mountains, Robertson would plant a crop of corn there before returning for the others.

The five men were well outfitted for their dangerous expedition. Each carried a Deckard rifle, a long flintlock firearm handmade in Lancaster County, Pennsylvania, which was state-of-the-art in 1769. The inside of a Deckard rifle barrel had twisted grooves that made the lead ball spin as it exited, offering greater accuracy than the smooth-bore muskets widely used at the time. Each man's waistband held a knife with an eight-inch blade and an iron tomahawk. A powder horn, cartouche, and a leather bag were slung over their shoulders, completing the necessary accessories.

As the small group moved higher into the mountains, the air became cooler and a dense fog enveloped the riders, obstructing their views. At times they could not see beyond the next rider in front, and they proceeded slowly in the eerie atmosphere. Although James Robertson was a religious man, his belief in divine guidance and protection did not always provide complete comfort in such dangerous situations.

The men reached an altitude where game was almost nonexistent, and they made camp. Earlier that morning one of the men had shot a deer at a lower altitude, and this kill provided welcome meat. The group built a fire and placed the deer's two hind quarters on the glowing embers, covered them, and allowed them to slowly bake. After the meat was cooked and cleaned off, it was served with "hoe cakes," made of ground corn and water that was cooked in the same fashion. The remainder of the venison was cut in thin strips, salted, and allowed to air dry. The "jerked" meat and parched corn would be their main provisions until another kill could be made on the western side of the mountains.

As they rode, none of the men likely realized how their journey would profoundly influence westward expansion. They seemed an odd lot. Robertson was the youngest and had less life experiences than the others. Nevertheless, he was bold, brave and willing to learn. He had a keen mind and was an exceptional judge of character. The Boone brothers were poorly educated, but they were known to be men of good character who could be trusted. All were men of few words. When Robertson spoke, his words were carefully measured and meaningful.

As the group continued upward, Robertson pondered his journey. Was he seeking the opportunities that lay ahead or simply escaping the uncertainties and unrest of the North Carolina backwoods? He concluded that both reasons were true and valid, and he felt satisfied with his decision to explore for new opportunities.

A few days later, as the men were descending the western slope, Robertson began to feel hopeful and excited. The opportunities that existed in the boundless wilderness seemed unlimited when he first saw the vast new territory. It was filled with beautiful forests and rolling hills that stretched before him as far as the eye could see.

Before arriving at the valley floor, Robertson spotted some buffaloes. A huge herd grazed in the distance. When he got closer, he was amazed at their size. These beasts were large; each adult appeared to be nearly twice the size of a cow. He saw numerous deer and elk wandering through the area, drawn by the valley's lush vegetation and plentiful water flowing from the many streams and rivers.

At the end of the long journey, the men finally arrived at the Watauga Valley. Following a short ride, they came to a solitary log cabin in the wilderness. There they encountered a man named Honeycutt who was acquainted with the Boones. Honeycutt seemed genuinely pleased to see them as he welcomed them into the relative comfort of his cabin.

That night, the men gathered around the hearth inside Honeycutt's small cabin and shared news from the outside world. They also told stories, some just for the joy of repeating and others meant specifically for the benefit of the newcomer Robertson. Most of the stories centered around experiences of the hunters in the areas known as Kentucky and the more distant Cumberland River region, which they referred to as the Great Salt Lick.

The next morning, the men arose early. During breakfast Boone and his companions shared a few last-minute tips and admonitions with Robertson before they headed northwest to hunt in what is now the state of Kentucky. Before leaving, Boone asked Honeycutt to look after his friend, Jamie, as James Robertson was often called by his friends.

The men said good-bye, and the small pack train slowly trailed off into the distance, eventually disappearing into the forest. The immense trees seemed to swallow up the men and horses, which appeared small and insignificant by comparison.

After the others disappeared from sight, Robertson began to feel lonely. The feeling frightened him at first, but then he remembered that Honeycutt was there to help him establish his homestead. And the exciting promise of a new life soon displaced any feelings of apprehension.

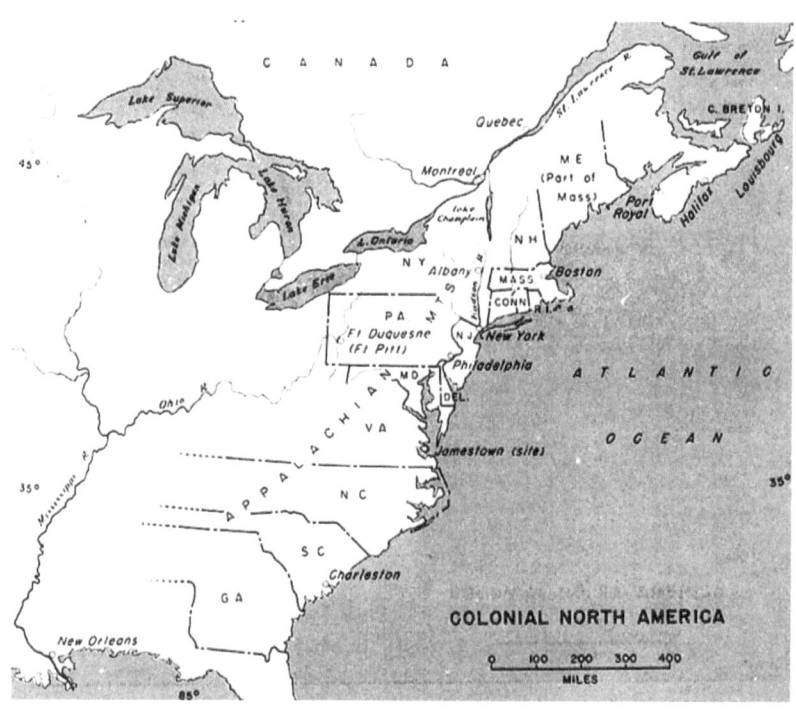

Map of the Thirteen Colonies.

Chapter 2

ESTABLISHING A SETTLEMENT

Honeycutt guided Robertson around the Watauga Valley. The valley was previously inhabited long before they arrived. He showed Robertson stone foundations and gravesites of the early inhabitants. An ancient race of Indians once lived there, but they either died off or abandoned the region. Long-hunters named the place Watauga Old Fields because of the people who once lived there for many generations before vanishing.

Robertson listened intently as he surveyed the ruins and took mental notes of some of the best locations for a homestead. Eventually he chose a good spot near the Watauga River where there were fewer trees to fell. He selected a home site on a knoll that would give him a good field of view, making it easier to defend against possible Indian attacks.

Honeycutt introduced Jamie to the Bean family who lived nearby at the mouth of Boone's Creek. William Bean and his wife, Lydia, came to settle there a year earlier and they decided to name the creek near their cabin in honor of William's friend and hunting companion, Daniel Boone, who once had a hunting camp at that site. Like Honeycutt, the Beans were very friendly toward Robertson, and they helped him as much as possible.

The young explorer began clearing brush and cutting trees to build a simple lean-to shelter. As soon as that was done, he started preparing a plot of land for cultivation. He had brought an ample supply of seed corn, and he soon began plowing and planting in order to have a good fall crop to sustain the group of settlers that he planned to bring back with him.

After finishing the planting, Robertson packed a supply of parched corn that Honeycutt had given him and some jerked (dried) venison for the long journey back to North Carolina. He said good-bye to Honeycutt and the Beans and departed on horseback, leaving his pack horse behind in Honeycutt's care. He reasoned that traveling with one horse would make the trip much easier and faster. Besides, horses were in short supply; and the young explorer planned to bring more horses when he returned with the settlers.

Robertson set out in clear weather, but after a few days it started to rain. The rain grew heavier, becoming a torrential downpour that soaked his clothes, provisions, and gunpowder. With his visibility limited by the heavy rain, Robertson lost sight of the trail and eventually found himself stranded on a dangerous precipice. He could not move forward or back without risking a fall. In order to extricate himself from the dangerous situation, he was forced to turn loose his horse and proceed on foot.

The journey seemed endless. For fourteen days Robertson trudged over the mountains without food or the ability to shoot game because his gunpowder was useless after getting wet. He grew progressively weaker and more discouraged. Finally, after he had nearly completed the crossing, he was too weak to continue any further. After collapsing, he propped himself against a rock, delirious and waiting to die. Eventually, he saw two figures approaching. Drifting in and out of consciousness, he had difficulty comprehending who or what they were. When they came closer and spoke to him, he realized that it was two hunters.

The men stopped and gave him food, water, and a horse to ride as they guided him most of the way back. When it was time for the hunters depart, Robertson sincerely thanked them for their kindness. After he arrived home, his strength began to improve and he started to feel much better.

While many men would have forsaken the wilderness after such a near-death experience, James Robertson was not deterred. Shortly after he arrived at his North Carolina home, he began organizing his family and friends for the return trip to Watauga. He made extensive preparations for the trip; about thirty-eight families would accompany him. They would need pack horses, provisions, utensils, and as many cattle, pigs, and chickens as they could handle on such a difficult trek. He assigned some of the women and older children to care for and herd the animals along the way.

The long journey westward over the mountain to Watauga was difficult, but relatively uneventful. The settlers arrived in late fall—just in time to harvest the corn that he had planted. The men set about selecting farm sites, clearing the land and building log shelters—simple lean-tos for single men and log cabins for families. A communal spirit developed under Robertson's leadership. The settlers learned that they could accomplish a lot more by working together building cabins and harvesting corn, than by working individually.

Life was hard and gritty as the settlers' cut trees and cleared brush from the fields. After felling the trees, the men would roll them into position to hew them to build cabins. By early spring, the cleared fields were ready to be plowed and planted.

Despite all of the hard work, the settlers managed to have fun in the evenings after the chores were completed. When a new cabin was finished, a cabin-raising celebration would begin. The sounds of laughter, music, and dancing would fill the evening air, and sometimes the merriment would continue until dawn.

Romanticized Portrait of a Frontiersman in Buckskin.

Chapter 3

DANGEROUS NEIGHBORS

The newcomers settled in Cherokee territory, and Robertson set out to establish good relations with the tribe. He possessed a unique gift, the ability to put himself in someone else's shoes (or moccasins). His timing was perfect.

The Cherokees had migrated to the region more than 800 years before Robertson and the white settlers arrived from the eastern side of the mountains. The tribe was divided into three sub-tribes: the Otari who resided on land that is present-day east Tennessee; the Etari who lived in the high Appalachian plains of present-day east Tennessee, the Carolinas and Georgia; and the Chickamaugas who occupied the area around present-day Chattanooga in southeast Tennessee.

The beloved town of Chota was the seat of power for the Cherokee nation; it was located in the Otari region. The capital was a city of refuge, situated on the banks of the Little Tennessee River about twenty miles from present-day Knoxville. It provided immunity to outcasts who had committed offenses. The offenders could escape tribal justice or retribution as long as they remained within the borders of Chota.

By the time Robertson and the settlers arrived, the Indians' population had been reduced by smallpox and intertribal warfare.

They had suffered the loss of many of their warriors during the French and Indian War from 1755 to 1763. Afterward, warfare with the neighboring Creeks and Chickasaws further reduced their numbers. Due to those events, the Cherokees were in a state of decline when Robertson and the other white settlers arrived. And the tribal chiefs were not inclined toward engaging in any new conflicts with outsiders.

Before the French and Indian War, the chiefs' respect for British power led to harmonious relations with the whites. Trade flourished between the Cherokees and Virginians; and South Carolina traders even lived among the Indians.

The Cherokees allowed the British to build forts on Cherokee lands to protect against French encroachment and to provide the Indians with valuable trade goods. The crown authorized the governor of South Carolina to construct an over-hill fort near the Cherokee village of Tuskegee in what is now east Tennessee. Fort Loudin was under construction in 1756, one year after war broke out between Britain and France.

During the French and Indian War, French agents went among the Cherokees trying to sow discontent. Most of the other Indian tribes were allied with the French. Despite French attempts to win their allegiance, Cherokee warriors fought loyally alongside the British, most notably during skirmishes along the Ohio River.

However, cultural and language difficulties gradually arose between the British and their Cherokee allies. The breakdown in relations eventually caused resentment among the Indians. One group of warriors stole horses from some Virginia frontiersmen while returning home after fighting for their British allies.

Another blow to English and Cherokee relations occurred in 1760, when the Cherokee supreme leader named Old Hop died. Attakullakulla, "The Little Carpenter," an Old Hop protégé, then became supreme leader.

By that time, relations between the British and Cherokees had become strained beyond recovery. The Cherokees were increasingly discontented with their white allies after French agents spread rumors that the British intended to make them slaves and take away their land.

In January of 1760, Cherokee warriors conducted several raids against white settlers in South Carolina and Georgia. In late February, Oconostota led a band of over-mountain Cherokees to Fort Prince George in present-day South Carolina. The wily war chief opened fire on the whites, killing their commander. Afterward, the remaining defenders inside the fort killed several captive Cherokees who resisted being placed in irons. Fort Prince George's supplies began to run low after the Cherokees laid siege to the fort for several weeks before finally retreating.

Shortly thereafter, the Cherokees besieged Fort Loudin near their capital at Chota. The British sent out two relief parties to rescue the fort's defenders, but neither group reached them in time. By August 6, 1760, the inhabitants of the fort were starving, and morale was low. In desperation, Captain John Stuart and Lt. James Adamson met with Oconostota, Attakullakulla and other chiefs at Chota to negotiate terms for surrendering the fort.

The Cherokees agreed to spare the lives of everyone inside the fort if they would surrender. They promised that all of Fort Loudin's inhabitants would be allowed to safely depart under Indian guard. The whites could take their rifles, but their cannons and powder were to be left behind for the Cherokees.

On the first day of their escorted march out of the area, the evacuees and their Indian guards traveled about fifteen miles. They set up camp near the mouth of Cave Creek on the Tellico River. During the night, all of the Cherokee guards slipped away. At daybreak, the whites found themselves surrounded by hostile

Indians who immediately opened fire. After a twenty-minute battle, most of the whites were killed.

Captain Stuart and twenty other survivors surrendered. The Cherokees made them prisoners and marched them back to Cherokee towns where several were tortured to death. Stuart, who was well-liked by the Cherokees, and a few others were spared. Later, they were released after South Carolina and Virginia paid their ransom. Stuart, however, was set free by his close friend Chief Attakullakulla. A year later, the British appointed the well-liked leader as Indian Agent for the southern colonies.

Oconostota, who previously attacked the British at Fort Prince George, planned to attack the fort once again. However, advancing armies from South Carolina and Virginia soon dissuaded him.

The French and Indian War continued until 1763, when the Cherokees witnessed the defeat of the French. Victorious Britain acquired by treaty all lands east of the Mississippi, thereby firmly cementing British power in the new world. Attakullakulla and Onconostota were once again in awe of Britain's might. Thirteen years later they would side with the British during the American Revolution. That decision would prove to be one that they would regret.

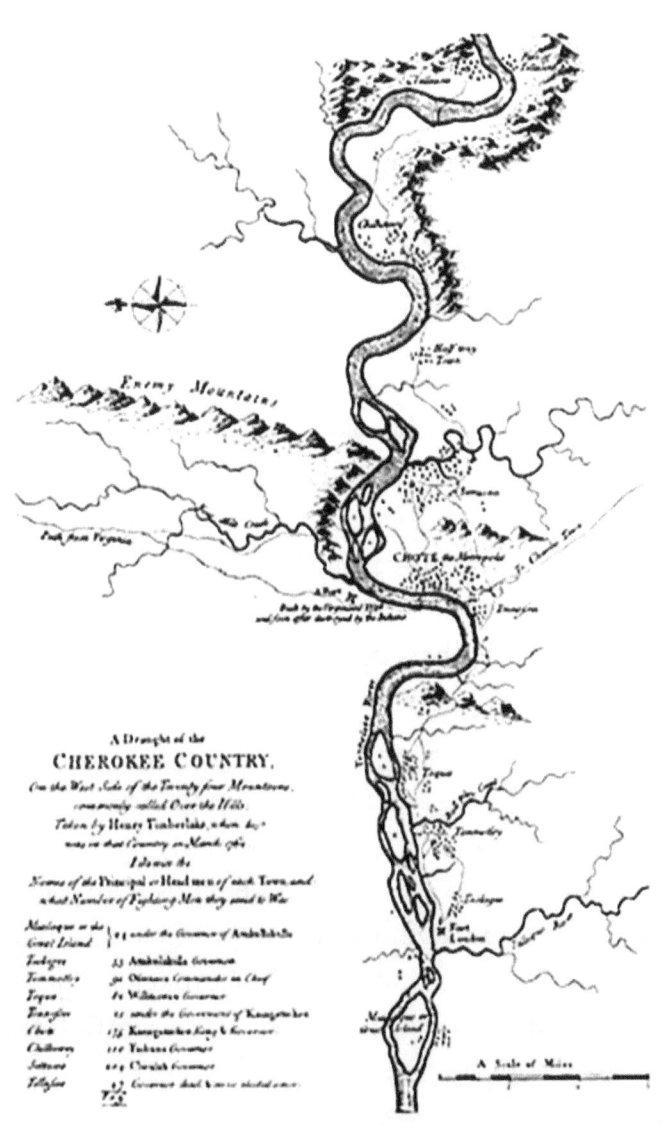

Old Map of Cherokee Towns.

Chapter 4

NANCY WARD-POCAHONTAS OF THE WEST

One battle between the Cherokees and the Creeks in 1755 proved costly, but it also brought to light the bravery of a squaw who would eventually become one of the most powerful women in the Cherokee Nation. Known as the Battle of Taliwa, the conflict was for control of North Georgia, and it is remembered as one of the bloodiest conflicts between the two tribes.

A young woman named *Tsistuna-Gis-Ke*, Wild Rose, accompanied her husband, King Fisher, into battle. During the fighting, she hid behind a log and assisted him by loading his rifle and pistol. After her husband was shot by the enemy, she picked up his rifle and returned fire against the Creeks as her spouse lay mortally wounded. Wild Rose fought bravely, and it was said that she helped rally the vastly outnumbered Cherokees. They won the battle and drove the vanquished Creeks from north Georgia, leaving the Cherokees firmly in control of the region.

When the victorious Cherokees returned to Chota, the warriors who witnessed Wild Rose's bravery praised her exploits. Soon the tribe held celebrations in her honor at Chota and other villages throughout the Cherokee Nation.

After she became a widow, Wild Rose met and married a white trader who lived among the Cherokees named Bryant Ward. From that day forward, she became known as Nancy Ward.

Nancy Ward was the niece of Attakullakulla, who would become the Peace Chief of the Cherokee Nation. She was also the cousin of Dragging Canoe, who later became an implacable foe of the white settlers.

As a result of her elevated status in the tribe, tribal elders selected Nancy Ward to fill the position *Ghighan*, meaning Beloved Woman. That honor placed her in a lifetime position that held great power. As a leading woman of authority, she would sometimes disagree with her male counterparts when she felt the need to do so. She had the power to pardon anyone convicted of a crime, even an offender who had been sentenced to death.

As Beloved Woman, Nancy Ward was the supreme leader of the Women's Council. She also sat with the Peace and War Chiefs during meetings and ceremonies held in the Council House at Chota. Her duties included both ceremonial and civil responsibilities. One of her ceremonial tasks included the mixing of various herbs and spices for the sacred "Black Drink" that they drank for purification during religious ceremonies.

From all accounts, Nancy Ward was a tall, beautiful woman who was highly intelligent and friendly to everyone, Indian or white. James Robertson described her as "queenly and commanding," who resided in a lodge with "barbaric splendor as befitted her rank in the nation." Future events would provide the opportunity for her to demonstrate that she was a genuine friend of the white settlers and earn her the title of "Pocahontas of the West."

Portrait of Cherokee Chiefs Visiting England in 1762.

Chapter 5

CREATING A FRONTIER COMMUNITY

Life on the frontier was difficult for the settlers. Home sites and farms had to be cleared by hand, and homesteaders endured the physically demanding process of removing trees and brush before planting corn, wheat, vegetables, and fruit trees. Each family typically cultivated about 400 acres. Tree stumps were left in the ground because it was too difficult to remove them, and crops and fruit trees were simply planted around the stumps. As the land was cleared and cultivated, the area once dubbed Watauga Old Fields began to come alive again.

From the beginning, the communal spirit flourished among the settlement's pioneers. Instinctively they seemed to know that their survival under those harsh conditions depended upon the success of the entire nascent community. There were practical reasons for cooperation as well. Many tasks could be more effectively completed by individuals working together. They had log-rolling parties to clear fields of felled trees and quilting parties to make clothing and household goods for their cabins.

Those events encouraged socialization and often culminated in lively parties after the day's work was done. The men and women played as hard as they worked. The men would also amuse themselves with horse races, wrestling matches, tests of strength, and shooting contests. The gatherings brought some fun to an otherwise arduous and isolated existence.

A typical pioneer family lived in a one-room log cabin. The fireplace hearth was used for cooking, as well as heat and light. Family members slept on crude rope beds. The beds had hardwood frames with fiber ropes or leather straps strung across to support mattresses made of plant fibers or animal skins. Creature comforts were rare because there were no roads over which wagons could transport manufactured goods across the mountains from North Carolina.

Everything brought to Watauga had to be packed in on horses. A few enterprising individuals recognized the opportunity and ran pack trains across the Mountains. Animal skins were sent east where they could be sold or traded for salt, iron products and other manufactured goods that were then packed for the return trip to Watauga.

In time, life on the frontier improved as families built cabins and harvested crops. A typical farm would raise corn, wheat and vegetables. Some also planted apple, peach and other varieties of fruit trees. Most families owned livestock; usually chickens, hogs, sheep and cows. They usually owned two or more horses for travel and transport.

On the frontier, chores were sometimes shared when necessary. Women usually performed the tasks around the home, such as child-rearing, cooking, gardening, milking and making clothes. Many used homemade spinning wheels and looms to weave flax or wool into clothing, blankets and household items.

Men typically assumed the more physically demanding chores such as farming and hunting. Men and older boys were expected to muster for militia duty to defend against Indian attacks or raids by bands of white criminals who occasionally crossed the mountains in search of plunder.

By 1771, events were occurring in North Carolina that would profoundly affect the Watauga community. Governor Lord Tyron built a lavish governor's mansion that was the most luxurious one in the thirteen colonies. He paid for its construction by imposing excessive taxes on the citizens. Most colonists were impoverished, and the higher taxes created undue hardships. Many people resented the governor's lavish lifestyle. Their anger was further compounded by the behavior of a wealthy class of Scottish merchants from the affluent Piedmont region who flaunted their wealth by wearing extravagant clothing and displaying haughty mannerisms. The Scotsmen treated the impoverished backwater residents as inferiors. The poor were further alienated by corrupt sheriffs and clerks who demanded bribes and exorbitant charges for taxes, probate costs and recording fees.

Eventually, the colonists grew restless and rebellious. Armed resistance soon followed; and today some call those skirmishes the first shots fired in the American Revolution. Governor Tyron called out the North Carolina militia to quell the rebellious colonists who became known as Regulators. Their leader, Herman Husband, had hoped that a show of armed resistance would gain concessions from Governor Tyron. But he and the other rebels underestimated Tyron's will.

On May 16, 1771, Tyron led his army of 1,000 men to the Alamance River to confront 2,000 armed Regulators who were encamped there. When Tyron arrived, he sent word to the Regulators to disperse immediately. They refused to disband and the battle soon began.

The Regulators were disorganized and Tyron's well-trained army won the battle. Herman Husband eventually fled the battlefield with many of his men. In the end, there were about 200 casualties on each side, but Tyron's more disciplined and better equipped army held the field. They took fifteen prisoners, six of whom were later hanged for insurrection. The Battle of Alamance virtually ended the Regulator Rebellion.

Following their defeat, many of the Regulators fled over the mountains to Watauga. The flood of new arrivals brought benefits as well as challenges to Watauga. More settlers meant greater security in case of Indian attacks. And the population increase provided more manpower for communal projects.

However, the influx of refugees included some escaped indentured servants, fugitives, and common criminals; thereby introducing an unsavory element that would eventually cause problems for the Wataugans. Some of the new arrivals were intent on stealing horses, livestock, and any other items of value. The criminals preyed on the settlers as well as their Cherokee neighbors.

Their activities caused problems beyond the simple loss of possessions. Revenge was ingrained in the Cherokee culture, and Cherokee warriors were known to travel great distances to exact revenge for a theft or murder. Unfortunately for the Wataugans, when criminal bands stole from the Indians, they usually fled the area. The white settlers living nearby sometimes became the focus of the Indians' wrath. Cherokees who were intent on revenge sometimes attacked innocent frontier families, either by mistake or simply out of frustration.

As those types of incidents increased, Robertson and other community leaders decided to establish an independent written legal system to protect themselves from criminals and vengeful Indians.

At the time, there were three small over-mountain settlements in what is now East Tennessee. Watauga was the largest. To the north was Carter's Valley, named for John Carter who established a trading post there with his partner, William Parker. The

Nolichucky Settlement, established by Jacob Brown, was south of Watauga. The leaders of all three settlements understood the urgent need to establish an effective legal means to handle criminal and civil matters. They came together to create an independent legal system.

John Carter was the eldest and most educated member of the group, and the settlers chose him to chair the convention that would establish laws for the region. He was born in Virginia and crossed the mountains in 1771 when he discovered the beautiful valley later named after him. Following an Indian raid on his trading post, Carter moved his family to Watauga in 1772.

Robertson, Carter and the other leaders believed that their homes were located within boundaries of Virginia. In fact, many of the settlers had migrated to Watauga from southwest Virginia. Therefore, they based the articles of the Watauga Compact on the laws of Virginia. In reality, the area where they had settled was south of the Virginia boundary and would therefore eventually come under the authority of North Carolina. Their ignorance of that fact would last for several years before an accurate survey revealed their mistake.

The leaders recognized that they lived too far from any established government that could provide dependable protection. Additionally, they knew their settlements were illegal because they had violated the terms of the King's Proclamation Line of 1763 which forbade settlements on the western side of the Appalachians. Considering the settlers' illegal status as squatters on Indian land, they could not depend on protection from the Crown, Virginia or North Carolina. Some scholars regard the Watauga Compact as a precursor to the Declaration of Independence because it was the first written compact of a free people in America.

The Articles of the Watauga Compact created the Watauga Association, which consisted of thirteen original commissioners: John Carter, James Robertson, Charles Robertson, John Sevier, Zach Isbell, Jacob Brown, William Bean, James Smith, George Russell, John Jones, Jacob Womack, Robert Lucas, and William Latham. The first court had five magistrates: John Carter, James Robertson, Charles Robertson, John Sevier, and William Bean. There is some controversy surrounding Charles Robertson's relationship to James Robertson. Some say that Charles was James' uncle, while others insist that he was his older brother; which seems more likely because family records clearly indicate that James Robertson had an older brother named Charles.

After the framework of government was established, the people elected office holders to begin the process of governing. The sheriff was Valentine Sevier. He was assisted by the militia, and he performed his duties with a strong determination to maintain an orderly society. Lawless behavior was severely punished. There was a pillory for whippings, brandings and the cutting off of ears as punishment for more serious offenses. Executions were reserved for the most heinous crimes. Because of the severity and certainty of the punishments, it did not take long for the authorities to purge the region of outlaws.

As the Watauga settlements became more secure, the population grew. Some settlers started to enjoy a modest level of prosperity, and James Robertson was among those who prospered. He was successful in farming, animal husbandry, and other activities. Robertson was fond of horses, which were considered to be a source of wealth at that time. He became moderately successful at breeding them and selling them to his neighbors.

Typical Log Cabin of that Era.

Chapter 6

THE MASSACRE

Several miles north of Watauga, in southwest Virginia, Captain William Russell established a frontier outpost named Castlewood. Russell was an officer in the Virginia militia and a veteran of the French and Indian War. His father, who shared the same name, was a member of the "Knights of the Golden Horseshoe," a group of men who years earlier had joined Governor Spotswood's exploration of the uninhabited regions of western Virginia.

The father and son each received generous western land grants for their services, as did many other Virginians. Lord Dunsmore, governor at the time, and George Washington were two prominent Virginians who were eager to settle the new territory. Each wished to acquire the wealth that he anticipated from his land grant when the new territory (present-day West Virginia and Kentucky) eventually opened for settlement.

But the King's Proclamation Line of 1763 prevented the occupation of that land in order to prevent further violent outbreaks between the settlers and Indians. Despite the line, white Indian traders and long hunters in search of pelts crossed into the over-mountain territory. A scattering of illegal white settlements already dotted the southern bank of the Ohio River.

In 1768, the Iroquois Indians, who lived northeast of the region, signed a peace treaty with Britain. In it, the Iroquois ceded all lands east and south of the Ohio River to England. However, the Iroquois had no rights to the land, which was inhabited or controlled by a number of other tribes, including the Delaware, Mingo, Miami and Shawnee. By signing the treaty, the Iroquois set the stage for more warfare. Whites poured into the area, believing that the treaty opened the region for settlement. Those encroachments infuriated the resident tribes because they were neither party to the treaty nor consulted about its terms. And they did not want white settlers in their territory.

When William Russell arrived and settled in the area of southwestern Virginia known as Castlewood, nothing but wilderness and Indians existed to the west. Shawnee Indians were the primary inhabitants, but no single tribe claimed the vast, game-filled Kentucky wilderness as its own. Therefore, Shawnee, Delaware, Miami, Mingo, and other tribes hunted there; as well as Cherokees who ventured north. Small bands of Indian hunters would roam the Kentucky region during the milder seasons and retreat to their distant villages in winter. Longhunters also entered the territory to exploit its bounty.

Occasionally, Indians from different tribes or white long hunters would encounter each other. Sometimes the different groups would be cordial to one another. Other times, there would be violence between different groups. Attacks could occur without warning or provocation.

Due to the danger and uncertainty associated with chance encounters, most tribes avoided contact with outsiders. The Indians remained vigilant while hunting in the Kentucky region. They tried to avoid armed conflict, except during periods of intertribal warfare. In peaceful times, Indians and white long hunters could usually to go about their business without incident, but it was always wise to be cautious and vigilant.

Daniel Boone, his brother Squire, and their friend Michael Stoner hunted in Kentucky with other long hunters on several occasions. During one of those trips, the Boones and Stoner became acquainted with Captain William Russell at his trading station at Castlewood.

Russell believed that the Boones and Stoner had the necessary experience and frontier skills to lead a settlement expedition into Kentucky; and he eventually hired the three men to do so. By then, Russell's father had passed away, leaving his Kentucky land grants to his son. Despite the fact that the Kentucky region was Indian land and was considered to be off limits for white settlers, he was eager to settle the large tracts of land that he had been granted, as well as the ones that he inherited from his father.

Extensive logistical arrangements had to be made before the expedition could start. The party would have to travel single file on horseback because no wagon roads had been cut through the vast wilderness. Large baskets had to be woven to hold pots, pans, domestic goods, axes, and saws. The baskets would be tied on wooden packs on horses. Food items, such as parched corn and jerked meat, also had to be placed in baskets for the long journey by pack train.

Daniel Boone returned to North Carolina and brought his wife, Rebecca, and his family to Castlewood, Virginia, to begin the expedition. Squire Boone also moved his family there. Michael Stoner and other friends and relatives from Yadkin, North Carolina, joined them in search of a better life. Several of Russell's Virginia neighbors rounded out the party.

Altogether, between forty and fifty people departed early in the morning on October 8th, 1773 to begin a journey that they hoped would lead them toward new and more prosperous lives. Because preparations had taken longer than expected, Russell and Boone were eager to begin the long trek. They knew that at journey's end, hard work would have to be done to ensure their survival. They would have to select suitable home sites, clear the land, erect cabins and prepare for a long, cold winter.

When the main body departed, the voices of men, women, and children mixed with the sounds of livestock and clanking utensils creating a cacophony of sounds in the forest. The men rode horses and towed pack horses behind them; while some of the women and children took turns walking and herding the livestock along the narrow winding trail.

William Russell had carefully planned the expedition. He made certain that the settlers had everything they would need to start a successful frontier settlement. He stayed behind at Castlewood to attend to some final business after the Boones and Stoner started moving the main party west into the wilderness. He planned to catch up with them as soon as possible.

Later that afternoon, Russell sent a few hands ahead with more cattle and supplies. He hoped his men would reach the expedition by nightfall and relay a message that he expected to catch up with them next day. Isaac Crabtree led the small group of eight that consisted of Russell's eldest son, Henry; Boone's eldest son, James; the Mendenhall brothers, John and Richard; a young man named Drake; and two slaves, Adam and Charles. They moved as quickly as possible along the difficult trail in an effort to reach the others. Near sunset, Crabtree realized they could not catch up with the main body; so, he decided to stop and make camp for the night at the eastern edge of Powell's Valley.

That night, the small group sat around their campfire on the north side of Walden Creek, while wolves howled in the distance, frightening the young Mendenhall brothers. Crabtree made light of their fears, and eventually calmed the young men by telling them stories. After a good meal, everyone bedded down for the night.

They were unaware that a small band of Indians had followed them and was lurking nearby in the darkness, watching and waiting. It was a mixed band of Indians consisting of fifteen Delawares, two Shawnees and two Cherokees. The Indians were returning from a council of local tribes that gathered to discuss mutual concerns over white intrusions into their territory. They saw the horses, cattle and supplies that the men brought with them, and they patiently waited for the right time to attack and steal everything of value.

Just before dawn, the Indians fired on the slumbering group, hitting Boone, Russell, the Mendenhall brothers, and Drake. The Mendenhall brothers were killed outright, and the mortally wounded Drake ran off into the darkness. Only Crabtree, Charles, and Adam were untouched. Crabtree escaped and Adam hid behind a nearby fallen tree. From his hiding place, Adam could see the horrifying events as they occurred.

The Indians grabbed the elderly slave Charles who stood there petrified with fear. They bound him so they could take him with them as a slave. Boone and Russell lay seriously wounded in their bed rolls after each had been shot in the hip. As they lay on the ground watching the Indians gather their livestock and supplies, young Boone recognized a large Shawnee named Big Jim, whom he and his father had befriended during a previous hunting expedition. Suddenly, some of the Indians tried to stab the wounded men with knives. Boone and Russell grabbed the blades as they tried to defend themselves, and in the process their hands were badly cut and mangled. In desperation, James Boone called out to Big Jim begging for mercy.

Instead of helping his young friend, Big Jim strode over and began to slowly and methodically torture both him and Henry Russell. Using his knife, the merciless Indian tore out their fingernails and toenails one by one as they screamed in agony.

From his hiding place, Adam watched the men cry and plead for mercy as Big Jim continued his grim barbaric torture. Finally, the young men begged to be killed after realizing that it would be their eventual fate. When the Indians had collected all of their booty and were packed and ready to leave, they granted the young men's pleas by shooting them with arrows and crushing their skulls with tomahawks.

The Indians fled north with their stolen goods, livestock and Charles. Crabtree soon found his way back to Castlewood, but Adam wandered in the wilderness for several days before finding his way back. Once he was home, Adam related the grisly details of the massacre.

The morning of the massacre, a young man from the main group slipped out of Daniel Boone's camp to return to Castlewood because Boone and others had severely reprimanded him for a theft he had committed the day before. About a mile or so from camp, he came upon the massacre site and hurried back to warn Boone and the others. Sadly, Crabtree had been unaware that they were so close to the main body. If they had pushed forward a bit longer, they would have reached the safety of the larger camp, and it is unlikely that the same Indians would have risked attacking such a large group.

Once they heard about the massacre, Boone's group threw themselves into preparations for an Indian attack. They passed out weapons to anyone who could shoot and began building a crude breastwork of wood for protection. Squire volunteered to take a burial party back to the site, while Daniel stayed with the others to defend their camp.

Captain Russell and Gass were the first to arrive at the grisly scene. They left Castlewood in a hurry that morning so they could catch up with the others. There in the forest lay the mangled corpses of four able-bodied young men whose lives had been filled with such promise and ambition. The discovery of the bodies drove the men to tears. As Russell and Gass stood there frozen with sorrow and disbelief, Squire Boone and his men arrived. Wanting to spare his brother and the others from the ghastly sight, Squire came to bury the dead. He wrapped his nephew and young Russell in a single blanket and buried the two friends together in an eternal embrace. Squire never forgot the awful scene, and some said it haunted him for the rest of his life. But at least he had spared his brother from witnessing the carnage. The men also properly buried the young Mendenhall brothers.

Many of the people who remained in camp with Daniel Boone panicked during Squire's absence. Having heard about the thefts and murders, they wanted to return to the relative safety of the homes they left behind. Later, when Squire returned with Russell and Gass, everyone attended a meeting to discuss the situation. Despite his grief over losing his son, Daniel Boone wanted to press on, but most wanted to turn back. Boone was outvoted and soon the melancholy group left to return to Castlewood. Captain Russell and Daniel Boone sent a few scouts to follow the Indians' trail, and hopefully take revenge. After following them for several miles, the scouts came upon the body of Charles.

They later learned that two of his Indian captors had argued over who could keep Charles as his slave. Their leader settled the issue by striking Charles on the head with his tomahawk. The fatal blow ended the dispute. The scouts eventually lost the Indians' trail and returned to Castlewood where they recounted Charles' sad fate.

Portrait Of Elderly Daniel Boone.

Chapter 7

CHEROKEE BILLY

Isaac Crabtree sat among a group of merry men in a tavern in Wolf Hills, Virginia. The men drank whiskey and told jokes and a few engaged in arm wrestling matches. While in their midst, Crabtree seemed detached from the group and refused to join in their merriment.

Ever since he returned from Powell's Valley in October of 1773, Crabtree was a changed man who had become quiet and withdrawn. His friends tried to cheer him up, but without success. They all knew about the massacre of several men and boys during the failed expedition to settle Kentucky; yet none knew how deeply that event affected Crabtree.

The more whiskey Crabtree drank, the less comfort he received from its intoxicating effects. He sat and ruminated about the events leading to the tragedy and wondered what went wrong. He pictured the young men at Castlewood preparing and packing for their journey. He visualized their faces as they enthusiastically worked alongside Charles and Adam getting everything ready.

Captain Russell had thought of everything needed to establish a settlement in Kentucky. He had even sent books so that the settlers could be entertained as they sat around the fire at night. Books were a luxury then because most frontiersmen were considered fortunate if they owned even one book; and if they did, it likely would be the Bible. However, Russell was from a prominent Virginia family and was well-educated.

Crabtree liked and respected Russell, and he felt a strong affection for the young men and boys who were placed in his care. Russell had given him a lot of responsibility in asking him to lead the small group. After the massacre, Crabtree felt guilty about stopping before they reached their destination. It haunted him that such promising young men had lost their lives, and he told himself that if he had only pushed a bit further, his group would have reached the safety of Boone's camp. Questions ran through his mind on a regular basis. Was it really the sound of wolves howling that had frightened the Mendenhall brothers, or the noise made by Indians signaling each other? If so, why hadn't he recognized it? Should he have posted a sentry before the group bedded down for the night? What else might he have done to protect his unsuspecting companions?

As the guilt intensified, no amount of liquor could wash it away. Over time, his self-doubt evolved into anger, and eventually rage. Crabtree began to hate Indians; not just those responsible for the massacre, but all Indians.

About six months after the massacre, the Watauga settlers gathered for fun and games with their Indian neighbors. Food and whiskey were served; and Crabtree and some friends came down from Wolf Hills, Virginia to enjoy the festivities.

During a foot race, Crabtree grabbed his rifle. His hatred toward Indians, fueled by the liquor he consumed that afternoon, caused him to fire at one of the Indian contestants. Cherokee Billy fell dead in his tracks. He was the innocent victim of Crabtree's malicious act. Afterward, Crabtree and his companions made a hasty retreat to Wolf Hills.

At first, some of the spectators did not realize what happened. When the Indians figured out what occurred, they turned sullen and abruptly gathered their belongings and left. Their afternoon merriment was spoiled by Crabtree's gunshot and their shock quickly turned to anger and a desire for revenge against the white settlers.

The whites feared for their lives. They understood that one of their own had murdered a Cherokee for no apparent reason. To make matters worse, the hapless victim was related to one of the tribe's sub-chiefs. The unprovoked violent act moved the Cherokee leaders to convene a war council, and begin making plans for an attack against the local settlers. It was a cultural imperative for them to avenge the murder of Cherokee Billy.

The settlers hastily called a meeting to discuss the situation. They realized that they were alone in the wilderness with little hope of any outside military assistance. North Carolina was too far away and separated by high mountains. Governor Tyron disapproved of their settlements and would probably be unwilling to send troops. Time was on the Indians' side because they would probably attack before a message could even reach the unsympathetic governor.

What should they do? Everyone realized that they would be slaughtered unless they acted quickly. At that moment, James Robertson stepped forward and offered to go to Chota to meet with the Cherokee chiefs. He promised to explain that the killer was not a Wataugan and that the whites would track down Crabtree and punish him for his crime. Robertson asked a Cherokee trader named William Faulin to accompany him and serve as his interpreter.

When Robertson and Faulin arrived at Chota, they saw that the Cherokees had already convened a war council and were preparing to attack. At first, the Cherokees were hostile, and

Robertson feared that they might be killed on the spot. Or even worse, they might be subjected to unspeakable torture. Rather than allowing his fears to overtake him, Robertson strode directly to the council house where the chiefs were meeting. Once inside, the white men sat among the chiefs and Robertson began to speak while Faulin interpreted.

The Indians were surprised by Robertson's courage. Seldom had they witnessed such bravery; and it prompted them listen to what he had to say. Robertson carefully chose his words, speaking slowly and deliberately. He told the chiefs how shocked and sad he and the others were about the senseless murder of Cherokee Billy. He related the whites' affection for Billy and their disdain for the outsider from Wolf Hills who had killed him.

The chiefs held talks with Robertson over several days. His sincerity and integrity impressed them, and they came to realize that he was an honest man. In the end, Robertson convinced them that Cherokees and whites were brothers who should live side-by-side in peace. He assured the chiefs that Crabtree would be tracked down and punished for his crime.

Upon his return to Watauga, Robertson was greeted by anxious settlers eager to learn the outcome of his mission. Robertson related what had transpired, and everyone was relieved and grateful for what he had done to save the white settlements.

Unfortunately, Robertson was unable to keep his promise to the Cherokees that Crabtree would be punished for his cowardly act. Most frontiersmen were not inclined to arrest one of their own for a crime against an Indian. Crabtree's friends understood what made him snap, and they justified his crime. They also protected him from being arrested. Due to the circumstances, Crabtree was never apprehended or tried for his crime. He got away with murder.

Chapter 8

PRELUDE TO WAR

Many members of Russell and Boone's ill-fated group abandoned their dreams of settling in Kentucky after the bloody massacre at Powell's Valley. For the Boone brothers, Michael Stoner, and other brave frontiersmen, the dream was merely postponed.

Most of the Boone clan, which included Daniel's in-laws, the Bryants, decided to return home to Yadkin, North Carolina. Other prospective settlers retreated to their homes in Virginia and North Carolina after the massacre.

Daniel escorted his wife and family to Watauga where they rested for a few days before beginning the difficult trip over the mountains to Yadkin. While visiting Watauga, Boone and his family stayed at the home of James Robertson.

James and his wife, Charlotte, offered comfort and support to their grieving friends. During that sad time, the Robertson's provided spiritual counseling for Daniel and his wife, Rebecca. They also arranged for them to be baptized in their home by a Methodist circuit rider who was ministering to the people in Watauga. Daniel's newfound faith would help him cope with his grief while remaining on the frontier.

After Rebecca and the family headed east over the mountains, Daniel returned to Castlewood, Virginia and moved into a vacant cabin with Michael Stoner. Captain Russell hired both men to work as scouts for the militia. Their frontier skills were appreciated by the local settlers, who were fearful of Indian attacks. By then, news had arrived that other Indian attacks were occurring along the frontier. Because the small scattered settlements in southwest Virginia were so remote, the people needed places of refuge where they could defend themselves.

William Russell's fort at Castlewood was one such place. Russell was a captain in the Virginia militia, and his fort was located near the Great Warrior's Path. For centuries, Indians used the path for trade and intertribal warfare. Within the Clinch River Valley, Russell's fort at Castlewood, Moore's fort, and Blackmore's fort were the best places for nearby settlers to congregate for protection from marauding war parties.

Because Russell's immediate superior, Colonel Preston, was stationed far from Castlewood, Russell had a great deal of authority in making decisions and issuing orders. Captain Russell's militiamen had a good reputation and were proud to call themselves, "Russell's Rangers."

The settlers were fortunate that Captain Russell was a natural leader. He had an even temperament and was an excellent officer. To prepare for attacks, he encouraged settlers to either congregate inside the larger forts, or upgrade the fortifications at their stations. Typically, a remote station had a small two-story log blockhouse with portholes for shooting at the enemy. Russell ordered Boone, Stoner and the other scouts to constantly roam the outlying areas while searching for Indian war parties.

The likelihood of an Indian attack terrified most settlers. They had either heard stories of Indian cruelty or had witnessed them firsthand. When Indians attacked, they often killed everyone, including women and children. When they did take captives, they frequently subjected them to unimaginable, prolonged torture.

One method of torture was called "running the gauntlet." This method was usually reserved for male captives. Braves and squaws who were armed with clubs, tomahawks, or knives formed two parallel lines, and the captive was forced to run between the lines. The Indians would strike, club, and stab the prisoner while he ran. Often, he would succumb to his injuries before reaching the end of the lines.

Burning at the stake was another common type of prolonged Indian torture. The victim would be bound to a stake atop slow-burning ember. The Indians frequently scalped the captive and burned his skin and body with red hot sticks. Squaws typically performed most of the torture and would give special attention to burning or cutting off the genitals and burning out the victim's eyes. After completing the torture, they let the victim slowly burn at the stake, thereby prolonging the agony until death.

Skinning a person alive was a particularly excruciating form of torture. Another heinous technique was to subject the captive to slow cuts. That method involved making slow, numerous cuts on the prisoner's body over an extend time. White women were not exempt from Indian cruelty. At best, they might be raped or enslaved. Children, who were not tortured or killed, were made slaves.

The best outcome for any Indian captive was to be adopted into the tribe, but such cases were rare. Sometimes women or children were abducted for ransom. If the ransom was paid for their release, they were the truly fortunate ones.

Amid the atmosphere of fear and hysteria, Boone and Stoner quickly became popular militiamen in the Clinch River Valley district. Boone distinguished himself as a scout; roaming the woods tirelessly, looking for signs of Indians. The local people appreciated his services and praised him, as well as the other scouts, for protecting them. Because of his exceptional service as a scout,

William Russell promoted Boone to lieutenant in the Virginia militia. Boone gladly accepted his appointment; and legend has it that he proudly carried the commission document with him wherever he went during the remainder of his active live.

Boone's role in the failed Kentucky expedition was the beginning of his notoriety. When survivors of the failed Russell Expedition returned to Yadkin, North Carolina, they quickly spread the news about the massacre at Powell's Valley. A North Carolina newspaper picked up the story and printed an account that documented Boone's participation. It also chronicled the barbaric murders of his son and his companions. The article was the first printed account of Daniel Boone's exploits.

At about the time Boone received his first publicity, other important events were happening on the frontier. Soon, another bloody encounter took place. In that unpleasant incident, friendly Indians were the innocent victims. It happened on the banks of Yellow Creek in Pennsylvania. In early 1774, a group of white men led by Daniel Greathouse invited some Mingo Indians to join them for food, drink, and entertainment. Eager to become acquainted with their frontier neighbors, the Indians accepted the invitation. The whiskey-fueled gathering included a shooting contest. No one knows exactly what happened next, but a survivor recounted that the white hosts suddenly turned on their Indian guests and started killing them, without provocation.

Some of the dead Indians turned out to be relatives of Chief Logan of the Mingo tribe. Their deaths caused the Shawnee, Delaware, Wyandot, and Mingo tribes to unite with them for war against the whites. After hearing about the Indians' agitation over the massacre, leaders from the Watauga, Nolichucky, Carter's Valley, Holston, and Clinch River settlements mobilized their militias to prepare for the worst.

Further complicating the volatile situation, a group of surveyors hired by wealthy Virginia land speculators were far out on the western frontier. Captain Russell received word that they were out and likely unaware of recent events as they went about their work far from civilization.

Concerned about the surveyors' safety, Russell ordered Daniel Boone and Michael Stoner to go find the men and bring them back to Castlewood. Boone and Stoner went to locate them, but they returned much later empty handed. Eventually, it became known that the surveyors had already heard about the Indian uprising and decided to return on their own.

Chapter 9

THE BATTLE OF POINT PLEASANT

As a result of several violent encounters between whites and Indians, the Kentucky frontier was a tinder box ready to ignite. In contrast, the Tennessee frontier was relatively peaceful due to the efforts of British Indian agents who lived among the Cherokees. Indian Superintendent John Stuart's careful supervision of his agents helped them maintain peaceful relations between the Cherokees and the growing population of white settlers.

In 1774, the Cherokees were in no mood to disobey the Crown's authority after having been chastised by British soldiers for their earlier rebellion during the French and Indian War. In fact, the Cherokees went so far as to punish one of their own braves who was involved in the massacre during the Russell-Boone expedition. Upon Stuart's orders, the brave was captured and executed by his own tribe. Afterward, the Tennessee settlers were more confident that their Cherokee neighbors were under good supervision.

However, in Kentucky there was no effective management of the various tribes roaming the area. The Shawnee and Delaware were the most powerful of those tribes. A third tribe, the Mingos, led by Chief Logan, were formerly staunch allies of the whites until the unfortunate Greathouse massacre of some of the chief's relatives. Immediately after that terrible deed, Chief Logan wanted revenge, and he called for war against the white settlers. He was able to persuade Chief Cornstalk of the Shawnees and other tribal chiefs to wage war and drive the whites away from their hunting lands. To his credit, Cornstalk was against going to war, but he was bound to do so after he was outvoted in council by the other Shawnee chiefs.

In Virginia, Governor Lord Dunmore had determined that an Indian war was inevitable in the western region. He called out the militia and sent recruiting agents to the border settlements in Virginia and Watauga. Volunteers eagerly signed up from both areas.

Watauga volunteers were proud, hardworking men who would fight to defend their Virginia neighbors. They were committed to the cause and in no mood to be trifled with. When they overheard a British recruiting officer making disparaging remarks about the over-mountain men, they became very angry. Although the settlers might have seemed strange to the officer because of their buckskin clothing and coarse behavior, the leaders felt that he had no right to ridicule them. James Robertson and William Cocke tarred and feathered the officer and evicted him from their settlement. That act typified the Wataugan spirit of independence from outside authority.

Despite that incident, the Wataugans and settlers from surrounding areas continued to volunteer. The impending war was not really their fight because they had not been attacked by any of the northern tribes. However, they understood the need to help the Virginians. If the Indians drove them off their lands, the Wataugans might be next.

On September 11, 1774, about 1,100 militiamen under the command of General Andrew Lewis marched toward Point

Pleasant, located at the confluence of the Ohio and Kanawha rivers in what is now West Virginia. James Robertson and Valentine Sevier were sergeants under Captain Evan Shelby as part of the Fincastle County Battalion. Captain William Russell led another Fincastle County Battalion of militia volunteers from the Clinch River Valley settlements. The militia was under orders to promptly march to Point Pleasant and wait there for the arrival of a second army commanded by Lord Dunmore.

Earlier, after returning from their mission to bring home the surveyors on the frontier, Daniel Boone and Michael Stoner had asked Captain Russell for permission to go on the expedition to Point Pleasant. He denied their request because they were two of his best scouts and he believed that they would be of better use patrolling the Clinch River Valley region in search of marauding Indians. It was really a sign of confidence in the two men because Russell and his militiamen needed capable men to protect family and friends who would be left behind during their absence.

When General Lewis' army arrived at their destination on October 3, 1774, everyone was exhausted from the long difficult journey. They began setting up camp, and hunters went out to secure meat to feed the men. The day of their arrival, Colonel Lewis received a dispatch from Lord Dunmore ordering him to immediately march his men from Point Pleasant to rendezvous with his army at Pickaway Plains. The news did not set well with the men who had already journeyed through difficult terrain for nearly a month before reaching their destination. They were fatigued and needed to rest.

However, before General Lewis had to deal with his angry subordinates, some of his scouts came in to report that there were large numbers of Indians nearby. Not wanting to get ambushed on the way to Pickaway Plains, General Lewis decided that it would be prudent to delay their departure from Point Pleasant.

His men could rest for a while, and he would have time to gather more intelligence as to the enemy's strength and intentions.

One week after their arrival, on October 10, 1774, James Robertson and Valentine Sevier left camp before sunrise to go hunting. In the dim pre-dawn light about a mile from camp, they spotted a massive force of Indians moving in the opposite direction.

Led by Shawnee Chief Cornstalk, the warriors were headed toward the camp in a line that stretched nearly a mile wide covering the distance between the Kanawha and Ohio rivers. Warriors from the Shawnee, Delaware, Mingo and other tribes comprised the attacking force of over 800 Indians.

Robertson and Sevier shot at the closest Indians and then ran back to camp to warn the others. After receiving fire, the Indians stopped in their tracks, fearing a possible ambush.

The warriors' pause gave Robertson and Sevier sufficient time to make it back to camp and alert the sentries. The sentries awoke their sleeping comrades, who hurriedly began to assemble and prepare for an attack. The sound of drum signals filled the air as the various units formed and received orders from their officers.

General Lewis ordered the formation of two lines to move forward and confront the enemy. One force was led by the General's brother, Colonel Charles Lewis, and the other was commanded by Colonel William Fleming. The two lines were comprised of more experienced officers and men while the less experienced were ordered to stay behind and guard the camp. James Robertson and Valentine Sevier served as sergeants under Fleming and Captain William Russell went out under Colonel Lewis.

The two lines encountered the Indian phalanx about 400 yards from camp. Both sides opened fire immediately and the sounds of hundreds of gunshots broke the early morning silence. Soon the air was filled with smoke from the rifles. Officers' shouts and Indian war whoops could be heard among the din, as well as the anguished cries of the wounded and dying.

The battle continued as Shawnee Chief Cornstalk ran among his warriors, directing their advances and retreats. Sharpshooters from both sides hid behind trees, targeting their adversaries from a distance. Other combatants engaged in hand-to-hand combat, striking one another with rifle butts, clubs, tomahawks or knives.

During brief lulls in the fighting, combatants from each side tried to remove their dead and wounded from harm's way. Around noon there was a brief pause while each side regrouped and rested. Officers in camp supervised the building of breastworks and the treatment of wounded men. After a brief respite, the fighting resumed.

General Lewis tried to outmaneuver the Indians. He sent Captain Isaac Shelby and a group of Wataugans up the Ohio River to flank the Indians. Other officers led similar flanking maneuvers, but each attempt failed. In every case, the men were eventually forced to withdraw.

By late afternoon, Chief Cornstalk surveyed his casualties. Many of his warriors lay motionless on the field. The weary leader reluctantly ordered his braves to collect the dead and wounded to begin a covered retreat. They eventually withdrew to an area where there were many fallen trees and high weeds, making a continued pursuit perilous and nearly impossible in the approaching darkness. In the end, General Lewis' men were victorious because they had driven the enemy from the field.

The whites claimed victory, but it was won at a high cost. They sustained more than one-hundred dead or wounded in the battle. The General's brother, Colonel Lewis, was mortally wounded early in the fighting. Several other officers fell while leading their men. Captain Russell was on the front throughout the day, but survived unscathed. Sergeants James Robertson and Valentine Sevier fought bravely with their forward units and were frequently under fire during the battle. They came back alive, but several of their men fell during the brutal fight.

The Battle of Point Pleasant helped bring about peace between the Indians and the settlers. Chiefs Cornstalk and Logan realized that the whites had larger numbers of men who were willing to fight. They understood that too many Indian braves had died that day, and they had precious few replacements.

Following the battle, General Lewis led his men toward a rendezvous with Lord Dunmore's army. Before leaving, he left Captain Russell in command at Point Pleasant with orders to supervise the treatment and protection of the wounded soldiers. Russell was also given the task of building a fort at that location. Russell oversaw the construction and it was eventually completed. Afterward, the fort was used for many years to protect settlers from Indian attacks

By the time General Lewis' army was near its destination, Lord Dunmore sent word for him to return and subsequently disband because he had already secured a peace treaty with the Indians. But the Indians were aware of Lewis' advance and they feared an attack. Not wanting to risk renewed hostilities that might jeopardize his treaty, Dunmore thought that it would be best to remove General Lewis' men from the area.

Lewis' men were angry because they had marched a long distance without being given the chance to do more fighting and finish the job. They wanted to completely defeat the Indians so that they would not be able to resume their attacks. In the end, General Lewis and his men reluctantly followed orders and withdrew. However, future events would soon reveal that their concerns were well-founded.

On the way home, Robertson thought about his role in the battle. He wondered what might have happened if he and Valentine Sevier had not gone hunting that morning. Would he and his comrades have been slaughtered as they slept?

As he traveled, he also recalled his near-death experience five years earlier when he got lost in the wilderness while crossing the mountains from Watauga to North Carolina. Knowing that he had already cheated death twice served to reinforce Robertson's faith in divine intervention. He believed that God had more in store for him. And he was right.

Chapter 10

THE TRANSYLVANIA PURCHASE

Valentine Sevier's brother, John, was also a close friend of James Robertson. John Sevier moved his family from New Market, Virginia to Watauga in early 1772. Shortly thereafter, he purchased a homestead on the Nolichucky River from Jacob Brown, founder of the settlement. Robertson and other leaders soon came to appreciate his talents. He was a well-educated man with dashing good looks and a charming personality. He was a natural born leader and an experienced Indian fighter.

John Sevier became a lieutenant in the local militia and a commissioner under the provisions of the Watauga Compact. As such, he worked closely with James Robertson on military and civil affairs. Both men's mutual respect for one another formed the basis for a lifelong friendship that would profoundly impact the future of the frontier region.

Their friendship flourished in part because their personal attributes complemented each other so well. Both men were highly intelligent and possessed strong leadership skills. Each was ambitious and audacious, with the ability to recognize fortuitous events and boldly exploit them. Both men were unusually brave and each would perform numerous courageous acts in the years ahead.

However, their educational backgrounds and personalities were very different. Sevier had a formal education and briefly attended what is now Washington and Lee University. Robertson lacked a higher formal education, but he was considered reasonably literate for that era. He could also perform arithmetic computations in his head faster than most could on paper. Sevier was charming and loquacious, while Robertson was cordial and somewhat reserved. When he spoke, he chose his words carefully for maximum effect.

Robertson's intrepid spirit flowed from an unwavering Presbyterian belief in divine guidance. He was an early advocate of Thomas Jefferson's principle of Manifest Destiny. A few years later, Robertson would encourage his fellow American frontiersmen by stating, "Our way is to the sea". He was resolute in his advocacy for American expansion all the way to the Pacific Ocean.

Less is known about Sevier's religious beliefs. As the son of Huguenot immigrants who fled Catholic persecution in France, he was a Protestant believer.

A third man who profoundly influenced the settlement of the over-mountain lands arrived in Watauga three years after Sevier. Judge Richard Henderson from Yadkin, North Carolina formed a land speculation company to acquire a huge tract of virgin land in the wilderness of Kentucky and Tennessee. Judge Henderson likely met Daniel Boone while he was serving as the presiding judge in Hillsborough, North Carolina. While not much is known about the friendship of the two men, Henderson was captivated by Boone's glowing accounts of the rich over-mountain territory and was eager to acquire land there.

The jurist's life in North Carolina had grown difficult during the social upheaval created by the Regulator Movement in North Carolina's back country. On one occasion, Henderson was forced to run out the back door of his courthouse to escape an angry mob of Regulators. Another time, an angry mob of Regulators attacked the judge's home and burned it to the ground.

Amid that turbulent atmosphere, Henderson quit the bench in 1773 and formed the Transylvania Land Company. Like other prominent men of his time, including George Washington and Thomas Jefferson, Henderson believed that the Kentucky wilderness would soon be open for settlement, and he hoped to acquire a huge portion of the area before others could stake their claims. After creating his land company, Henderson eventually became the most ambitious land speculator of his time.

Richard Henderson logically selected the frontiersman Daniel Boone to serve as his over-mountain agent for the Transylvania Land Company. Then he formulated a bold plan to acquire the vast amount of land he desired. He devised a plan to make a treaty with the Cherokee tribe that would allow him to purchase land from them in areas encompassing large portions of present-day Kentucky and middle Tennessee in exchange for trade goods. After Henderson formulated his plan, he sent Boone to confer with James Robertson.

Boone arrived in Watauga in 1775 to discuss strategy with his friend. By then, Robertson was the most influential leader among the local settlers. More importantly, he had earned the trust and respect of his Cherokee neighbors and the two most powerful chiefs of the Cherokee Nation, Attakullakulla and Oconostota. Oconostota once said of Robertson, "He has winning ways and makes no fuss."

With Robertson by his side, Boone began negotiating with the Cherokees on behalf of Henderson. After some time had passed, Henderson joined his agent to finalize the details and strike a final deal. Ultimately, he paid over two-thousand pounds sterling in trade goods that consisted of iron cooking implements, cloth, jewelry, vermillion, knives, tomahawks, rifles, gunshot, powder, and sundry other items for the land.

However, there were major legal problems with Henderson's land acquisition treaty that were never addressed. Only official agents of the British colonial government were authorized to negotiate and sign treaties with Indian tribes. A second technicality was that all of the white settlements west of the Proclamation Line of 1763 were deemed illegal. The final and most serious flaw in Henderson's treaty was that the land that the Indians sold him was neither occupied nor claimed by the Cherokee Nation. The Chickasaws had defeated the Cherokees in battles over the region that eventually became middle Tennessee. And the Shawnee, Delaware, Wyandot, and Mingo tribes had stronger claims on the land in the Kentucky wilderness. Henderson's purchase was clearly illegal under British colonial law, and the Cherokees sold land to which they had no legitimate claim. If the timing had not been so fortuitous, due to mounting colonial unrest, such an absurd treaty would have never been sanctioned or completed.

Before the treaty was even finalized, Henderson sent Daniel Boone and more than thirty axmen to widen the Warriors' Path leading through the Cumberland Gap into Kentucky. The path needed widening to accommodate wagons.

As soon as the treaty was consummated, a wagon train of settlers began their journey over the newly widened road. Shortly after they crossed the Cumberland Gap, they heard about an Indian attack against Boone and his men who were still widening the last portion of the Warriors' Path. The report of the attack came from a survivor who fled the scene. The news caused several of the travelers to panic and consider turning back. When Henderson heard about the trouble, he paid a large bounty to one of his scouts to ride ahead and escort Boone back to the area where the settlers had stopped. Boone returned with Henderson's well-paid scout and they calmed everyone's fears before escorting the wagon train safely to its destination. Their journey ended at a site on the Kentucky River known as Big Lick, now called Boonesborough.

Earlier on March 17, 1775, hundreds of Indians dressed in their finest clothing had gathered at Sycamore Shoals to share the bountiful feast provided by Henderson and his associates. The white settlers joined their Cherokee neighbors at the social gathering that preceded the treaty-signing ceremony.

Henderson and the Cherokee chiefs signed the treaty later that day. The Transylvania Land Company had purchased nearly twenty-million acres of land encompassing the entire region between the Cumberland and Kentucky rivers.

The signing of the illegal treaty took place one month before the battles of Lexington and Concord, the conflicts that ignited the American Revolution. Some believe that the spirit of rebellion that inflamed the colonies and over-mountain areas created a void in official authority, allowing Henderson to finalize his transaction. In doing so, he sealed the largest and most audacious private land purchase on American soil. Richard Henderson was a man with big dreams. His original objective was to create a new nation on the frontier, with himself as its leader. Unfortunately for Henderson, there were people who would stand in his way.

Earlier In 1774, James Harrod and a group of adventurers had already arrived in the Kentucky region and began to lay out a town that would become Harrodsburg. When they learned of Henderson's land purchase, those frontiersmen already living in Kentucky had strong doubts about the newcomer. They could not reconcile the former judge's goals with their own. Despite his intelligence and superb oratory skills, Henderson would have a difficult time convincing the earlier pioneers that he owned the land they had developed. That difference of opinion would eventually lead to confrontation.

A man named George Rogers Clark proved to be particularly vexing for Henderson. Clark was a fearless frontiersman who first ventured into the Kentucky region in 1772 as a 20-year-old surveyor. It was four years after the Treaty of Fort Stanwix had ceded most of present-day Kentucky to the crown without any prior input or consent from the Indian tribes that hunted there.

Clark did not recognize Henderson's land acquisition or his authority over the Harrodsburg settlement. He had been hired by wealthy land speculators, who were eager to acquire western lands that were previously prohibited from settlement by the King's Proclamation Line of 1763. Lands west of the line had been set aside for various Indian tribes to avoid future conflicts between them and the white settlers, as noted earlier. However, settlers did not obey the demarcation line and often forayed into or squatted on Indian Territory; especially after the Treaty of Fort Stanwix in 1768 clouded the issue of western settlement on Indian Lands.

Clark became an accomplished frontier scout during his long forays into Kentucky, first as a surveyor and later as a ranger on patrol to keep out hostile Indians. By 1775, he had settled in Harrodsburg, shortly before Richard Henderson's land purchase from the Cherokees.

In June of 1776, Henderson, Boone, and their compatriots met at Harrodsburg to vote on the status of the Kentucky region. Clark and Harrod convinced their fellow frontiersmen that everyone would be safer and better off if Kentucky became a western county of Virginia. Becoming a separate state had too many drawbacks. The area would be vulnerable to Indian attacks and many suspected that Henderson wanted to create his own empire. That kind of autocracy did not mesh well with the democratic mind-set of the fiercely independent frontiersmen.

Therefore, the Harrodsburg settlers voted to override Henderson's questionable land claims. Afterward, they drew up a petition and selected George Rogers Clark and John Gabriel Jones to travel to Virginia and deliver it to the General Assembly. The petition formally requested that Virginia's western boundary be extended to include Kentucky.

Clark, Jones, and a few other settlers set off for Virginia. Clark felt energized and excited to be entrusted with such an important mission. When the group passed through Point Pleasant, Clark recalled the epic battle that had taken place there two years earlier.

Further on, the group passed through Powell's Valley, where the Russell Expedition had tragically ended with the deaths of several men, including William Russell's and Daniel Boone's sons. Clark wondered how he would have felt had his own son been ambushed while sleeping and then slowly tortured to death.

As Clark pondered the pain and anguish the young men had suffered at the hands of their tormentors, he realized that he had no idea how he would have reacted had he been in similar circumstances. He concluded that the Russell Expedition's tragic end was a horrific event.

Clark felt the burden of his mission. He knew that the settlers who had remained behind were at the Indians' mercy. His expedition's gunpowder supply was low, and he knew that he had to secure more for the return trip.

The group stopped at Castlewood, Captain William Russell's frontier fort. They received a warm welcome and were given food and shelter for the night. The group discovered that Castlewood's residents had already made extensive defensive preparations. Early the next morning, the group headed up the Clinch River Valley where they passed other forts that were on high alert with defenses prepared to fend off Indian attacks.

When they arrived in Williamsburg, Virginia, Clark and Jones received an audience with Revolutionary Governor Patrick Henry who persuaded the State Assembly to establish Kentucky County, Virginia. To reinforce his intent, the governor appointed Clark as major in the Kentucky County militia and gave him 500 pounds of gunpowder to defend the settlements from Indian attacks after his return to Kentucky. The annexation, as well as the gunpowder, encouraged the settlers' who desperately wanted more security and protection from Indian attacks.

Governor Patrick Henry's actions in June 1776 effectively ended Richard Henderson's designs on Kentucky. Virginia and North Carolina subsequently nullified Henderson's Cherokee Treaty and his massive land acquisition. However, Virginia did grant Henderson a sizable amount of land in Kentucky in recognition of his efforts to settle the wilderness.

Stymied by his opponents, Henderson then set his sights on starting a settlement in the Tennessee wilderness along the Cumberland River. The site was known as French Lick, site of an old abandoned French trading post.

Meeting of the Transylvania Delegates in Kentucky.

Chapter 11

EVENTS LEADING TO WAR

American colonists became increasingly dissatisfied with their British masters after a series of events occurred between 1765 and 1775. In 1765 the Stamp Act imposed a tax on every piece of printed paper American colonists used, including ships' papers, legal documents, licenses, playing cards, newspapers, and other publications. The money collected from the tax was used to help pay off massive debts incurred in the French and Indian War. The colonists objected to the new tax because it was imposed by the British Parliament and colonial representatives were not given the authority to vote for or against it.

The Boston Massacre, five years later, further enraged the colonists. On March 5, 1770, a crowd of colonists gathered around soldiers of the 29th British Regiment. The crowd taunted the soldiers, hurling verbal insults and snowballs. The scene grew volatile as the crowd closed in on the soldiers. One soldier gave the order to fire. Three civilians were killed and two others were mortally wounded.

The Battle of Alamance in 1771 also contributed to the colonists' rebellious spirit. Western North Carolina settlers had grievances with the colonial government over excessive taxes, illegal fees, and dishonest sheriffs. They formed an association of

Regulators, mentioned in Chapter 5, to oppose the unfair practices through negotiation.

After peaceful attempts to settle their differences failed, the frustrated Regulators resorted to violence and lawlessness to further their cause. Governor William Tryon called out the militia to quash the rebels. The Regulators and militia fought for two hours on May 11, 1771, but the Regulators were no match for the well-supplied and better-organized militia.

The Tea Act of 1773 increased colonial grievances and culminated in the Boston Tea Party. The Tea Act grew out of the Townshend Acts, in which Parliament levied import duties on articles of everyday use in America. These included tea, lead, glass, and colors for paint. As a result, the colonists boycotted British tea. The Townshend Acts were repealed, except for the tax on tea. Consequently, the colonists refused to import tea from England, which caused a major loss of revenue to the East India Company.

The East India Company asked Parliament to pass a law giving it permission to import tea directly to America. Since many members of Parliament owned stock in the East India Company, the law passed in 1773 was called the Tea Act. It upheld the tax on tea but actually lowered tea prices. The colonists objected to this act because it gave them no say in the decision-making process.

In late 1773, several colonists disguised as Indians boarded ships anchored in Boston Harbor that were carrying tea and heaved nearly 350 casks of tea into the water. That event became known as the Boston Tea Party, and it drew widespread attention in the colonies and abroad.

In retaliation, the British passed four laws called the Coercive Acts. The colonists referred to them as the Intolerable Acts, as they were attempts to wield power over the rebellious American colonists. In its determination to enforce those acts, Britain appointed General Thomas Gage governor of Massachusetts. Gage already served as commander-in-chief of the British armed forces in America, and his appointment was intended to intimidate the colonists and suppress the growing spirit of rebellion.

Most of the colonists opposed the Intolerable Acts, while many remained loyal to Great Britain. On September 5, 1774, the colonists convened the First Continental Congress to compile a list of requested changes to British policies. If these changes were not made by January 1775, the group agreed to convene again in spring 1775.

The battles of Lexington and Concord in April 1775 effectively ended the colonists' attempts at peaceful negotiations with their British overlords and started the American Revolution.

After the outbreak of hostilities, the colonists formally declared their independence from Britain on July 4, 1776. Following the Declaration of Independence, the British initiated contingency plans to crush the growing rebellion. The most notable preplanned strategy that would affect the western frontier was the Anaconda Plan.

Conceived before the Declaration of Independence, the Anaconda Plan was designed to strangle the rebellious colonies with a two-pronged attack, by sea and from the interior. The British would attack a number of eastern seaboard targets and move their troops inland. Indians along the western frontier would attack the over mountain-settlements. Once they defeated the frontiersmen, the various Indian tribes were to move east across the Appalachians and eventually link up with the British forces moving inland. The plan was for the two groups to strangle the rebels in the same manner that an anaconda slowly coils around its prey and crushes it.

General Gage first devised the Anaconda Plan along with high-level members of the British War Department. He then worked out the details with Henry Hamilton, British lieutenant-governor at Detroit, and John Stuart, British Superintendent of Indian Affairs for the southern district.

They in turn delivered instructions to British agents in the field. The most notable was Alexander Cameron, British Agent for Cherokee Indian Affairs. He lived among the Cherokees in their capital of Chota and supplied them with rifles, lead, powder, and other arms, as did British agents living among other tribes. The various agents made a number of promises to the Indians in exchange for helping the British drive out the over-mountain settlers. Those assurances included allowing the Indians to keep any clothing or other valuables they could plunder from their victims, and reclamation of their lost hunting grounds once they had driven off the settlers. The last inducement was probably the stronger, since the tribes had become increasingly concerned about white encroachment on western Indian lands. Traditional Indian hunting grounds were disappearing at an alarming rate during the prior six years leading up to the American Revolution.

Awed by British military power and persuaded by promises of endless supplies and recovering lost lands, many Indian tribes made the fateful decision to ally themselves with the British. The most appalling aspect of their unholy alliance was that the British fully understood the types of atrocities the Indians would commit against innocent white settlers.

Fortunately, the series of events leading to the Declaration of Independence had also given the colonists advance knowledge that a violent rebellion was in the making. That awareness gave the frontier settlers adequate time to prepare their defenses.

In Virginia, William Russell and most of his fellow settlers in the Clinch River Valley decided to join the revolution. They made the necessary repairs and improvements to the forts along the Clinch and Holston rivers and replenished them with arms, munitions, and stores of food. Because lead was used to make bullets, Russell's Rangers seized and secured the lead mines at Fort Chiswell to ensure a steady supply of ammunition to fight the British and their Indian allies.

While their Virginia neighbors prepared for war, the settlers in Watauga made ready as well. Before the Declaration of Independence, James Robertson and John Sevier oversaw the construction and outfitting of a fort at Sycamore Shoals.

Like most forts of that era, it had palisades constructed of logs buried upright with the tops carved to sharp points. Two-story log block houses stood in each corner of the fort's walls. The block houses featured gun ports in the sides and in the floor of the second story. The latter served as a redoubt in case the Indians entered the building's first floor. Those upstairs would have a last chance to defend themselves by being able to shoot down through the floor at the intruders.

Chapter 12

THE DECLARATION OF INDEPENDENCE

By the July 4, 1776 signing of the Declaration of Independence, the American Colonies announced their freedom from British rule. That document formalized the war with Britain that effectively began fifteen months earlier at Lexington and Concord. The time between the initial outbreak of hostilities on April 19, 1775 in Lexington, Massachusetts and the signing of the Declaration of Independence gave each side ample opportunity to prepare for open warfare.

Committees of Safety were established along the western frontiers of Virginia and North Carolina with William Russell and James Robertson serving as leaders in their respective settlements. Rangers from the local militias roamed the countryside searching for British loyalists and Indian raiding parties.

The colonists who bore allegiance to the crown, known as Loyalists or Tories, were forced to swear their support for independence or be banished from their land. The Patriots, also known as Whigs, often administered stern frontier justice to those who refused to join their cause. Some Loyalists who refused to join the rebellion were whipped, hanged, or shot by the rebels in their fervor to break away from the crown's authority.

When independence was finally declared, the frontier settlements in Virginia, Kentucky and Tennessee were prepared to fight. They had already strengthened their fortifications and secured ample supplies of food, gunpowder and lead to sustain them during an attack.

James Robertson commanded Fort Watauga, also known as Fort Lee, with Lieutenant John Sevier serving as second-in-command. Many settlers from outlying homesteads abandoned their homes and banded together at the fort. They brought their livestock and household supplies to the fort where they found a safe haven.

While many of the Patriots congregated at Fort Watauga and fortified stations, the over-hill Cherokees assembled nearly 750 warriors to attack them. Alexander Cameron, the British Indian Agent stationed at Chota, distributed the stockpiled arms and ammunition to them. The Cherokees organized their raiding parties into two groups. The first was led by Dragging-Canoe, a chief known for his hatred of the white settlers. The second group was led by Chief Old Abraham of Chilhowie, a wily, seasoned warrior.

Two occurrences gave advance warning of Indian attacks. The first involved Charles Robertson's interception of a letter indicating that the British planned to attack. The British strategy was to incite the Cherokees in conjunction with the Creeks, Chickasaws, and Choctaws. The settlers knew that all of these tribes shared a cultural affinity for warfare and could be induced to fight with promises of trade goods, armaments, plunder and the prospect of retaking their land. They hoped to rid their lands of the white interlopers who had encroached on their land over the previous six years. The letter was reviewed and considered valid; so the Patriots prepared to fight.

The second warning came from Cherokee Beloved Woman, Nancy Ward. In tribal council she spoke out against going to war, but she was outvoted. Afterward, she secretly freed four white traders who were being held hostage and told them to warn James Robertson of the imminent attack. In doing so, she betrayed her own tribe.

Nancy Ward's motives were varied. She truly believed that the whites were the Indians' brothers, and that a war against them would be a disaster for the Cherokees. She knew that James Robertson was an honest and sincere man, and she believed him when he spoke to the Cherokee chiefs about the whites' desire for peace. In addition, she had developed friendships with the white traders who were being held, and she feared that they might be executed. While her allegiance to her own people was strong, she believed that the slaughter of innocent settlers was morally wrong.

In the spring of 1776, Colonel William Russell sent a letter to Daniel Boone, urging him to advise the Kentucky settlers to return to Virginia where they would be more secure. Many settlers heeded his warning and returned, but Boone and the majority of his men remained at Boonesboro to fight for their land.

Most in Kentucky had already prepared their defenses due to prior sporadic attacks by Shawnees, Mingos, and others. After Boone received Russell's letter, he made sure that the settlers took additional precautions.

Russell's superior, Colonel William Preston, ordered more fortifications in the Clinch River Valley. He also authorized additional troops to protect the recently commandeered lead mines at Fort Chiswell.

In July, the Cherokees showed their savage nature after capturing one of Watauga's residents, Lydia Bean, wife of William

Bean. She was taken to Chota and sentenced to be burned at the stake. Mrs. Bean was tied to the stake and a bundle of twigs was lit under her feet. Nancy Ward intervened by stepping forward and kicking aside the burning sticks. As Beloved Woman, she proclaimed amnesty through her right to pardon the condemned. Once again, her compassion was displayed through her actions. Afterward, she proclaimed that Mrs. Bean would remain at Chota and teach domestic skills to the Cherokee women.

Nancy Ward's display of kindness did not deter the Cherokee warriors from preparing to attack Fort Watauga. Fortunately, the hostages she freed arrived in time to warn the settlers of the Indians' plans. On July 11, 1776, John Sevier sounded the alarm by writing a letter to his compatriots in Fincastle County, Virginia.

Fort Lee (Watauga)
July 11, 1776

Dear Gentleman:

Isaac Thomas, William Falling, Jarot Williams, and one more have this moment come in by making their escape from the Indians, and say six hundred Indians and whites were to start for this fort, and intend to drive the country up to New River before they return.

John Sevier

The letter served two purposes. It was a warning and an indirect plea for assistance because Fort Watauga was the first line of defense.

Nine days after Sevier's warning, Captain James Robertson sent a letter to Colonel William Russell in Virginia.

July 20, 1776

Sir:

Our scouts this moment (some of them) come in, William Fording in particular and have discovered the tracks of about one hundred Indians coming right along the path from Brown's making towards our fort; the scouts then left the road and pushed in and as they came in they discovered the tracks of several parties supposed to be 15 or 20 in a party and making towards the fort.

I am sure they will attack the fort in the morning.

Myself and the other officers are in good spirits and will do all we can and hope we will be able to give them a warm reception and keep them out until you can assist us with more men.

Farewell
James Robertson

Robertson's letter showed that the thirty-four-year-old had matured after his experience at the Battle of Point Pleasant. He took the scouting report seriously, recalling how it was only by chance that he and Valentine Sevier discovered the Indians at Point Pleasant. That discovery had saved the army from possible annihilation.

As soon as Robertson became aware of the Indians' plans, he went into action and oversaw every detail, from storing food and ammunition to sending out scouts in search of the enemy. The seasoned young leader knew that he and his men were greatly outnumbered. He had only forty riflemen to defend the fort against over 300 Indians.

While Robertson's letter to Russell seemed to exude confidence, his use of "farewell" in the ending betrayed his resignation to the very real possibility that he and the others would be killed in the upcoming battle.

At the beginning of the Battle of Fort Watauga, John Sevier saved Kate Sherill by pulling her over the wall.

Chapter 13

CHEROKEES ATTACK

As the Cherokees prepared to attack Fort Watauga (Fort Lee), Chief Dragging Canoe led another force of about 350 warriors toward Heaton's Station, located about five miles from what is now Kingsport, Tennessee. Their attack was coordinated to occur at about the same time as Old Abraham's assault on Fort Watauga.

Like their compatriots at Fort Watauga, the settlers near Heaton's station had advance warning of an attack. Captain William Cocke was in charge and led the effort to repair and reinforce a nearby abandoned fort that served as a safe haven for nearby settlers.

Five small militia companies arrived to assist. Some were sent by Colonel William Russell of Virginia and others were sent by Colonel Isaac Shelby, commander of a fort a few miles north of Watauga. After a spirited debate, William Cocke persuaded the other officers to send a force of 170 men under Captain Thompson to leave the fort and intercept the advancing Indians. Thompson's band soon departed toward Long Island Flats near Kingsport.

As they neared their destination, an advance group of twelve scouts encountered Dragging Canoe's war party, and both sides exchanged fire. The scouts quickly retreated to the main body where an immediate council was held that resulted in a decision to return to the fort. After they started their return march, a scout came in to report that the Indians were about to attack from the rear.

Captain Thompson immediately ordered his men to halt and form two battle lines facing the approaching Indians. While the men were moving into position, Lieutenant Robert David spotted a group of Indians trying to outflank them. He quickly moved a small contingent to a nearby slight ridge to block their maneuver. As soon as they fired on the approaching warriors, the Indians returned fire and the battle commenced.

In the beginning, some of Captain Thompson's men panicked and ran back to the fort, but most remained to engage the enemy. The battle was intense and at close range. In the midst of the battle, Dragging Canoe was shot in the thigh and seriously wounded. After witnessing their leader fall, the warriors began to lose spirit.

Later in the battle, there was a fight between Lieutenant Moore and another chief, who was a very large Indian. Moore shot him in the leg, but the wound did not deter him. The chief continued toward Moore, threw his tomahawk and narrowly missed the mark. Moore drew his knife and thrust it at his adversary who grabbed it by the blade. The two combatants embraced in a deadly struggle until Moore threw him to the ground, where the wounded man lay with his hand bleeding profusely. With his opponent finally down, Moore drew his own tomahawk and buried it into the chief's skull, killing him instantly.

After losing another chief, the Indians lost heart and retreated with their wounded. Nearly forty warriors lay dead and many more were wounded, based on the blood trails left by the retreating Indians. The Battle of Long Island Flats lasted only ten minutes, but the ferocity of the frontiersmen convinced the warriors to withdraw before suffering more casualties. There was a brief pursuit, but the scouts returned, fearing an ambush in the difficult, wooded terrain.

When Thompson's men returned to the fort, they were in high spirits. And they had good reason. They soundly defeated the enemy while suffering only five wounded men. All eventually recovered.

Although Colonel Russell had sent some of his Rangers to Heaton's, he had to keep most of his men in Virginia to protect the settlers there. Therefore, his strategic decision to send riflemen men only to Heaton's left Fort Watauga's defenders without any outside help.

The following day at dawn on July 21st, 1776, women from Fort Watauga went out to milk cows left outside to graze in the meadow. As they were milking in the open pasture, they saw Cherokee warriors approaching. The women immediately dropped their buckets and sprinted toward the fort, with the Indians in close pursuit.

Kate Sherrill was the last one back and found the gate closed. Lieutenant John Sevier witnessed her predicament and called to Kate as he reached over the fort's wall and extended his hand to her. With braves close on her heels, Sevier grabbed her extended arm, lifted her up and pulled her over to safety. Four years later, following the death of his first wife, Sevier would end up marrying "Bonnie Kate" Sherrill, the woman he saved.

There were only 40 riflemen defending the fort against over 300 Cherokees. Chief Old Abraham led the attack against Fort Watauga, commanded by Captain James Robertson with Lieutenant John Sevier second in command. The hotly contested battle lasted for several hours. As the men on the parapets bravely fought the hordes of warriors trying to breach the fort's walls, women and children joined in the fray by reloading rifles and passing them up to the besieged riflemen.

Throughout the battle, Robertson and Sevier directed their men to reinforce one wall or another as needed. Their decisive leadership throughout the battle prevented significant breaches of the walls, which could have been disastrous for the defenders. Every rifleman fought ferociously, fearing the cruel atrocities that would be inflicted on everyone inside, including their beloved women and children.

At one point during the battle, Indians set a blockhouse on fire to stop the defenders inside from shooting warriors who were trying to scale the adjacent wall. Robertson's sister, Anne, organized a bucket brigade using boiling wash water to put out the fire and scald the Indians who tried to relight it. Anne Robertson's quick thinking and leadership helped save the day.

Throughout the long battle, men, women and children pitched in to help save the fort. Most were fueled by fear and adrenaline as they pitched in. Each person's frenzied acts of bravery and courage served to strengthen the resolve of others. Everyone knew that their very survival depended on the outcome.

The Indians sustained significant casualties while trying to overrun the fort. By sundown, they retreated, taking most of their dead and wounded with them. Old Abraham kept the fort under siege for three more weeks, but he did not attempt any more full-scale attacks.

Several days after the battle, James Cooper took his son Tucker and a boy named Moore out of the fort to gather wood near the river. Indians ambushed them at the river and the victim's cries for help could be heard at the fort. John Sevier asked permission to lead a relief party to go to their aid, but Captain Robertson refused out of concern about a possible ambush.

James Tucker and his son were killed at the scene, but young Moore was captured and taken to a Cherokee village where he was tortured and burned to death at the stake.

The Portrait of Cherokee Chief displays his shaved head with a scalp lock. The knife in his hand and his grim expression shows the warrior spirit of the Cherokees. That is in contrast with the peace medals around his neck.

Chapter 14

RUSSELL'S RANGERS FIGHT THE RAVEN

A group of Cherokees led by The Raven, a chief who assumed command after Dragging Canoe was wounded in the Battle of Island Flats, headed northeast toward the Virginia settlements immediately after the Indians' defeat at the Battle of Long Island Flats. The Raven proved to be a capable warrior and tactician. Under his command, the Cherokees and their Shawnee allies fought a guerilla war against the Clinch River Valley settlers in southwest Virginia. The attacks were fiercest during July and August of 1776. The warriors split into small bands that scattered throughout the countryside, attacking isolated stations and ambushing unwary settlers who ventured outside the forts to tend crops and livestock. Settlers who ignored warnings to seek refuge in nearby forts made easy targets for roving warriors.

Whenever possible, the Indians killed the men and burned their homes and crops. Sometimes they kidnapped slaves, women, or children and held them for ransom or made them into slaves. Other times, the Indians killed everyone and mutilated their bodies after taking their scalps as war trophies. Unsuspecting settlers who arrived later at the burned out settlement would come across a gruesome scene. Although the Indians had some success with their small-scale raids, they were careful to avoid direct assaults against the larger, well-defended forts. They did so to avoid unnecessary casualties.

The Raven proved no match for Russell's Rangers, who continually patrolled southwest Virginia searching for Indians. Only three years earlier, Russell discovered the mutilated bodies of his son, Boone's son, and the other young men on their way to Kentucky. Afterward, he vowed to avenge their senseless deaths. Therefore, he commanded his rangers with an intensity born from vengeance.

Russell's Rangers were exceptional scouts who knew how and where to look for tracks and other signs of an impending attack. Daniel Boone and Michael Stoner had trained them well while serving in the Clinch River Valley after the massacre at Powell's Valley.

Soon the hunters became the hunted. Russell's Rangers ambushed roving bands of Indians and extracted a terrible toll. By early September, The Raven was unable to replace his casualties and retreated from Virginia.

Later that month, Russell obtained permission from his superior, Colonel Preston, to lead a detachment of militiamen to Long Island in Kingsport. He planned to build a fort there to block further Cherokee incursions northward along the Great Warrior Path, a well-worn trail used by the Cherokees and other tribes. A fort at that location would offer more security for nearby settlers and discourage Cherokee sorties into southwestern Virginia.

An experienced builder, Russell had designed and supervised the construction of Fort Blair after the Battle of Point Pleasant. That fort served as a barrier to large-scale Shawnee incursions from the northwest.

The new fort was planned to provide additional security for Virginians and their neighbors to the south. Russell and his men completed it in just two weeks and named it Fort Patrick Henry in honor of the new revolutionary governor of Virginia; although it was later found to be well south of the Virginia border in what is now East Tennessee. It is unclear whether he knew or cared that the fort was located outside Virginia's boundary. What Russell did know was that he had taken a proactive stance, effectively blocking the Indians' easy access from the south.

By October of 1776 the over-mountain men had dealt the Cherokees and their allies significant defeats in the three main battles: Long Island Flats, Fort Watauga, and the Clinch River Valley

Chapter 15

COLONEL CHRISTIAN'S CAMPAIGN

By the time The Raven's warriors retreated from Virginia, plans were already underway to mount a campaign against the Cherokees. James Robertson and his Watauga neighbors felt betrayed by their Cherokee neighbors. They had dealt with the Indians fairly by first leasing their land and later purchasing it from the tribe, rather than just seizing it. Both sides had pledged friendship and a willingness to be good neighbors.

All of that changed after Charles Robertson intercepted a letter from Indian Superintendent John Stuart to Agent Cameron at Chota. The letter not only revealed British intent, but also Cherokee betrayal. Once the patriots understood the Anaconda Plan, they realized they could play an important part in the War of Independence.

The Wataugans and their Virginia neighbors had three reasons to mount a large-scale military campaign against the Cherokees; revenge, security and the Revolutionary War. They wanted to avenge the Cherokees' betrayal. The settlers' goal was to subjugate the tribe so that everyone could live in peace and security. There was a high spirit of Independence among the frontiersmen, and most were enthusiastic in their willingness to fight the British and their Indian allies in order to win the war.

In early October of 1776, Colonel William Christian of Virginia mustered 1,800 Volunteers from Virginia, North Carolina and the Watauga settlements. William Russell, James Robertson and John Sevier served as officers during the campaign. The expedition departed from the newly completed Fort Patrick Henry in single file. There was a small contingent of cavalry, but most were foot soldiers. As the last soldiers passed through the gate, they were followed by men with a pack train of supplies and a herd of cattle to supply meat for the expedition.

Over a week later, as the army approached the French Broad River, a Cherokee emissary arrived to warn Colonel Christian that a large body of warriors was poised to attack if they dared to cross the river. Colonel Christian listened to the Indian's warning before sending him away. When the army reached the French Broad, Colonel Christian ordered the column to halt and set up camp. That evening, he convened a meeting of his officers to discuss tactics for the next day's battle.

On the other side of the river, the Cherokees were having their own council. According to legend, a white Indian trader named Starr stood up to speak to the assembled warriors. He delivered a prophetic speech to his superstitious Indian companions that profoundly affected them. He told the assembled warriors that the Great Spirit created Indians out of red clay and the whites out of white clay. Furthermore, he said that it was destiny for the white man to rule the world. The orator went on to warn them that if they fought the white army, they would certainly be destroyed. After hearing his prophesy, the superstitious chiefs ordered a retreat, even though they outnumbered the whites that were camped on the other side of the river.

The militia crossed the French Broad at daybreak in a well-planned, two-pronged attack only to discover an abandoned camp. The men were expecting a fierce battle, but once they reached the other side, the only evidence of Indians was traces of smoke floating from their abandoned fire pits.

Colonel Christian and his men were undeterred by the apparent setback. The army cautiously proceeded onward toward the Cherokee villages. One after another, the villages they came upon were deserted. The army burned the villages of Tamotlee, Great Island Town, Neowee, Telico, Chilhowie and Tuskega. There were almost no Indians found in any of the villages. Only two or three braves were encountered and killed during the entire campaign. The few women and children that they encountered were spared.

Once Colonel Christian was convinced that the Cherokees had been sufficiently chastised, he sent out scouts with white flags to find the Indians and arrange for a treaty. The Cherokees were located, and they agreed to meet at Fort Patrick Henry the following May to sign a peace treaty.

After Colonel Christian received positive assurances of peace from the Cherokee chiefs, he marched through their capitol at Chota and other Indian settlements, leaving them unmolested as his army marched back to Fort Patrick Henry.

Upon their arrival at the fort, most of the army was disbanded. A garrison of soldiers remained at the fort to guard against any future hostilities. Their campaign had lasted nearly three months and was believed to be successful because they had incurred no casualties; and the Cherokees agreed to sign a peace treaty.

However, a significant body of Cherokees remained determined to continue fighting. Dragging Canoe, who was seriously wounded at the Battle of Island Flats, fled south with his warriors to Chickamauga Creek near present-day Chattanooga, Tennessee. Some of the warriors who fled Colonel Christian's army and wanted to continue to fight against the whites joined Dragging Canoe's band. His settlement continued to grow as

Tories, outlaws and runaway slaves joined up with him. The renegades under Dragging Canoe soon became known as Chickamaugas to distinguish them from other Cherokees. They would be the whites' formidable foes for many years to come.

Chapter 16

ASSASSINATION OF CHIEF CORNSTALK

The subjugation of the Cherokee Nation severely weakened the British Anaconda Plan for winning the Revolutionary War. The defeat of the Cherokees caused other tribes to rethink their attachment to the British cause. The Creeks initially planned to join the British, but changed their minds after the defeat of their Cherokee neighbors.

The pacification of the Indians on the southwestern frontier would have been accomplished if Chief Dragging Canoe had not rallied his group of warriors who wanted to continue to fight. He and his motley band of Chickamauga renegades continued to stage attacks from their villages along Chickamauga Creek.

To the north, the Shawnees would have been pacified if not for one disastrous event. Chief Cornstalk, Indian leader during the epic Battle of Point Pleasant in 1774, came to Fort Randolph in the spring of 1777 to negotiate a peace treaty for his tribe. Fort Randolph was constructed on the site of the battle by William Russell after the conflict. Cornstalk had learned English and understood the white man's customs from his experiences as a British prisoner for several months during the French and Indian War. At Point Pleasant, he had witnessed the frontiersmen's bravery in battle and recognized them as formidable foes.

Cornstalk believed that further conflict would be disastrous for the Shawnee Nation, and he wanted to negotiate a favorable peace treaty for his people.

Chief Cornstalk and Red Hawk approached Captain Arbuckle, commander of the Fort Randolph garrison, to discuss peace. Captain Arbuckle was worried because the fort was undermanned and running low on supplies. Out of worry about a possible Indian attack, he decided to arrest the Indians and hold them as hostages to prevent further attacks against the fort. Arbuckle was eagerly awaiting the planned arrival of General Hand with additional men and supplies. Unfortunately, General Hand's arrival was delayed due to rapidly evolving engagements in the Revolutionary War.

Due to General Hand's delayed arrival, Cornstalk, Red Hawk and another Shawnee remained prisoners in the fort for over two months. By all accounts, their confinement was lax, and they had amicable relations with their captors. If General Hand had arrived in time, it is likely that Chief Cornstalk and the General would have successfully negotiated a peace treaty.

An unfortunate turn of events precluded that outcome. Two young men named Hamilton and Gilmore left the fort one morning to hunt deer on the opposite side of the Kanawha River. Once there, they were ambushed by Shawnee warriors who killed Gilmore. The attack occurred within earshot of the fort, and a canoe full of men crossed over to rescue Hamilton. The rescuers drove off the Indians and returned in the canoe with Hamilton and the scalped corpse of Gilmore. When they arrived at the fort, the sight of Gilmore's dead body enraged his friends who were aware that Shawnees had massacred Gilmore's family years earlier. As the men's anger intensified, Captain Arbuckle tried to calm and restrain his subordinates.

Soon an angry mob formed and approached Cornstalk's cabin as Captain Arbuckle stood in front of the crowd trying to stop them. At that moment, one of the men ordered Arbuckle to step aside or be shot. That was typical of frontier militia rules; a commander's authority only came from the consent of his subordinates. At that instant Arbuckle realized that he had lost control of his men, and he stepped aside. It was clear that he could do no more to protect the Indians who had come to make peace.

Hearing the commotion, the Indians awaited their fate inside the cabin. Cornstalk's son, Elinipsico, had recently arrived at the fort to check on his father's welfare and was inside with his father, Red Hawk and another Indian. When the angry mob reached their cabin, Cornstalk opened the door. At that moment, seven simultaneous shots rang out, and Cornstalk fell dead in the doorway. The crowd stepped over his body and killed his son where he sat. Red Hawk tried to conceal himself in the chimney, only to be discovered and shot dead in his hiding place. A worse fate awaited the fourth unfortunate Shawnee who was taken outside and cruelly tortured to death by the angry mob.

When word reached the Shawnees that Chief Cornstalk and his companions were murdered by their white captors, they were outraged. Afterward, they allied themselves with the British and vowed to avenge the deaths of their esteemed chief and his fellow Shawnees.

The senseless massacre profoundly affected the course of Indian relations along the Kentucky frontier. If Chief Cornstalk lived to negotiate a peace treaty, a lot of bloodshed would have been avoided during the Revolution, and for many years afterward. The Shawnees would remain implacable foes of the frontiersmen until after the end of the War of 1812.

Chapter 17

WAR ON THE WESTERN FRONTIER

The year 1777, known as "the year of the three sevens", was an eventful year for the frontier patriots. As battles raged in the colonies to the northeast, the frontiersmen were busy with their own Revolutionary War conflicts against Indians and Tories. It was a time of warfare, upheaval and intrigue along the vast western frontier. While most of the rugged settlers living there chose to revolt against the Crown; some remained loyal, causing a certain amount of distrust between neighbors. The Patriots viewed newcomers with suspicion because of the possibility that they might be British spies. All Indians, regardless of tribe, felt the close scrutiny of their white neighbors.

Early that year, William Russell accepted a commission as colonel in the 13th Virginia Regiment. He received orders to lead a force of one hundred men to Fort Pitt, located at what is now Pittsburgh, Pennsylvania. At the time, Fort Pitt was a remote western frontier outpost. Because of the demand for supplies to support soldiers fighting in the east, the fort was a miserable place with meager supplies. The garrison was surrounded by hostile Shawnees and their Indian allies. Little is known of his service there, other than his inability to pacify the Indians. Perhaps his lifelong hatred of Indians after the massacre of his son and others at Powell's valley guided his leadership decisions at Fort Pitt. It is likely that he directed his efforts toward protecting the fort and conducting raids, rather than negotiating peace terms with the Indians.

Colonel Russell commanded Fort Pitt until May 12, 1778 when General George Washington ordered him to take command of the 6th Virginia Regiment, as part of Woodford's Brigade. Colonel Russell subsequently led his troops in battles against the British in several of the former colonies.

George Rogers Clark was a frontier patriot who made enormous contributions to the American Revolution. Following his defeat of Richard Henderson's grand scheme to create the state of Transylvania, Clark became a delegate to the Revolutionary Virginia Legislature. As mentioned earlier, Clark met with Patrick Henry and other leaders and was successful in convincing them to support his plan to incorporate Kentucky into county of Virginia.

On a second trip from Kentucky to Virginia, Clark again met with the legislature and governor to discuss his strategy to eliminate Shawnee attacks against Kentucky settlements. He was commissioned as Lieutenant-Colonel in the Virginia militia on January 2, 1778 and was provided with currency, rifles, powder and lead. His mission was to recruit a small force of about 175 men to attack British forts in the northwest. British control over what is now Indiana allowed them to use the Mississippi River as a supply route for goods and munitions.

Clark was a natural leader who managed to recruit his small force from rugged Virginia and Kentucky frontiersmen. As soon as they were outfitted and supplied, they set out for Fort Pitt. While there, he and Colonel Russell conferred about frontier conditions and the strategy of Clark's campaign. As fellow Virginians, they shared stories about Lord Dunmore's War and the Battle of Point Pleasant. Clark and his men marched out early the next morning amid the cheers from the men of Fort Pitt who urged them on to victory.

In May of 1778, Clark's expedition arrived at the falls of the Ohio in what is now Louisville. From there they proceeded to Fort Kaskaskia on the Mississippi River. With the help of local French inhabitants, they were able to take Fort Kaskaskia and Fort Cahokia, also on the Mississippi. After befriending a local French priest, Father Gibault, Clark used his assistance to take Fort Vincennes on the Wabash River.

The daring exploits of Clark severely disrupted British supplies and influence over the region, and helped prevent the Shawnees from mounting significant attacks against the former colonies. By doing so, Clark dealt another blow to the British Anaconda Plan. Shawnee attacks were limited to frontier settlements and forts in Kentucky. Despite their setbacks, the Shawnees remained staunch British allies.

The notorious Simon Girty, his two brothers, George and James, and Alexander McKee worked as Tory agents among the Shawnees and their Indian allies. Their efforts to drive Boone and the other Kentuckians out of the area were almost successful.

Earlier, under the leadership of George Rogers Clark, Boonesborough, Harrodsburg and Logan's station mustered their Militias on March 5, 1777. Daniel Boone was one of the men selected to serve as an officer in the militia. Quite naturally, he was stationed at Fort Boonesborough where nearby settlers had sought refuge from Indian attacks. Boone's family, including his brother Squire, and his friend Michael Stoner, were among the fort's one hundred or so inhabitants.

On Sunday July 14, 1776 Boone's daughter, Jemima, tired of months of confinement in the fort, persuaded two friends to take a canoe out on the river. She and the Calloway sisters, Betsy and

Fanny, took a dugout canoe and paddled out. Before long, the current drew the canoe nearly five hundred yards downriver. As they attempted to paddle back, they were swept to the bank on the opposite side of the fort. Indian scouts lurking in the bushes spotted the girls and captured them. Without delay, the Indians left with their captives and headed toward the Upper Blue Licks. They were careful to stay off the warrior trail to avoid being followed.

Daniel Boone and others at the fort heard the girls' screams as they were captured. He immediately formed a rescue party. Boone knew the Indian ways and his party was soon on their trail. He had surmised their route and probable destination. Jemima cleverly left pieces of clothing and other signs, knowing that her father would attempt a rescue.

Boone's relentless pursuit through the wilderness finally paid off. The Indians relaxed on the third day, believing that they had eluded any pursuers. If not for Boone's wilderness skills and dogged determination, they would have been correct. That morning, the Indians shot a buffalo to prepare their first good meal in days. As they started building a fire to cook the meat, Boone and the others carefully moved into position by using hand signals to direct their movements without being detected. When everyone was in place, the ambush began. Two Indians were killed in the initial volley and the others were so surprised that they ran off and left their captives behind.

After a brief tearful reunion with the girls, Boone led the party on a rapid retreat back to Boonesborough. When they arrived, everyone was greeted with a joyful welcome. Boone and his party were heroes, and the tale of the daring rescue soon became legendary and enhanced Boone's growing reputation.

The year of the three sevens proved to be a bloody one for Kentuckians. In the preceding December, a Mingo chief named

Pluggy led a raiding party of about fifty warriors who ambushed ten whites who were traveling through the Lower Blue Licks. The Indians killed two of them and took two prisoners, while the rest managed to escape.

A few days later, Pluggy's band of warriors attacked McClelland's Station. The fort's defenders fought off the Indians and killed Pluggy. Unfortunately, Captain John McClelland and several others were killed during the battle, and the station had to be abandoned in early January of 1777.

Enraged by the killing of his ally, Pluggy, Shawnee Chief Blackfish (Chief Cornstalk's successor) was determined to drive the whites out of Kentucky. In early March, Blackfish led a party of seventy warriors who ambushed four white men near Harrodsburg. They killed and mutilated a settler named William Ray, but his brother and the other two men managed to escape. Four other settlers were also killed in separate attacks at about the same time. A day or two later, a group of men were making sugar outside Fort Harrodsburg when they were attacked and killed. Among those killed was a stepson of a settler named Hugh McGary; it was his second stepson killed by Indians in a matter of days.

The following day, Indians burned several cabins outside the fort. After the fighting, one of the dead Indians was found wearing the shirt of Hugh McGary's second slain stepson. McGary was enraged by the discovery, and his mind snapped. With his knife and tomahawk he chopped and slashed the warrior's body to pieces and fed it to the dogs. Onlookers were horrified by the savagery displayed by one of their own, but fearing for their own safety, no one dared to interfere with his fiendish rage. After all, the Indian was already dead and if it made McGary feel better, so be it. That was their rationalization.

On April 24th of the same year, Daniel Goodman and a companion left Fort Boonesborough to tend livestock grazing nearby when Indians attacked. The other man made it back, but Goodman was injured within sight of the Gate. When a warrior attempted to scalp the downed man, Simon Kenton shot and killed the Indian.

Daniel Boone, Michael Stoner and about ten others followed Kenton in pursuit of the Indians. About a hundred Indians were hiding nearby and fired at the pursuers. Soon after, some of the Shawnees quickly maneuvered themselves between the whites and the fort.

Simon Kenton proved to be the hero of the engagement. Having already killed one Indian, he shot another who had Boone in his sights. When the men decided to make a desperate charge against the Indians who stood between them and the fort, Boone was shot in the ankle and fell down. As a brave prepared to finish him off with his tomahawk, Kenton shot him as well. After reaching Boone, Kenton fought off another Indian with the butt of his rifle before lifting Boone on his shoulder and running back to the fort. Michael Stoner was shot in the hip and wrist, but he managed limp back and was the last one in before the gate was closed.

Everyone fought bravely, but Kenton had saved both Goodman and Boone. In Boone's case it was actually three times. The first two Shawnees were about to kill Boone when Kenton shot them, and the final rescue came when he beat another Indian assailant with his rifle butt before carrying Boone back to the fort.

Once inside, Boone made a point of thanking Kenton for saving his life. Boone's and Stoner's wounds were serious, but both men later recovered. Boone was fortunate to avoid a crippling wound because the musket ball had flattened against his ankle bone, rather than shattering it. Due to the scarcity of gunpowder, Indians would often give their muskets a light charge. More than a few frontiersmen received less serious wounds than they otherwise would have because of the light charges.

Afterward, Blackfish and his warriors prowled the area seeking another opportunity to strike. Their next attack took place in May when some settlers were outside Fort Boonesborough planting corn under armed guard. One of the sentries spotted a glint of sunlight reflecting off an Indian gun barrel, allowing him to fire the first shot and alert the others. By the time the skirmish ended, everyone made it back to the fort with only three wounded. However, the Shawnees sustained seven dead due to the frontiersmen's superior marksmanship.

In September of 1777, the settlers at Fort Boonesborough received some relief when militia volunteers arrived from Yadkin, North Carolina and Watauga. Indian scouts observed their arrival, and the Shawnees decided to abandon their siege. They had already suffered a number of casualties and they wanted to return to their villages before winter.

The year of the three sevens was also a harrowing year for the Watauga settlers. They were threatened by attacks from renegade Indians, Tory agitators and common criminals who had migrated there to prey on the isolated settlers. James Robertson and John Sevier organized committees of safety and sent out scouts to roam the area searching for troublemakers. While the scouts were not entirely successful, whenever miscreants were located and apprehended, justice was swift. Sometimes the scouts would kill offenders outright or return them for trial. Convictions for capital offences were usually followed by a swift execution. Judges would order that the condemned person be hung or shot immediately after the conviction. There were no appeals.

The authorities used pillories to whip, brand or slice off the ears of the offenders who were convicted of lesser crimes.

Captured Tories were forced to choose between being executed or signing a pledge of allegiance to the Revolution. Not surprisingly, most decided to sign the pledge.

On July 10, 1777, a large band of renegade Indians shot and scalped Frederick Calvert. Captain James Robertson and nine men pursued the Indians and took back some horses they stole from Calvert. They had nearly made it back home when they found themselves surrounded by Indians, and vastly outnumbered. Robertson quickly ordered his men to charge, and they successfully broke through the Indian line. Two of his men were wounded and some of the horses were shot, but all of the men made it back alive.

On July 20, 1777, the over-hill Cherokees met with representatives of Virginia and North Carolina at Fort Patrick Henry to sign a formal peace treaty that they had agreed to during Colonel Christian's campaign. Colonel Anthony Campbell, Isaac Shelby, Captain James Robertson and Lieutenant John Sevier were among the many frontier representatives who attended. The Raven, who had recently been elevated to supreme chief, led the delegation of Cherokees. It was a colorful affair with some of the militia officers wearing their uniforms and swords, and the frontiersmen dressed in buckskins. The Chiefs and braves were dressed in their finest attire, displaying intricate bead-work on their otter pelt-trimmed buckskins. They wore feathers, necklaces and silver earrings. The whites displayed flags, banners and other accoutrements which were intended as a show of authority that was meant to impress the defeated Cherokees.

During the negotiations, the vanquished Cherokees agreed to cede some of their lands to North Carolina, and they pledged to remain at peace. Ominously, neither Dragging-Canoe nor any of his renegade followers came to the treaty grounds. His motley band of Cherokees, Tories, escaped slaves and white outlaws remained at their Chickamauga hideouts. From then on, his hostile band was collectively known as Chickamaugas as a way of distinguishing them from the Cherokees who had opted for peace (at least for awhile).

James Robertson learned the language and customs of the Cherokees and had earned their trust. Governor Richard Caswell observed Robertson's exceptional abilities during the treaty negotiations and decided to offer him an appointment to be Superintendent of Indian Affairs for North Carolina. Robertson accepted the assignment on July 27, 1777 and immediately established a part-time residence in the Cherokee capital at Chota, located about 25 miles up the Tennessee River from present-day Knoxville. Living among the Cherokees helped him maintain the peace by keeping out outside agitators (such as Tory agents and Indians from hostile northern tribes who would want the Cherokees to re-join their cause).

In November of 1777, the North Carolina legislature enacted legislation creating the Washington District (in honor of General George Washington) that encompassed the Watauga settlements in what is today East Tennessee. The legislation made allowances for land that was already settled and it established favorable terms for new settlers. It was meant to encourage western expansion by populating the lands that the Cherokees had ceded in the treaty.

Portrait of an Elderly Daniel Boone with his Rifle and Dog.

Chapter 18

PEACEKEEPING

For the next two years, the Watauga frontier was relatively free from Indian warfare, due to the 1777 Treaty of Long Island. From the south, Dragging-Canoe's Chickamaguas ventured north and made sporadic raids against some of the more isolated farms, stealing horses and livestock and sometimes murdering or kidnapping innocent settlers. Sometimes white criminals who fled justice in North Carolina were just as predatory and bloodthirsty as the occasional roving band of Chickamaugas.

James Robertson, John Sevier and other leaders remained busy with infrequent Indian raids and law enforcement, but the treaty with the Cherokees gave the whites an advantage. Their numbers swelled due to a large influx of refugees escaping the Revolution and turmoil in the former colonies. Others came with the simple goal of acquiring their own land to start a new life. In addition to his responsibilities as Indian Agent for the Cherokees, Robertson served as Justice of the Peace for the over-mountain settlements.

When North Carolina established the Washington District in 1777, there was a framework for legitimizing land claims. The legislation created legal guidelines for earlier settlers to record their existing land claims, and provisions for newcomers to record their claims as well.

Robertson formed scouting parties to patrol the region looking for signs of trouble, and to track down miscreants and bring them to justice. Criminals who were apprehended received fair trials and those who were found guilty got harsh frontier punishment.

His relative, Charles Robertson, served as chairman of the Washington District, and the first meeting of the leaders was held in his cabin at Jonesboro.

John Sevier was clerk for the Washington District and his brother, Valentine, was elected sheriff. A few years earlier, John Sevier had purchased land south of Watauga on the Nolichucky River from Jacob Brown. Thereafter, Sevier's compatriots nicknamed him, "Nolichucky Jack".

James Robertson developed lifelong friendships with the Sevier brothers out of respect for their intelligence, likeability and courage. They fought bravely together at the Battle of Point Pleasant and at the Battle of Fort Watauga. Later, the three served together during Colonel William Christian's campaign against the Cherokees. There were numerous other skirmishes and events that bonded their friendships.

In late 1777, James Robertson moved his residence to what is now Rogersville, Tennessee. He and his family erected a station at the mouth of Big Creek. Their station was a two-story log house with shooting ports built into the walls and the second story floor to make it highly defensible in the event of an Indian attack. That type of highly defensible structure saved many frontiersmen living in outlying locations from being slaughtered during Indian attacks.

Whenever Robertson was away performing his duties, he could always depend on his trustworthy brothers, Elijah and Mark, to protect his wife, Charlotte, and their children. At that time, he and Charlotte had four children. Jonathan, age 9, was the oldest, next was James, age 7, followed by Delilah, age 5, and

Peyton, 3. In-laws from his wife's family, the Reeves, also lived with them.

Even though the new station was isolated, there were always enough men there to provide a good defense. Robertson selected that location because it was closer to Chota where he was serving as Indian Agent. As previously stated, there was a legitimate concern that renegade Shawnees, their Indian allies, or Tory agents might come to incite the Cherokees once again. The new location made it easier to intercept troublemakers and maintain close contact with Cherokee leaders.

During Robertson's time as Indian Agent, the Cherokees remained peaceful while under his supervision. He had a unique gift for dealing with Indians. Perhaps it was because he viewed them as fellow human beings, rather than sub-human savages worthy of extermination, as was the case with many whites during that era. His Presbyterian beliefs guided him in his contacts with all Indians, regardless of tribe. He had acquainted himself with the Cherokee language and customs through many earlier interactions. Soon after he settled at Watauga, he had successfully negotiated the lease of Indian lands. Later, his intervention and careful diplomacy succeeded in placating the Cherokees after the unfortunate murder of Cherokee Billy. Lastly, he actively participated in the 1777 Treaty of Long Island negotiations at Fort Patrick Henry that resulted in his appointment as Indian Agent.

From the Cherokee perspective, those interactions gave them the opportunity to measure Robertson as a man. They found him to be an even-tempered person who carefully chose his words. They trusted him and believed what he said. He kept his word and seldom, if ever, made promises he could not keep. It is recorded that the old chief, Oconostota, once said of James Robertson, "He has winning ways and makes no fuss".

The new supreme chief, The Raven, called Robertson "Brother" and trusted him to be fair and just. On one occasion, Robertson returned horses that white outlaws had stolen from the Cherokees. Because of his acts of kindness and fairness, he gradually earned their respect and admiration. Under his careful guidance and watchful eye, the over-hill Cherokees remained at peace.

The pacification of the Cherokees, followed by Agent Robertson's skillful supervision to maintain the peace, dealt another blow to the British Anaconda Plan by allowing the patriots from Virginia, the Carolinas and Georgia to battle the Redcoats without having to fight the Indians as well.

Chapter 19

THE FRENCH LICK

As a result of the lobbying of George Rogers Clark and Patrick Henry, Virginia invalidated Richard Henderson's Transylvania Purchase. Most of that purchase encompassed lands that were subsequently incorporated into that state as the County of Kentucky. For his efforts, Virginia granted Henderson 20,000 acres in Kentucky. All that remained of his grand land scheme was the lesser portion of lands purchased from the Cherokees that were located in what is now Middle Tennessee. Because of the setback in Kentucky, Henderson sought to lay claim to the Tennessee portion of the Transylvania Purchase to avoid losing it as well. Henderson believed that he could still salvage what remained of his 1775 treaty purchase at Sycamore Shoals because the remainder was south of Virginia's jurisdictional authority.

His first frontier land scout, Daniel Boone, stayed in Kentucky and was unavailable to continue working as his agent. Boone's friend, James Robertson, seemed like a good replacement. Robertson and Henderson had become acquainted during the Sycamore Shoals Treaty negotiations, and they subsequently renewed their friendship at Fort Patrick Henry during the negotiations for the Long Island Treaty of 1777. John Donelson also came to help negotiate the treaty as a representative of Virginia. While the details are unclear, it is believed that while the three men were together at Long Island, preliminary discussions took place regarding the establishment of a settlement at the French Lick (also known as the Great Salt Lick).

Located in what is now Nashville, the French Lick was the site of a long-abandoned French Indian trading post on the Cumberland River. Daniel Boone and other long-hunters had visited there during their hunting expeditions in the late 1760's. Boone and his companions returned with glowing accounts of vast herds of buffalo, plentiful deer, bear and other game.

Adding to the mystery of the region were stories of a vanished race of people who had cultivated large areas, leaving behind rock walls surrounding the fields and stone foundations of deserted dwellings near springs. There were also many unusual above-ground ancient burials covered in thick layers of moss.

As in Kentucky during the 1700's, middle Tennessee had no permanent Indian settlements. It served as a vast game reserve used by several Indian tribes who visited the area to hunt during spring, summer and fall. In winter, the Indians would return to their distant villages to seek shelter from the cold weather and enjoy the primitive comforts in their villages. Fires warmed their homes and they were able to feed their families with food stores previously collected for the winter.

Chickasaw Indians came from the west near what is now Memphis to hunt at the French Lick and other parts of middle Tennessee. The Choctaw hunters migrated from the southwest in what is now Mississippi; while Creek hunters came from present-day Alabama. The Cherokees residing in what is now East Tennessee visited the region from the east. There was usually an uneasy truce between hunting parties from different tribes. The Chickasaws were the dominant tribe among those who hunted there. Earlier, they had gone to war against the Cherokees, Shawnees and their allies, and had soundly defeated them. Following their victory, the Chickasaws were magnanimous in allowing the vanquished tribes to resume hunting there under an uneasy truce.

That was the state of affairs in the region when Robertson, Henderson and Donelson were formulating plans to establish a settlement there. The French Lick seemed to be an ideal spot because of its location on the banks of the navigable Cumberland River. The site would be well suited for the shipment of goods to and from the settlement. That was a critical consideration because the French Lick was completely isolated, and was over two hundred miles west of the nearest settlement at Jonesborough.

Each of the three men had his own reasons for wanting to establish the settlement. Henderson and Donelson were experienced land speculators and they wanted to open land offices. Henderson's Transylvania Purchase included Middle Tennessee lands east of the Cumberland River. There is some evidence suggesting that Donelson's primary interest was in eventually starting a settlement at Muscle Shoals, near the Big Bend of the Tennessee River in what is now Alabama. That area was south of Henderson's Purchase. Because the land on the west side of the Cumberland River was just outside the Transylvania Purchase, Robertson could settle there without concern about encroaching on Henderson's land claim.

Of the three, there is ample evidence to suggest that Robertson's motives were more complex, and perhaps loftier, than his two compatriots. There is no doubt that he wanted a better life for himself and his family. Subsequent actions during his lifetime clearly demonstrate that the acquisition of wealth, while of some importance to him, was not his primary motive. Understanding him within the context of his Scotch-Irish Presbyterian upbringing allows a greater appreciation for his underlying motives.

James Robertson was an early advocate and believer in the philosophy of Manifest Destiny. Born in Virginia and living there during most of his early life before moving to North Carolina, he was aware that Virginia's original Colonial Charter extended all the way to the Pacific Ocean. Even at that early date, the British Crown envisioned an audacious westward expansion. Therefore, Robertson's belief in Manifest Destiny, combined with his religious philosophy of Divine Guidance and Free Will, gave him the certitude and confidence needed to undertake such an ambitious and dangerous enterprise. Like many of his contemporaries, he advocated settling the wilderness and sharing western civilization with its inhabitants. Robertson liked and respected most Indians and he devoted much of his life trying to assist them in adapting to the benefits of the white culture; while also trying to protect them from some its shortcomings.

Chapter 20

MAKING PLANS

The collaboration between James Robertson, Richard Henderson and John Donelson continued from 1777 to 1779 as they put together their plans to establish a settlement at the French Lick. Each man had abilities, experiences and assets that would be needed for the project.

The youngest, James Robertson, had become an exceptional woodsman, Indian fighter and negotiator since he crossed the mountains with Daniel Boone in 1769. The leadership and judicial experience he gained at Watauga would be useful for the new settlement. His surveying skills would be used to mark land boundaries. Additionally, Robertson was an excellent horseman, experienced farmer and all-around capable person.

Richard Henderson was a retired North Carolina judge, land speculator and surveyor. He was well-educated for that time, and was an exceptional writer and orator. Whenever he spoke, he could be very passionate, as well as persuasive. His well-honed leadership abilities came from prior experience as a militia officer before the outbreak of the Revolution.

Like Henderson, John Donelson was an educated middle-aged man who was experienced in land speculation and surveying. A former militia officer, he was well-known and had connections to many of the leading figures in his home state of Virginia.

Of the three, Henderson probably had the most available assets to pay costs associated with their undertaking. Robertson and Donelson undoubtedly made significant contributions as well since each had acquired a modest level of prosperity. Donelson was wealthy before the Revolution, but afterward had fallen on hard times. To a lesser extent, Henderson experienced significant losses due to the collapse of the Kentucky portion of his Transylvania Purchase.

The three men complemented each other in ways that made them collectively well-suited for the project. Their plans began to coalesce in early 1778 after continually discussing various ideas and strategies. The French Lick was located over 200 miles west of civilization; and the distance required comprehensive logistics for transporting over 300 people, their possessions, livestock, tools and provisions that were needed to settle in such a remote location.

Eventually, they decided that a land journey would be too difficult for women, children and the elderly. They would be transported by boats along with additional supplies. The boats would follow a series of rivers leading to their destination. Several men and older boys would pilot the boats and serve as armed guards to protect the flotilla. The winding river route of over one thousand miles would take them on five different rivers before reaching the French Lick.

Most of the men and older boys would travel by land. Their journey would begin at the Wilderness Road made by Daniel Boone and his axmen in 1775 on their way colonize Kentucky.

After entering Kentucky, Robertson's expedition would travel over two hundred miles west through the wilderness until reaching a point above the French Lick. From there, they would head south to the French Lick.

Robertson would lead the land expedition and Donelson was to command the river flotilla. Each would soon demonstrate that he was well-suited for the challenges that lay ahead.

Before either group could depart, Robertson needed to lead a small advance group overland to the French Lick. They were to blaze a good trail on their way, and a plant a crop of corn after their arrival to sustain the main body of colonists who would come later along the same route.

Chapter 21

THE JOURNEY

There was no choice for James Robertson. He could not resettle at the French Lick and continue his duties as Cherokee Indian Agent. There would be hundreds of miles of wilderness between him and the tribal leaders who needed his guidance and supervision. Regular interactions with the Indians and careful monitoring were essential to maintaining the peace. Without it, warfare between the Cherokees and whites would likely resume. Keeping the peace with the tribe was no easy task. The Cherokees had a deeply ingrained cultural tradition of warfare that had existed for centuries. Robertson understood that as well as anyone.

The only choice was a timely resignation to allow the North Carolina governor and assembly sufficient time to appoint a qualified successor. That would also give Robertson enough time to introduce the new Agent to the Indians and provide for a smooth transition. With that in mind, he submitted his formal resignation in December of 1778.

In the early spring of 1779, James Robertson, his slave named Robert, Mark Robertson, George Freeland, William Neely, Edward Swanson, James Hanly, Zachariah White and William Overall left Watauga on an expedition to the French Lick to make advance preparations for the arrival of the main body of settlers.

They rode out on horseback with a few pack horses loaded with seed corn, foodstuffs and implements needed for the trip and for use after their arrival.

The men started out along the Wilderness Road and rode through the Cumberland Gap into Kentucky. Travel was easy as they rode along the road that Boone had widened enough to accommodate the wagons of settlers headed into Kentucky.

Once they arrived in Kentucky, the pack train turned westward where there were no roads or man-made trails. The terrain also changed after they emerged from the forested mountains. In Kentucky the landscape was relatively flat, punctuated by soft rolling hills. Much of the ground was covered with vast canebrakes over ten feet tall. Whenever possible, they followed buffalo trails. When those were not available, they were forced to cut paths through the dense cane.

On most days they traveled from sunrise until sunset through the difficult terrain. Whenever possible, they camped near a spring or creek where fresh water and game were plentiful. Buffalo, elk, deer, bear and turkeys provided an abundant supply fresh meat that could be shot and prepared as needed. Some of the meat was roasted over an open fire. Thin slices of meat were jerked (dried) to carry and eat during the day. Whenever they encountered signs of Indians or anticipated possible danger, they avoided a fire for cooking and resorted to a "cold camp" with a supper of parched corn and jerky.

They slept next to their loaded rifles with knives and tomahawks close at hand, while leaving one man awake to guard against Indian attacks. The seasoned frontiersmen were capable of defending against a raiding party several times their number. They were expert marksmen with their Deckard rifles; while Indians were usually armed with less accurate English or Spanish smooth-bore trade muskets.

Aside from the physically demanding trail blazing, they made their way west along a good portion of southern Kentucky without any serious incidents. Then they turned south toward the French Lick.

When the men finally arrived, they saw great herds of buffalo congregated around the immense salt lick for which the area was named. There was no time for leisure. Robertson immediately began supervising the work that needed to be done. Everyone pitched in while they planted a large plot of corn and felled trees to build fences to keep out roaming animals. They constructed corn cribs and lean-tos for shelter.

Robertson scouted the area for the suitable locations for forts and stations. He selected a place for himself that became known as the Bluffs. The Bluffs was so named because of its location at spring just overlooking the Cumberland River. The location offered fresh water, proximity to the river for navigation and a commanding view to defend against Indian attacks.

After completing most of the necessary tasks for the settlers' arrival, two men remained behind to protect the corn crop and complete other assigned chores.

Some of the men returned along the previously forged trail. Robertson, his slave Robert, and his brother Mark headed north by river in a pirogue hollowed out from the trunk of a poplar tree. Their destination was Kaskaskia in the Illinois country.

Robertson wanted to confer with George Rogers Clark about buying his "cabin rights" (land grants) received for prior military service. The grants were for land in Kentucky, a western county of Virginia. Robertson, Henderson and Donelson mistakenly believed part of the French Lick would be in Virginia, pending the completion of a western survey of the boundary between Kentucky County, Virginia and western North Carolina (present-day Tennessee). All three preferred to be under the jurisdiction of Virginia, rather than North Carolina because Virginia was more prosperous and had a better style of government.

In Kaskaskia, Robertson purchased a herd of Spanish mares to be used for the settlers as mounts and pack horses for the expedition to the French Lick. Because the herd was too large for three men, Robertson hired two men to help them drive the horses to Watauga. It was no small undertaking. If they had encountered Indians along the way, the Indians would likely have attempted to kill the men and steal their horses. Fortunately, the final leg of their return trip to Watauga was uneventful, and they returned unscathed.

Chapter 22

MANIFEST DESTINY

The pack train was over a mile long, with over two hundred riders and their pack horses heading north along the Wilderness Road toward Kentucky. James Robertson was in the lead while his 11-year-old son, Jonathan, and other boys herded sheep and cattle in the rear. The line moved forward slowly amid the sound of human voices intermingled with snorts from the horses and the occasional bleating sheep and mooing cattle. Adding to the noise was the sound of chickens and other fowl protesting their confinement in small wooden cages tied to packs on the horses.

The size of the group eliminated any possibility of stealthy movement. Roving bands of Indians who might encounter such a large group would likely evade it to avoid any sort of conflict. At least that was the hope of Robertson and his men.

When they departed Watauga in November of 1779, the men and boys said good-bye to the women, children and elderly who would depart later by boat. Everyone hoped to safely reunite at the French Lick.

By the time the pack train traversed the Cumberland Gap and headed westward, the weather turned cold. In fact, the coldest winter of the century was setting in. Deep snow and bone chilling cold made their travel slow and difficult. Blankets or coats made from buffalo hides were their only real protection from the wind and snow. It was so cold that a few of the livestock froze to death after bedding down at night.

Despite the hardships, Robertson led the group steadily toward their destination. When they finally arrived at the French Lick on Christmas Day, they found the Cumberland River frozen over so solid that they were able to drive their livestock over the surface. As they crossed, the sound of the ice cracking under the weight of the animals' hooves pierced the frigid air. When they reached the other side, their long, arduous journey had ended. The men paused there to give thanks to the Lord for their safe arrival.

More settlers arrived at the French Lick than had departed Watauga because of a chance encounter with John Rains in Kentucky. Rains was leading a group of settlers who were planning to relocate in Kentucky before Robertson convinced them to join his party heading to the French Lick.

The number of new arrivals was enhanced even more by a separate group of settlers led by the intrepid long-hunter, Kasper Mansker. Mansker had previously explored the area during earlier hunting expeditions. The exact number of new arrivals is unknown, but there were nearly three hundred men and boys who made the long journey.

There was no time for rest. Despite the extremely cold weather, the immigrants began to spread out in groups searching for suitable locations for their homesteads.

After selecting a place to settle, the hard work began as the frontiersmen felled trees to erect stations for shelter and defense. Despite the harsh weather, there was a lot of pressure to complete as much work as possible in preparation for the arrival of the women, children and others who were expected to arrive with the fleet of boats commanded by John Donelson.

Chapter 23

THE VOYAGE

On December 22, 1779, the loved ones that were left behind gathered at Long Island on the Holston River. Wives, children, slaves and the elderly brought their meager possessions. A small fleet of flat-bottom boats, pirogues and canoes awaited them. John Donelson, leader of the voyage, supervised the loading of passengers, their possessions, livestock, fowl and barrels packed with foodstuffs. A hand-picked group of men were doing most of the physical labor. James Robertson and the men who departed for the French Lick a month earlier entrusted the safety and welfare of their relatives to Donelson and his men. As it would turn out, their trust was well-placed.

Donelson made sure that Robertson's wife, children and other relatives joined his family aboard the Adventure, the largest boat in the fleet. It was big enough to accommodate several families.

The weather was bitter cold, but there was an air of excitement as each of the vessels was pushed off, allowing the current to draw it downriver. However, their enthusiasm soon subsided when several of the boats grounded on immense slabs of ice that had formed a few miles downriver from where they launched. They were forced to remain there for nearly two months waiting for the ice to melt. When it finally did, they pushed off again.

Another flotilla commanded by John Blackmore came down the Clinch River and joined Donelson's at the mouth of Cloud's Creek. It was good to have them along because a larger group would afford better security for everyone.

What followed was an epic river voyage of over a thousand miles. It was a winding route along several rivers; first down the Holston and Tennessee, then up the Ohio and down the Cumberland. They journeyed as far south as present-day Alabama and as far north as Kentucky, before heading south to the French Lick.

Fortunately, John Donelson kept a journal to record events along the way. It would prove to be one of the most harrowing river voyages in American History. The complete journal is presented here:

> JOURNAL OF A VOYAGE, intended by God's permission, in the good boat Adventure, from Fort Patrick Henry, to the French Salt Springs on Cumberland River, kept by John Donelson.
>
> December 22, 1779 – Took our departure from the fort, and fell down the river to the mouth of Reedy Creek, where we were stopped by the fall of water and most excessive hard frost; and after much delay, and many difficulties, we arrived at the mouth of Cloud's Creek on Sunday evening, the 20th February, 1780, where we lay by until Sunday, the 27th when we took our departure with sundry other vessels bound for the same voyage, and on the same day struck the Poor Valley Shoal, together with Mr. Boyd and Mr. Rounsifer, on which shoal, together with Mr. Boyd and Mr. Rounsifer, on which shoal we lay that afternoon and succeeding night in much distress.
>
> Monday, February 28th, 1780 – in the morning, the water rising, we got off the shoal, after landing thirty persons to

lighten our boat. In attempting to land on an island, received some damage, and lost sundry articles, and came to camp on the south shore, where we joined sundry other vessels also bound down.

Tuesday, February 29th, 1780 – Proceeded down the river and camped on the north shore, the afternoon and following day proving rainy.

Wednesday, March 1st – Proceeded on and camped on the south shore, nothing happening that day remarkable.

March 2nd – Rain about half the day; passed the mouth of French Broad River, and about 12o'clock Mr. Henry's boat being driven on the point by the force of the current was sunk, the Whole cargo much damaged and the crew's lives much endangered, which occasioned the whole fleet to put on shore and go to their assistance, but with much difficulty bailed her, in order to take in her cargo again. The same afternoon Reuben Harrison went out a hunting and did not return that night, though many guns were fired to fetch him in.

Friday, 3rd – Early in the mourning fired a four-pounder for the lost man, sent out sundry persons to search the woods for him, firing many guns that day and the succeeding night, but all without success, to the great grief of his parents and fellow travelers.

Saturday, 4th – Proceeded on our voyage, leaving old Mr. Harrison with some other vessels to make further search for his lost son; about ten o'clock the same day found him a considerable distance down the river, where Mr. Belew took him on board his boat. At 3 o'clock, P.M. passed the mouth of Tennessee River, and camped on the south shore, about ten miles below the mouth of Tennessee.

Sunday, 5th – Cast off and got under way before sunrise; 12 o'clock passed the mouth of Clinch; at 12 o'clock, M. came up with the Clinch River Company, whom we joined and camped, the evening providing rainy.

Monday, 6th – Got under way before sunrise; the morning proving very foggy, many of the fleet were much bogged- about 10 o'clock lay by for them; when collected, proceeded down. Camped on the north shore, where Capt. Hutching's negro man died, being much frosted in his feet and legs, of which he died.

Tuesday, 7th – Got under way very early, the day proving very windy, a S.S.W., and the river being wide occasioned a high sea insomuch that some of the smaller crafts were in danger; therefore, came to, at the uppermost Chicamauga Town, which was then evacuated, where we lay by that afternoon and camped that night. The wife of Ephraim Peyton was here delivered a child. Mr. Peyton has gone through by land with Capt. Robertson.

Wednesday, 8th – Cast off at 10 o'clock, and proceed down to an Indian village, which was inhabited, on the south of the river; they insisted on us to "come ashore," called us brothers, and showed other signs of friendship, insomuch that Mr. John Caffrey and my son then on board took a canoe which I had in tow, and were crossing over to them, the rest of the fleet having landed on the opposite shore. After they had gone some distance, a half-breed, who called himself Archy Coody, with several other Indians, jumped into a canoe, met them, and advised them to return to the boat, which they did, together with Coody and several other canoes which left the shore and followed directly after him. They appeared to be friendly. After distributing some presents among them, with which they seemed much pleased, we observed a number of Indians on the other side embarking in their canoes, armed and painted with red and black. Coody immediately made signs to his companions, ordering them to quit the boat, which they did, himself and another Indian remaining with us and telling us to move off instantly. We had not gone far before we discovered a number of Indians armed and painted proceeding down the river, as it were to intercept us. Coody, the half-breed and his companion, sailed with us for some time, and telling us that we had passed all the towns and were out of danger, left us. But we had not gone far until we had come in sight of another town, situated likewise on the south side of the river, nearly opposite a small island. Here they again invited us to come on shore, called us brothers, and observing the boats standing off for the opposite channel, told us that "their side of the river was better for boats to pass." And here we must regret the unfortunate death of young Mr. Payne, on board Capt. Blackmore's boat, who was mortally wounded by reason of the boat running too near the northern shore opposite the town, where some of the enemy lay concealed, and the more tragical misfortune of poor Stuart, his family and friends to the number of twenty-eight. This man had embarked with us for the Western country, but his family being diseased with the small pox, it was agreed upon him and the company that he should keep at some distance in the rear, for fear of the infection spreading, and he was warned each night when the encampment should take place by the sound of a horn. After we had passed the town, the Indians having now collected to a considerable number, observing his helpless situation, singled off from the rest of the fleet, intercepted him and killed and took prisoners the whole crew, to the grief of the whole company, uncertain how soon they might share the same fate; their cries were distinctly heard by those boats in the rear.

We still perceived them marching down the river in considerable bodies, keeping pace with us until the Cumberland Mountain withdrew them from our sight, when we were in hopes we had escaped them. We were now arrived at the place called the Whirl or Suck, where the river is compressed within less than half its common width above, by the Cumberland Mountain, which juts in on both sides. In passing through the upper part of these narrows, at a place described by Coody, which he termed the "boiling pot," a trivial accident had nearly ruined the expedition. One of the company, John Cotton, who was moving down in a large canoe, had attached it to Robert Cartwright's boat, into which he and his family had gone for safety. The canoe was here overturned, and the little cargo lost. The company pitying his distress, concluded to halt and assist him in recovering his property. They had landed on the northern shore at a level spot, and were going up to the place, when the Indians, to our astonishment, appeared immediately over us on the opposite cliffs, and commenced firing down upon us, which occasioned a precipitate retreat to the boats. We immediately moved off, the Indians lining the bluffs along continued their fire from the heights on our boats below, without doing any other injury than wounding four slightly. Jenning's boat is missing.

We have now passed through the Whirl. The river widens with a placid and gentle current; and all the company appear to be in safety except the family of Jonathan Jennings, whose boat ran on a large rock, projecting out from the northern shore, and partly immersed in water immediately at the Whirl, where we were compelled to leave them, perhaps to be slaughtered by their merciless enemies. Continued to sail on that day and floated through the following night.

Thursday, 9th – Proceeded on our journey, nothing happening worth attention to-day; floated till about midnight, and encamped on the northern shore.

Friday, 10th – This morning about 4 o'clock we were surprised by the cries of "help poor Jennings," at some distance in the rear. He had discovered us by our fires, and came up in the most wretched condition. He states, that as soon as the Indians discovered his situation, they turned their whole attention to him, and kept up a most galling fire at his boat. He ordered his wife, a son nearly grown, a young man who accompanied them, and his negro man and woman, to throw all his goods into the river, to lighten their boat for the purpose of getting her off, himself returning their fire as well as he could, being a good soldier and an excellent marksman. But before they had accomplished their object, his son, the young man and the negro, jumped out of the boat and left them. He thinks the young man and the negro were wounded before they left the boat. Mrs. Jennings, however, and the negro woman, succeeded in unloading the boat, but chiefly by the exertions of Mrs. Jennings, who got out of the boat and shoved her off, but was near falling a victim to her own intrepidity on account of the boat starting so suddenly as soon as loosened from the rock. Upon examination, he appears to have made a wonderful escape, for his boat is pierced in numberless places with bullets. It is to be remarked, that Mrs. Peyton, who was the night before delivered of an infant, which was unfortunately killed upon the hurry and confusion consequent upon such a disaster, assisted them, being frequently exposed to wet and cold then and afterwards, and that her health appears to be good at this time, and I think and hope she will do well. Their clothes were very much cut with bullets, especially Mrs. Jennings'.

Saturday, 11th – Got under way after having distributed the family of Mrs. Jennings in the other boats. Rowed on quietly that day, and encamped for the night on the north shore.

Sunday, 12th – Set out, and after a few hours' sailing we heard the crowing of cocks, and soon came within view of the town; here they fired on us again without doing any injury.

After running until about 10 o'clock, came in sight of Muscle Shoals. Halted on the northern shore at the appearance of the shoals, in order to search for the signs Capt. James Robertson was to make for us at that place. He set out from Holston early in the fall of 1779, was to proceed by the way of Kentucky to the Big Salt Lick on Cumberland River, with several others in company, was to come across from the Big Salt Lick to upper end of the shoals, there to make such signs that we might know he had been there, and that it was practicable for us to go across by land. But to our great mortification we can find none-from which we conclude that it would not be prudent to make the attempt, and are determined, knowing ourselves to be in such imminent danger, to pursue our journey down the river. After trimming our boats in the best manner possible, we ran through the shoals before night. When we approached them, they had a dreadful appearance to those who had never been seen them before. The water being high made a terrible roaring, which could be heard at some distance among the drift-wood heaped frightfully upon the points of the islands, the current running in every possible direction. Here we did not know how soon we should be dashed to pieces, and all our troubles ended at once. Our boats frequently dragged on the bottom, and appeared constantly in danger of striking. They warped as much as in a rough sea. But by the hand of Providence, we are now preserved from this danger also. I know not the length of this wonderful shoal; it had been represented to me to be 25 or 30 miles. If so, we must have descended very rapidly, as indeed we did, for we passed it in about three hours. Came to, and camped on the northern shore, not far below the shoals, for the night.

Monday, 13th – Set out early in the morning and made a good run that day.

Tuesday, 14th – Set out early. On this day two boats approaching too near the shore, were fired on by the Indians. Five of the crew were wounded, but not dangerously. Came to camp at night near the mouth of a creek. After kindling fires and preparing for rest, the company were alarmed, on account of the incessant barking our dogs kept up; taking it for granted that the Indians were attempting to surprise us, we retreated to the boats; fell down the river about a mile and encamped on the other shore. In the morning, I prevailed on Mr. Caffrey and my son to cross below in a canoe, and return to the place; which they did, and found an African negro we had left in the hurry, asleep by one of the fires. The voyagers returned and collected their utensils which had been left.

Wednesday, 15th – Got under way and moved on peaceably the five following days, when we arrived at the mouth of the Tennessee on Monday, the 20th, and landed on the lower point immediately on the bank of the Ohio. Our situation here is truly disagreeable. The river is very high, and the current rapid, our boats not constructed for the purpose of stemming a rapid stream, our provision exhausted, the crews almost worn down with hunger and fatigue, and know not what distance we have to go, or what time it will take us to our place of destination. The scene is rendered still more melancholy, as several boats will not attempt to ascend the rapid current. Some intend to descend the Mississippi to Natchez; others are bound for the Illinois–among the rest my son-in-law and daughter. We now part, perhaps to meet no more, for I am determined to pursue my course, happen what will.

Tuesday, 21st – Set out, and on this day labored very hard and got but a little way; camped on the south bank of the

Ohio. Passed the two following days as the former, suffering much from hunger and fatigue.

Friday, 24th – About 3 o'clock came to the mouth of a river which I thought was the Cumberland. Some of the company declared it could not be-it was much smaller than was expected. But I never heard of any river running in between the Cumberland and Tennessee. It appeared to flow with a gentle current. We determined, however, to make the trial, pushed up some distance and encamped for the night.

Saturday, 25th – Today we are much encouraged; the river grows wider; the current is very gentle, and we are now convinced it is the Cumberland. I have derived great assistance from a small square sail which was fixed up on the day we left the mouth of the river; and to prevent any ill-effects from sudden flaws of wind, a man was stationed at each of the lower corners of the sheet with, directions to give way whenever it was necessary.

Sunday, 26th – Got under way early; procured some buffalo-meat; though poor it was palatable.

Monday, 27th – Set out again; killed a swan, which was very delicious.

Tuesday, 28th – Set out very early this morning; killed some buffalo.

Wednesday, 29th – Proceeded up the river; gathered some herbs on the bottoms of Cumberland, which some of the company called Shawnee salad.

Thursday, 30th – Proceeded on our voyage. This day we killed some more buffalo.

Friday, 31st – Set out this day, and after running some distance, met with Col. Richard Henderson, who was running the line between Virginia and North-Carolina. At this meeting we were much rejoiced. He gave us every information we wished, and further informed us that he had purchased a quantity of corn in Kentucky, to be shipped at the Falls of Ohio for the use of the Cumberland settlement. We are now without bread, and are compelled to hunt buffalo to preserve life. Worn out with fatigue, our progress at present is slow. Camped at night near the mouth of a little river, at which place and below there is a handsome bottom of rich land. Here we found a pair of hand mill stones set up for grinding, but appeared not to have been used for a great length of time.

Proceeded on quietly until the 12th of April, at which time we came to the mouth of a little river running in on the north side, by Moses Renfroe and his company called Red River, up which they intend to settle. Here they took leave of us. We proceeded up Cumberland, nothing happening material until the 23rd, when we reached the first settlement on the north side of the river, one mile and a half below the Big Salt Lick and called Eaton's Station, after a man of that name, who with several families, came through Kentucky and settled there.

Monday, April 24th – This day we arrived at our journey's end at the Big Salt Lick, where we have the pleasure of finding Capt. Robertson and his company. It is a source of satisfaction to us to be enabled to restore to him and others their families and friends, who were entrusted to our care, and who, sometime since, perhaps despaired of ever meeting again. Though our prospects at present are dreary, we have found a few log cabins which have been built on a cedar bluff above the Lick, by Capt. Robertson and his family.

Robertson and the others were anxiously awaiting Donelson's arrival. They were overjoyed when the boats landed below the Bluffs. Unfortunately, the joy was tempered with some sadness over the loss of life that occurred during the journey. Families and friends of the survivors were united again and ready to make new lives for themselves in the wilderness. As whole, these were not ordinary people. They were extraordinary in the sense that they had the courage and sheer toughness to journey so far west from the comfort and safety of civilization.

Image of Indians Attacking Donelson's Flotilla.

Chapter 24

A NEW GOVERNMENT

Soon after Donelson's arrival, the leaders met at Robertson's station at the Bluffs to devise a suitable form of governance. It is likely that many of the details had been decided earlier in Watauga during the planning phase. On May 1, 1780 the Article of Agreement, or Compact of Government, was established. It eventually became known as the Cumberland Compact. It was a set of administrative, legislative, legal and military structures and laws to govern the newly arrived settlers residing throughout the expansive Cumberland Region.

On May 13, 1780 additional resolutions were added, and the entire Cumberland Compact was ratified by an assembly of the adult male settlers. Nearly all of the men were sufficiently literate to sign their names at the bottom. Only one person used an X rather than signing his name.

The system of government was clearly democratic and positions were filled by nominations followed by a vote. As was the custom of that era, militia officers were elected to their positions. Officers could be voted out by their subordinates in a system where true leadership was required for an officer to keep his rank and maintain his men's loyalty.

The authorship of the Cumberland Compact is uncertain, but it seems likely that Richard Henderson was the one who actually penned the document. It is known that Henderson wrote the Transylvania Articles in Kentucky. That document was decidedly autocratic, whereas the Cumberland Compact was democratic and similar to the Watauga Compact. That leads to the conclusion that Robertson likely played a significant role in formulating articles of the Cumberland Compact. Even if Henderson wanted a form of government similar to the one that he created in Kentucky, Robertson would not have allowed it. He had lived under the democratic Watauga Compact for eight years. After experiencing democracy, it is unlikely that he would have accepted anything less. Although Robertson had less education and scholarly experience, he likely played a greater role than Henderson in formulating the actual terms of the Cumberland Compact. However, at least one modern handwriting analysis has concluded that Henderson actually put the words on paper. That is not surprising because his education, judicial experience and writing skills were likely superior to most, if not all, of the other participants.

John Donelson's degree of input is less certain. His arrival was so close to the May 1 date that there was limited time for his participation. However, it is likely that he contributed to the May 13 additions to the document. There were 244 male settlers aged twenty-one or older who signed the Cumberland Compact on May 13, 1780.

Robertson's fort at the Bluffs became the center of civic activity due to its size, location and defensibility. Another reason was due to Robertson's status among the settlers. He was soon elected to the position of chief judge as well as colonel in command of the militia. Those appointments by his peers confirmed that he was the most influential leader in the Cumberland settlements.

There were eight initial forts erected in the Cumberland region. Robertson's Fort was named Nashborough in honor of Francis Nash, a North Carolina general killed during the Revolution. General Nash died on October 7, 1777, after being mortally wounded at the Battle of Germantown. Bestowing such an honor for a fallen revolutionary hero from his home state exhibited Robertson's patriotic zeal.

The other seven forts, or stations, were: Freeland's, Eaton's, Asher's, Stone's River, Mansker's, Bledsoe's and Fort Union. Each fort had a commanding officer in charge of his own militia that was formed from all able-bodied males aged sixteen or older. There was at least one judge appointed to serve at each location. The exceptions were Nashborough with three judges, and Mansker's and Eaton's with two apiece.

Chapter 25

TERROR AND BLOODSHED

In April of 1780, the settlers suffered their first Indian attack. Two hunters named Milliken and Keywood were returning to the Bluff when they stopped for a drink at Richland Creek. Indians, who were believed to be either Chickamaugas or Creeks, ambushed and killed Milliken as he stepped off his horse to get a drink. Keywood rode off and made it safely back to the fort. Milliken became the first, among countless others, who would be slaughtered by Indians over the next fifteen years.

Soon after the initial assault, the same band of Indians was believed to be responsible for other attacks. Joseph Hay was killed near Lick Branch. An old man named Bernard was attacked and killed near Freeland's Station. The Indians carried off his head as a trophy. Another young man from the Milliken family was killed near the same fort and, as with Bernard, the Indians took his head.

The next Indian attack was in July of 1780 by a band of Delawares. They attacked and killed Jonathan Jennings on a river island above Nashborough. The Indians proceeded farther north along the Cumberland River and killed Ned Carver. His wife and children managed to escape to Nashborough. The next day, the same band killed William Neely and carried away his daughter.

To their horror and dismay, the settlers endured Indian attacks at various places throughout the region. Small bands of warriors roamed the area attacking targets of opportunity; such as settlers living in isolated locations, hunting parties or people traveling between stations. Initially, the Indians avoided direct attacks against the larger stations out of concern about suffering too many casualties. Whenever the opportunity arose while roaming near the settlements, the warriors would steal the settlers' horses or kill their livestock.

Indian attacks were widespread and occurred as far north as present-day Clarksville, Tennessee. Renfroe's Station was built there by the settlers who had left John Donelson's flotilla for the Red River. The Chickasaws and their Choctaw allies committed atrocities there in retaliation for George Rogers Clark building Fort Jefferson on Chickasaw land at the intersection of the Ohio and Mississippi Rivers. Clark had built the fort there to block British access to the Ohio River.

After fleeing south toward Nashborough, some of the settlers decided to return to Renfroe's Station to retrieve some of the belongings left behind during their hasty retreat. On their way back, they stopped to camp for the night. Early the next morning, the Indians ambushed Joseph Renfroe and an old man named Johns, killing them both. Then they proceeded to slaughter most of the remaining men, women and children. Henry Ramsey and a woman named Mrs. Jones were the only survivors. Somehow, they managed to escape and make their way to Nashborough.

By the fall of 1780, food supplies were low because heavy rains in July had destroyed nearly all of the corn crops, and Indians had either stolen or killed most of their livestock. To secure much needed meat, twenty hunters went up the Caney Fork to Flinn's. They returned in canoes filled with meat and hides from one hundred and five bears, eighty deer and seventy-five buffaloes; enough to help them survive the upcoming winter.

After the floodwaters subsided that fall, John Donelson discovered that his corn crop at Clover Bottom had survived the inundation. He generously offered to share his crop with the settlers at the Bluff and surrounding areas.

Near the end of the day after his corn was harvested, Donelson separated from the others because he wanted to pick some cotton that he had planted nearby. Meanwhile, after the men and boys had finished loading their boats with corn and were preparing to depart, Indians suddenly ambushed them. Only two men survived; a free black man and a white man. Among those killed was James Robertson's nine-year-old son, James Randolph Robertson. Others killed by the Indians were Richard Henderson's slave named Jim, Abel Gower, his son, Abel Gower Jr. and a young white man. Three slaves, Jack Civil, his son and a man named George were captured and taken away by the Indians. The unfortunate incident became known as the Clover Bottom Massacre.

At about the same time, a party of Indians stole some horses from Fort Nashborough. About fifteen men commanded by Captain Leiper left to pursue of the Indians and caught up with them after they had stopped to camp for the night. Leiper's men ambushed the Indians who then quickly fled, leaving behind the stolen horses. Later, the victorious whites proudly returned to the fort with the horses they had retrieved after the brief skirmish.

Near the end of the year, Thomas Sharpe Spencer was returning to the Bluff with several pack horses loaded with meat and hides. Just before he made it back, Indians attacked and stole all of his pack horses and supplies. Fortunately, he got back to the fort unharmed. Spencer was a legendary long-hunter who had frequented the Cumberland region prior to the arrival of settlers.

A large man of huge proportions, Spencer had once reportedly camped there alone for several months, using a hollow tree trunk for shelter.

The same band of Indians who attacked Spencer proceeded to Asher's Station where they killed and scalped one man and wounded another before stealing several more horses. From there, the Indians headed toward Bledsoe's Lick until they came upon a hunting party that included Alexander Buchanan, James Manifee, William Ellis, Alexander Thompson and others. Buchanan shot and killed one Indian and another was wounded before the Indians fled, leaving behind all of the stolen horses, hides and meat to be reclaimed by the whites.

In late December of 1780, Robertson and his fellow settlers prayed that 1781 would be a better year; and that the violence and terror would come to an end.

This is an early French portrait of Chickasaw Indians with scalps. They were fierce warriors who were responsible for some of the earlier attacks against the Nashborough settlers.

Chapter 26

OTHER CONFLICTS

While Robertson and his fellow settlers were fighting for their personal survival, as well as the survival of their infant settlements, their compatriots in Kentucky had already endured conflicts of their own. Henry Hamilton, British governor of Detroit, continued arming the Shawnees and their Indian allies and encouraged them to attack white settlers in Kentucky.

Daniel Boone survived numerous harrowing events. On one occasion, he and some of his men were on an expedition to boil salt from brine when they were surrounded and captured by Shawnees. The men were taken to the Shawnee capital of Chillicothe where Boone was eventually adopted by the Shawnee chief, Blackfish.

After several months in captivity, Boone managed to steal a horse and escape. He rode and walked for four days at a distance of over 160 miles before reaching Boonesborough. He arrived just in time to warn the settlers about British and Shawnee plans to attack the fort. Boone immediately took charge of preparing the fort's defenses. He sent scouts to warn outlying settlers and nearby forts about the impending attack.

Soon afterward, on September 7, 1778, Chief Blackfish arrived at Boonesborough with his warriors and a small contingent of British militia from Detroit. Boone and several others were invited to parlay with Blackfish and his chiefs. They met in a clearing outside the walls of the fort. Besides Daniel Boone, the delegation of whites included Squire Boone, William Buchanan, Isaac Crabtree, William Smith, Richard and Flanders Callaway, John South and Edward Bradley.

Boone and Blackfish enjoyed a mutual bond of affection and both men sincerely wanted to reach an agreement that would avoid bloodshed. Blackfish tried to persuade Boone and the other leaders to surrender the fort in exchange for a promise of safe passage. However, Boone and his men were determined to stay. None of Blackfish's many assurances were sufficient to induce them to surrender and abandon the fort.

Before their third meeting, Blackfish had already concluded that further talks would be futile. He devised a plan for his warriors to kidnap Boone and the other leaders at the next meeting and hold them hostage to persuade the others inside the fort to surrender. At the final meeting, the Indians outnumbered Boone's party by two to one. When the third council ended without success, the Indians tried to capture the whites when they shook hands.

While the Indians struggled to hold them hostage, a melee ensued and Boone and his men were able to brake free. They sprinted toward the fort amid a hail of Indian gunfire. Sharpshooters in the fort provided cover fire and felled several of the Indians. In their flight toward safety, Squire Boone was the only one hit. He was shot in the shoulder, but managed to get up and run the final distance.

Once they made it back to the fort, the gate was closed and the siege of Fort Boonesborough commenced. The fighting continued on and off for twelve days. The attackers tried to burn the fort several times, and they even attempted to tunnel under the wall adjacent to the river. In the end, all of their tactics to take the fort failed.

On September 18, 1778, the Indians withdrew after suffering nearly forty dead and many more wounded during the siege. Fort Boonesborough's defenders only sustained two killed and several wounded during the conflict.

For some time afterward, the Shawnees split into small bands and raided nearby settlements. The smaller ambushes kept Indian casualties low while spreading terror throughout the Kentucky region. During that time, Boone and his compatriots mounted several scouting parties that killed a few of the marauding warriors.

In March of 1780, a large force of Shawnees, their Indian allies and a small British militia contingent with cannons began attacking the smaller Kentucky forts. With British cannons to batter the walls, they were able to secure the surrender of Ruddle's Station. From there they proceeded to Martin's Station and took that fort as well. Later, they destroyed two other stations that were already abandoned before their arrival.

Following those disastrous events, a retaliatory expedition was mounted under the command of George Rogers Clark in July of 1780. The Boones, Logan and other leaders served in Clark's army of over 800 men who went on to destroy the Shawnee capital of Chillicothe and several other Indian villages. During their attacks, the whites intentionally committed a few atrocities to warn the Indians that they could be just as brutal and inhumane as they had been. The militia returned from their mission and disbanded in late August of 1780. Their undertaking was largely successful and Indian attacks in Kentucky subsided for a while.

In that same year, George Rogers Clark made a strategic decision that would impact the Nashborough settlements. To block the transport of British armaments and supplies along the

Mississippi River, Thomas Jefferson convinced Clark of the need to construct a fort on the river. Clark accepted the orders from his fellow Virginian and chose a suitable location on the banks of the Mississippi.

Clark built a fort there on the extreme southwestern corner of what is now Kentucky. Clark named it Fort Jefferson in honor of his superior. It was situated on land that was claimed by the powerful Chickasaw tribe, a British ally. The tribe was incensed by the encroachment on their land and they not only attacked Fort Jefferson, but also the Nashborough settlements to the south. While the new fort was believed to be strategically important for the Revolution, the timing of its construction only added to the intensity and ferocity of Indian attacks against Robertson and his fellow settlers.

This portrait of George Washington by Charles Wilson Peale was made in 1776 when he assumed command of the Continental Army.

Chapter 27

ENCOURAGING NEWS

By December of 1780, the Cumberland settlers were running out of gunpowder and lead. Without the use of their rifles, they would be unable to shoot game for meat. And they would be defenseless against Indian attacks. It was a time of desperation; some of the original settlers had already fled the region due to hardships and the fear of being killed by Indians.

Decisive leadership was needed if the people were to survive. James Robertson calmed their fears and exhibited his usual selflessness and courage by volunteering to go to Kentucky to obtain gunpowder and lead from Daniel Boone.

Soon Robertson and his trusted slave, Robert, left Fort Nashborough on horseback for a long journey to Fort Boonesborough. The weather was very cold, but it was not as severe as the prior year, known thereafter as the "cold winter". Besides enduring the hardships associated with winter travel, they had to remain vigilant for signs of Indians along the way. Fortunately, they avoided any encounters with Indians because they had likely returned to their distant villages for the winter. Therefore, cold weather, ice and snow presented the greatest challenges for Robertson and his slave as they traveled through the wilderness.

When they finally reached Boonesborough, Boone and the others gave them a warm welcome. Later, everyone shared news about the Revolution and other current events.

Hearing reports about the great victory against the British at the Battle of Kings Mountain two months earlier lifted Robertson's sagging spirits. He was further heartened by accounts of his Kentucky compatriots surviving numerous Indian attacks. By all appearances, they seemed to be prospering. While listening to their stories, he gradually became confident that he could successfully lead his own settlers through their desperate circumstances. Assurances that he could take adequate supplies of powder and lead from the Boonesborough stores made the prospects of his own settlements' survival seem more likely.

The Battle of Kings Mountain in North Carolina was a significant victory for the Patriots because it helped turn the tide in the southern theatre of the war. Before the battle, the British were able to recruit Tories to fight for the crown. Following their stunning defeat, recruitment effectively ended in the Carolinas, and it signaled the beginning of the end of the Revolution. Robertson listened with great interest to accounts of that great event. He was very pleased to hear about the various acts of bravery shown by John Sevier, Charles Robertson and many other friends and relatives from Watauga who fought in that pivotal battle.

Following the British capture of Charleston in April of 1780 and their victory at Camden in August, British Colonel Patrick Ferguson sent a letter to the over-mountain settlers. He was in command of operations to eliminate what little resistance remained in the Carolinas. In his letter, Ferguson demanded that the over-mountain people abandon the Revolution and declare loyalty to the crown. If they failed to do so, he threatened to march his army over the mountains, lay waste to their settlements and hang their leaders. Unfortunately for Colonel Ferguson, he had miscalculated the toughness and independence of the frontiersmen who received his letter and took it to heart.

As soon as Isaac Shelby, to whom the letter was addressed, and other leaders read Ferguson's threats, they unanimously resolved to send riders throughout the Watauga and southwest Virginia settlements with a call to arms. The volunteers arrived at Fort Watauga within forty-eight hours.

On September 25, 1780, the frontiersmen left Fort Watauga to go after Colonel Ferguson. Nearly a thousand patriots marched out that day amid the cheers and tears of relatives and friends who stayed behind.

After crossing the Blue Ridge Mountains, the over-mountain army arrived at Quaker Meadows near present-day Morgantown, North Carolina. There they rendezvoused with Major Joseph McDowell who commanded an additional force of 400 volunteers from the Carolinas.

From there, the army headed south toward Gilbert Town where they initially expected to encounter Ferguson's force comprised of a small group of British regulars and a much larger contingent of well-trained Tory recruits. Both Colonel Ferguson, as well as his pursuers, sent out scouts to assess the other's strength, movements and location.

On October 5th, Ferguson sent a message to his commander, Lord Cornwallis, which betrayed his growing apprehension. He stated that he was marching toward Cornwallis' army at Charlotte, and he requested that a relief force of three to four hundred soldiers be sent out to bolster his ranks.

Shortly afterward, Ferguson decided to make a stand. Perhaps his men and horses were too fatigued to continue moving toward Cornwallis; or maybe he expected reinforcements to arrive at any moment. At the time, he was only 35 miles from Charlotte and the protection of Cornwallis' army.

Colonel Ferguson selected Kings Mountain, a wooded low rocky outcropping about 100 feet high, for the location for his encampment. He ordered extra sentries and other defensive measures while he awaited the arrival of his reinforcements, his pursuers, or both.

Meanwhile, part of the Whig army went on a forced march in the rain to catch up with Ferguson before he could reach the safety of Charlotte. On the morning of October 7, 1780, the patriots arrived at the base of Kings Mountain. Meanwhile, Ferguson's request for reinforcements was rejected by Cornwallis for reasons that remain unclear to this day.

The Whigs' officers hastily devised a battle plan for eight separate detachments to attack Ferguson's position from all sides. Robertson's friends, John Sevier and Isaac Shelby, each commanded a unit. Cleveland, Campbell, McDowell, Chronicle, Williams and Winston led the other six detachments.

The defenders were caught off guard; perhaps because they had not anticipated such a rapid advance during the rainy weather. When the attack started, Colonel Ferguson commanded the well-organized defense of his position.

The battle was essentially a contest between two distinct types of warfare. Ferguson's men were armed with smooth-bore muskets and bayonets, utilizing the classic European style of warfare. They fired one or more volleys that were followed by well-organized bayonet charges.

The Patriots charged uphill using Indian warfare tactics. They fired their more accurate Deckard rifles randomly, and often used trees or large rocks for cover as they fired and reloaded.

On more than one occasion, the British bayonet charges caused disorderly retreats among Shelby's and Cleveland's detachments. But the officers managed to regain control and return their men to the fight.

The superior rifles and marksmanship of the patriots gradually took a deadly toll on the more exposed defenders. It is believed that Ferguson's men were generally well-trained, but they were unaccustomed to making the necessary adjustments for shooting downhill. By failing to compensate by aiming slightly lower, many of the musket balls flew over their intended targets.

Throughout the battle, Ferguson rode his white horse back and forth while shouting orders and encouraging his soldiers. Toward the end, some of his men started to panic as their comrades fell next to them and the enemy advanced closer up the hill. As he was trying to stop his soldiers from waving white flags to surrender, Ferguson was suddenly shot off his horse by the impact of seven bullets simultaneously slamming into his body.

With Ferguson lying dead on the battlefield, his second in command, Captain De Peyster, tried to surrender. Unfortunately, once the Patriots reached the top of the hill, many were too excited and lacking in military discipline to quit firing. In the confusion and turmoil, they shot several British defenders who were trying to surrender. Colonel Campbell eventually calmed his men and got them to stop firing.

While Campbell was accepting De Peyster's official surrender, several of the over-mountain men stripped Ferguson's body of his clothes, silver whistle, pocket watch and other souvenirs. Afterward, they urinated on his naked corpse as one final insult. With losses of their own of only 28 killed and 62 wounded, they had almost annihilated Colonel Ferguson's detachment of 1,100 men. Only 600 of his men remained alive, and many of those were wounded.

After burying the dead and tending to the wounded, the patriots departed early the next day with their prisoners and some of the wounded. Those who were too seriously wounded to travel were left behind with volunteers to care for them. Concern about the possible arrival of British reinforcements dictated a forced march out of the area.

The retreat was slow because the men were fatigued and they had to forage for food along the way. On October 14th they camped at Red Chimneys, about ten miles northeast of Gilbert Town.

Angered by reports of prior atrocities committed by the notorious British Colonel Tarleton and Tory retaliations against Whigs, the Patriot officers decided that it was an appropriate time to try some of their prisoners for war crimes. A tribunal was assembled and thirty-six prisoners were tried for their alleged crimes. All were convicted and sentenced to death.

By the time the executions were ready to be carried out, it was dark. It was a grim scene when the men gathered around a large oak tree illuminated by their torches. Three prisoners at a time were brought forward and hanged. When the first nine men were hanging dead from the tree, the officers and men decided that the rest of the condemned should be pardoned. When the army departed the next day, the executed men were left hanging with note to serve as a grisly warning to passersby. News about the British defeat at Kings Mountain and the subsequent execution of Tory collaborators at Red Chimneys virtually ended Britain's ability to recruit new soldiers in the Carolinas.

The victory at Kings Mountain, punctuated by the executions, left a lasting impression on the residents of the Carolinas and marked the beginning of the end of the Revolution.

Portrait of the Over-Mountain Men Mustering at Fort Watauga.

Chapter 28

THE BATTLE OF FREELAND'S STATION

The return trip to Nashborough was as uneventful as the journey to Boonesborough. Robertson and his slave, Robert, arrived at Fort Nashborough, also known as Robertson's Station or the Bluffs, on January 14, 1781. He immediately inquired about his wife, Charlotte, and was pleased to learn that she had recently given birth to a healthy baby boy. She and the baby were staying with friends at nearby Freeland's Station.

Robertson briefly told everyone about the good news from Boonesborough as he shared some of the powder and lead that he brought back. Then he was off to Freeland's Station to see Charlotte and their new son, Felix, who held the distinction of being the first white child born in the region.

Once there, he shared the good news that he had heard in Boonesborough. Everyone was encouraged by reports of the bravery shown by their friends at Boonesborough in fighting off Indian attacks. They were also heartened by news of the stunning victory at the Battle of Kings Mountain where many of their friends and relatives had fought.

After dinner, everyone went to bed. James, Charlotte, baby Felix and a slave woman shared the same cabin. Robertson's slave, Robert, went to spend the night in Major Lucas' cabin.

Robertson was restless from the excitement of returning home and found it difficult to fall asleep. He lay in bed savoring the blessings of making it back alive and reuniting with family and friends.

At about midnight, he heard noise coming from the chain that secured the fort's gate. When he opened the cabin door to investigate, the light of the full moon illuminated the ghostly figures of Indians entering the fort through the open gate. Quickly, he grabbed his rifle, shot one of the intruders and yelled, "Indians!" to alarm the others. There were only eleven men inside the fort to answer his call. Each man grabbed his rifle and joined the fight. When Major Lucas stepped out of his cabin to take aim, he was shot and mortally wounded. Fortunately, the defenders' gunshots drove the Indians back outside and Colonel Robertson and his men were able to close and secure the gate.

After being repulsed from the fort, the Indians went to the outside wall of Lucas' unfinished cabin and started shooting through the gaps between the logs that had not been chinked with mud. They shot and killed Robertson's slave, Robert, who had been firing from inside the cabin. The fighting raged on for hours, and several Indians were shot during the battle. At sunrise, the defenders and Indians heard a cannon shot from nearby Fort Nashborough signaling that relief was on its way.

Sensing that they were already fighting at a disadvantage from outside the fort, the warriors soon quit firing and started to retreat. They carried off all of their dead and wounded, except the one that Robertson had killed inside the fort. Afterward, the defenders counted over 500 bullet holes in the fort's log walls.

The attackers were most likely Chickasaws because the assault occurred in winter when other more distant tribes were likely at home in their villages. The Chickasaws lived nearby, and the settlers were encroaching on their tribal land. They had already made several attacks against the newly constructed Fort Jefferson on Chickasaw land to the north. And they had also attacked Renfro's settlement on the Red River for the same reason.

After the battle, Robertson reflected on the likelihood that everyone in the fort would have been slaughtered if he had not heard the Indians making noise as they opened the gate. He mourned the death of his friend, Major Lucas, a trusted militia officer he relied on to provide security for the settlers. He was perhaps even more saddened by the loss of his trusted slave, Robert. The two men had spent a lot of time together and had developed a bond of trust and friendship, the likes of which was seldom experienced between a master and his slave. On the frontier, theirs was a much closer bond than the usual slave and master relationships that typically existed on large plantations to the east.

Robertson had narrowly escaped death several times before. That latest brush with death strengthened and reinforced his religious beliefs regarding divine intervention and protection. Those religious principles remained a part of his belief system and guided him throughout the rest of his life. He had the benefit of a tremendous sense of purpose, inner strength and courage that few others possessed.

Chapter 29

BATTLE OF THE BLUFF

The year began badly with the Battle of Freeland's Station serving as an omen of what was to come. The Indians were undeterred by their defeat at Freeland's. From there they proceeded to outlying homesteads, wreaking havoc wherever there was an opportunity. Although scouts were sent out to advise everyone to evacuate to the Bluff or Eaton's Station, many did not make it there in time.

War parties slaughtered settlers, burned their cabins and torched their crops. They either stole or slaughtered any remaining horses or livestock that they could find. In 1781, all of the stations were evacuated except for the two most defensible forts, Nashborough and Eaton's. Many of the original settlers were either dead or had fled the area. Some went downriver to New Orleans and others traveled north to the relative safety of the Kentucky settlements. With grim determination, the Indians had initiated an all-out campaign to drive the white settlers out of the region. And they nearly succeeded.

John Donelson, who commanded the flotilla to Nashborough, left and relocated his family to Kentucky. Richard Henderson, the grand speculator and initiator of the settlement plan, also fled the region.

When Mansker's Station was evacuated, David Goin and Patrick Quigley stayed behind an extra day to attend to some final chores. Then the Indians attacked; and that one extra day ended up costing them their lives.

A few days later, a young girl was scalped after she ventured outside Eaton's Station. Her mother, Mrs. Dunham, heard her screams and was shot when she went out to save her child. Fortunately, both were rescued and later recovered from their injuries.

Among his many accomplishments, James Robertson was a frontier surgeon. One of his specialties, the treatment of scalp wounds, he learned from a physician named Dr. Vance who had married one of his relatives while he was living in Watauga. The procedure involved the use of an awl to bore small holes into the exposed skull; thereby causing fluid seepage that would promote tissue growth over the affected area. Without proper treatment, a scalping victim would endure prolonged suffering, followed by a slow agonizing death. Over the next several years, Robertson would be called upon to treat many other scalping victims who were fortunate enough to survive the initial attack. However, the Indians often killed or mortally wounded their victims before scalping them.

In late March, an Indian ambushed one of Robertson's officers, Colonel Samuel Barton. He was shot in the wrist, but managed to make it back to Eaton's Station with an Indian in close pursuit. However, the warrior quickly retreated when he saw an armed soldier named Martin leave the fort to aid Barton.

Shortly thereafter on April 2, 1781, a large body of Indians, believed to be Dragging Canoe's Chickamaugas, set up an ambush outside Fort Nashborough. Also known as The Bluff, it and Eaton's Station were the only two occupied forts left in the western region to shelter and protect the remaining the settlers.

Nearly half of their original number had been killed by Indians, were missing (never to be seen again and presumed dead) or had fled to a safer location.

The Indians positioned themselves nearby in two lines under ample cover afforded by tall canebrakes and brush. Early that morning, three Indians showed themselves and fired at the fort before moving out of range. Their bravado was taken as an invitation to come out and fight. A brief council was held inside the fort. Captain Leiper and several others wanted to go out after the Indians. Robertson counseled caution and explained that it could be an ambush. However, he was outvoted. On the frontier, a militia officer could only lead and retain his commission with the support of his subordinates.

Outvoted and against his better judgment, Robertson finally agreed to lead a group of nineteen riders in pursuit of the three Indians. What followed would have been a disaster if not for a miraculous series of events that likely saved most of them from being killed by Indians who were indeed waiting to ambush them.

After the riders passed though the clearing surrounding the fort and entered the brush, the Indians sprang their trap. They closed their two lines behind the riders and blocked them from retreating to the fort. When the firing started, the riders dismounted and began returning fire. Their horses panicked because of the gunfire and commotion and bolted toward the fort, but the gate was closed.

Captain Leiper, Peter Gill, Alexander Buchanan, George Kennedy and Zachariah White were shot and killed by the gunfire from several hundred Indians. James Manifee and Joseph Moonshaw were wounded during the Indian's initial volley.

Fortunately, the Indian line between the survivors and the fort disintegrated when individual warriors broke ranks and went after the whites' fleeing horses. They lacked military discipline, and each Indian wanted to catch a horse to keep as his own war trophy.

Charlotte Robertson witnessed the events unfolding from the lookout tower at the fort. She reacted immediately by ordering a pack of dogs to be released from the fort.

The gate was opened and about forty ferocious dogs ran out and began attacking the Indians. The hounds were robust animals that were bred and trained to hunt Indians, as well as bears.

While the Indians were distracted by the horses and vicious dogs, the surviving whites took advantage of the situation and retreated through a gap in the Indians' broken line. While they ran toward the fort, marksmen positioned along the fort's walls provided cover fire.

While running back, Isaac Lucas received a shot in the thigh that dropped him to the ground. He managed to shoot the first warrior who came at him with a tomahawk. Others who wanted his scalp were either shot or driven off by the forts' sharpshooters until some men ran outside, picked him up and carried him inside to safety.

As Edward Swanson was running toward the fort, a pursuing warrior hit his back, causing him to drop his rifle. Swanson then turned and grabbed the Indian's musket to prevent him from firing. They struggled briefly until the large warrior managed to knock him to his knees. At that moment, John Buchanan was running from the fort to rescue Swanson. Witnessing Swanson's predicament, he stopped and shot the Indian. The mortally wounded warrior stumbled back and fell against a tree stump. Buchanan's well-placed shot allowed enough time for him to help Swanson back to the fort.

After all of the survivors were inside and the gate was closed, the firing subsided and the Indians carried off most of their dead and wounded. Of the nineteen whites who rode out, five were killed and three were wounded. Only Robertson and ten others were uninjured. If not for the Indians' attempts to catch the startled horses and having to fight off the dog attacks, all nineteen whites would have been killed; and the fort would have been overrun. Charlotte Robertson's husband and the other survivors were very grateful to her for releasing the dogs. Her decisive action helped save the day. Thereafter, Charlotte was fond of saying, "Thanks be to God, that he gave Indians a fear of dogs and a love for horses!"

Stung by their unlikely defeat, the Indians returned before sunset and began firing at the fort once again. Robertson powdered his small swivel cannon; and because there were no cannon balls, he loaded it with bits of lead, small rocks and pottery shards. After he fired it at a distant group of Indians, they retreated and the gunshots ceased. Taking it as a signal, people at Eaton's Station also fired their cannon to let them know that they were sending reinforcements. By the time the men from Eaton's arrived from the other side of the river, the warriors had already disappeared. Their earlier ill fortune, followed by the two cannon shots, had persuaded the Indians to give up the fight.

Chapter 30

ROBERTSON'S SPEECH

Robertson and his compatriots won two pitched battles in 1781 that they nearly lost. An Indian victory at either Freeland's Station or The Bluff would have resulted in the slaughter of the fort's inhabitants and encouraged the Indians in their ultimate goal of complete annihilation of all white settlers in the region.

Despite those victories, many settlers were disillusioned due to the Indians' barbarity and their own difficult frontier existence. Nevertheless, James Robertson was encouraged. He viewed the two victories in battle as clear signs that the hand of God had reached down and rescued them in their time of need. How else could he explain their miraculous survival?

At the time, there were only about 70 riflemen and their families left in the settlements. Nearly half of the 256 men who signed the Cumberland Compact had either been killed by Indians or moved to a safer region. Roaming war parties were so numerous that the settlers were unable to plant corn during the entire year of 1781. The only source of food was game meat, nuts and berries foraged by the few souls who were brave enough to venture outside either of the two forts that remained occupied. Several people paid the ultimate price while trying to obtain food.

That year Thomas Sharpe Spencer, the notable long-hunter, was wounded. Some of those killed during various incidents while hunting or foraging were: a man named Mason, Josiah Hoskins, George Aspie, William McMurray, Jacob Freeland, Joseph Castleman, Jacob Castleman, William Hood, Peter Renfroe and Timothy Terril. Many others, not listed here, were killed, wounded or captured during 1781.

By 1782, the settlers' morale was very low due to inadequate food supplies and the constant threat of Indian attacks. Long periods of confinement inside the forts added to their distress.

Because of the dire circumstances, a meeting of the remaining settlers was convened at Fort Nashborough to discuss their plight. Many wanted to abandon the settlements. As their leader, Robertson opened the meeting and allowed everyone the opportunity to express their fears and concerns. The meeting continued for some time while everyone who wanted to speak was allowed to do so.

When the final speaker finished, Robertson stood to address the crowd. By all accounts, it was a powerful and persuasive speech. Although Robertson was not a loquacious man, he was a gifted orator who chose his words carefully. Using undeniable reason and logic, he slowly and methodically made the case for staying and fighting it out.

Robertson carefully restated the aforementioned problems that the settlers were facing, as well as the suffering that everyone had endured. He openly acknowledged that evacuation was an option. But how would they travel? The Indians had stolen most of their horses. If they tried to walk to Kentucky, it was certain that the Indians would attack them along the way.

Another other choice would be to evacuate by river. But they would need boats. In order to cut trees to make boats, they would expose themselves to Indian ambushes.

After reciting the likely hazards for either type of evacuation, Robertson listed the reasons to stay. The Revolution had effectively ended after Cornwallis' surrender at Yorktown in 1781. Many former soldiers would soon arrive to claim land grants provided by North Carolina for their service during the Revolution. An influx of settlers would bring more experienced riflemen into the region, and their arrival would certainly enhance everyone's security.

Another argument was that the suffering and privation that they had already endured was reason enough to stay. Why give up after sacrificing so much and witnessing the deaths of their friends and loved ones? After all, even he and Charlotte had lost a son to the Indians. Nearly everyone there had lost relatives or friends in Indian attacks.

Robertson concluded his speech by telling the audience that it was their duty to stand for a cause greater than themselves. They had just become part of a new nation that would need to grow and expand its borders. They occupied good fertile land with abundant wildlife. It was their proverbial "promised land", and it was their duty to keep it.

Ever the visionary, he predicted that the infant nation would prosper and require more land as the frontier moved westward. With exuberance he proclaimed, "Our way is to the sea!" In making that bold statement, Robertson became one of the first Americans on record to promote the now well-known philosophy of Manifest Destiny.

Robertson closed his speech by exclaiming "I, for one, intend to stay and fight it out!" At that point, the crowd was aroused and some of the other leading men stepped forward and declared their determination to stay and fight it out. Others quickly followed by proclaiming their own willingness to stay. Robertson's inspiring speech had established a consensus among the settlers.

The matter of abandoning the settlements was settled once and for all. His stirring speech and moving display of personal resolve convinced everyone to stay and fight it out, regardless of the outcome.

Chapter 31

THE TREATY OF PARIS

The Treaty of Paris officially ended the American Revolution nearly two years after the surrender of Cornwallis at Yorktown. The treaty was signed on September 3rd 1783 and ratified by Congress on January 4th 1784. Its terms set the stage for a new rivalry with Spain, an American ally against Britain during the Revolution. Britain ceded its colonial holdings in Florida to Spain and granted it free navigation on the Mississippi River. As is often the case, the terms of the treaty had unintended consequences. A free and independent America replaced Britain as a direct competitor for Spain's colonial holdings in what is now the continental United States. Control of lands east of the Mississippi River, and rights of navigation on the river itself, were the initial sources of competing interests.

Spanish officials correctly surmised that the land hungry American frontiersmen in present-day Tennessee and Kentucky represented potential threats to Spain's colonial aspirations. Worries about their potential new rival prompted Spanish authorities to start implementing policies that were designed to weaken, and eventually eliminate, the western American frontier settlements. The means for accomplishing their goal was similar to Britain's during the Revolution; supply the Indians with firearms and trade goods, and incite them to drive the settlers out. The prevailing warrior cultures that existed among the various tribes, combined with the whites' encroachments on their lands, made them receptive pawns for Spanish intrigues.

In 1781, James Robertson made tentative peace overtures toward the Chickasaws who were reputed to be the fiercest warriors on the western frontier. With the Revolution effectively over, the Chickasaws no longer received British protection from the Spaniards, whom they despised. By 1782, Robertson's skillful diplomacy bore fruit, and he was allowed to open a trading post at Chickasaw bluffs. By pacifying the Chickasaws and their Choctaw allies to the south, he fostered peaceful relations with his closest Indian neighbors who respectively controlled the lands to the west and southwest of the Nashborough settlements.

In June of 1782, Chief Piomingo and a very large contingent of Indians met with Robertson and other leaders to sign a formal peace treaty. John Donelson and Joseph Martin were the officials who represented the interests of Virginia and North Carolina.

Donelson and his family had temporarily relocated to Kentucky where conditions were safer for his large family and numerous slaves. Beforehand, he had met with Chickasaw leaders that Robertson sent to Kentucky. After meeting with the Indians, Donelson contacted leaders in Virginia and North Carolina who consented to a formal treaty. He and Martin also arranged for Cherokee chiefs to be at the treaty grounds in order to sign a new treaty to settle land disputes with settlers in the eastern part of what is now Tennessee. It was necessary because Evan Shelby and John Sevier had fought several battles with the Cherokees after Robertson left to settle Nashborough in 1780.

There was quite a spectacle at the treaty grounds located about four miles northeast of Nashborough. The meeting place was on the site of Robertson's future plantation which would be named,

"Richland". Chickasaws, Choctaws Cherokees and others arrived dressed in their finest attire. The Chickasaws were the largest contingent with several hundred chiefs, warriors and squaws. The treaty negotiations lasted several days while the visiting Indians and whites feasted on bear meat, venison, fowl, corn and other frontier delicacies provided by the Nashborough settlers. Donelson and Martin handed out trinkets, trade goods and other commodities that were prized by the Indians, in exchange for their land. For their part, the Chickasaws ceded the land already occupied by the settlers, as well as a "trace" of land leading from Nashborough to the trading post at Chickasaw Bluffs.

The Indians enjoyed the lavish hospitality, and seemed satisfied with the terms of their respective treaties. Robertson and the settlers were grateful for the land they received, but they were even more pleased by the promise of a lasting peace with their Indian neighbors. For their part, the Chickasaws and Choctaws were impressed with the white settlers and their leaders. Robertson, in particular, made a good impression on his Indian neighbors that would last throughout his lifetime. They loved and trusted him like a father from then on.

The men and women of the settlement had worked hard to provide enough food and entertainment for several hundred Indian guests. There were horse races, foot races, wrestling, shooting contests, music, dancing and other activities that everyone enjoyed. When it ended, the participants from all sides went home with pleasant memories of the gathering.

The settlers were particularly hopeful that they would enter a new era of peace and prosperity. The Chickasaws and Choctaws remained at peace with the settlers from that time forward.

However, the settlers' desire for a lasting peace would prove to be elusive. Spanish machinations among the Creeks, Chickamaugas and others would result in renewed Indian attacks against the isolated settlements. But at least the settlers had their western flanks covered by their new friends and allies, the Chickasaws and Choctaws. That alone was a major accomplishment that would help them survive what was to come.

On December 23, 1783 George Washington formally resigned his commission as Commander-in-Chief of the Continental Army following the Treaty of Paris.

Chapter 32

NEW CIVIL AUTHORITY

The Cumberland Compact that had served the infant Nashborough settlements for the first three years of their existence faded into history by 1784. In 1783, North Carolina agreed to claim the distant region and brought it under its authority through legislation in the state assembly.

On October 6, 1783, North Carolina established the Inferior Court of Pleas and Quarter Sessions. The court's purpose was to serve the newly established Davidson County, with Nashborough as the county seat. Isaac Bledsoe, Samuel Barton, Francis Prince and Isaac Lindsay were the first judges to serve on the court. Andrew Ewing, who had served as clerk under the Cumberland Compact, was again appointed clerk in the new court.

Reflecting its new status as the county seat of Davidson County, Nashborough was renamed Nashville in 1784.

All of that progress resulted from the dogged determination of James Robertson. In late 1781, he made a hazardous four-hundred-mile journey (eight hundred miles round trip) to petition North Carolina legislators on behalf of his fellow settlers. That was the first of an incredible fourteen trips to the North Carolina capital that he would make during his lifetime. Ironically, his first trip was nearly a failure because the legislature was not in session due to the political and social turmoil that existed at the time. He returned home in early 1782 without having had the opportunity to address the state legislature.

However, during the first visit he made at least one important influential contact. William Blount was a wealthy and prominent member of the legislature. He was an ambitious man who immediately recognized that Robertson would make a good business partner for western land speculation. For his part, Robertson sensed that Blount might be the right person to help him pass laws to benefit the western settlers. Thus began an enduring and mutually beneficial relationship.

North Carolina was nearly bankrupt at the end of the Revolution and lacked the resources to pay veterans who had fought for the cause. However, western lands could be granted to them at almost no cost to the state. Therefore, in 1783 the legislature established a military reserve with Davidson County serving as the center for distribution of land allotments for state Revolutionary War veterans.

In that same year, legislation was enacted to allow preemption rights of 640 acres for 152 original settlers, including the heirs of those who were killed by Indians. There were only 67 surviving male settlers on the list. Also on the list were nineteen settlers who arrived a bit later or had come of age by 1784. The remaining 71 were the heirs of settlers who were killed by Indians. While the preemption rights were not outright grants, the legislation allowed the settlers to keep the land they settled in 1780 or shortly thereafter by paying only the recording fees. The legislation was a means to reward the hard work and suffering of the pioneers and the heirs of those who made the ultimate sacrifice. Their heirs were given the opportunity keep the land that their relatives had sacrificed their lives for. It was James

Robertson's first of many legislative accomplishments that benefited the Cumberland settlements.

The Revolution had ended. They made peace with their closest enemies, the Chickasaws and Choctaws. North Carolina formally acknowledged the settlers' existence by granting civil and judicial authority to the western settlements. With those accomplishments, Robertson and the other frontiersmen had every reason to be optimistic about the prospects for their safety and prosperity. Unfortunately, their hopes were soon dashed by a series of events that were beyond their control.

James Robertson was unaware that three Spanish governors met with the Chief of the Creek Indians, Alexander McGillivray, to sign a peace treaty with Spain in June of 1784. Their intent was to incite the Creeks to go to war against the western settlers. The Creeks, who lived in present-day Alabama, soon begin to attack the whites, along with Dragging Canoe's Chickamaugas. A new Indian war against the Nashville settlements erupted because America's former ally, Spain, wanted to prevent the new nation's western expansion.

The infant American nation was governed by the Articles of Confederation. It was a very flawed structure for governance due to a weak central government. The government did not have a reliable source of funding, it was unable to conduct a coherent foreign policy, and it lacked the authority to effectively regulate commerce. In that uncertain environment, North Carolina decided to cede its over-mountain western lands to the United States in order to unburden itself from the expenses of governing the western region. Although the cession was rescinded shortly afterward, it created uncertainty among the western settlers that sparked a movement to create a new western state.

Chapter 33

THE LOST STATE OF FRANKLIN

After James Robertson resigned as Indian Agent and relocated to the French Lick in 1780, a group of Cherokees went on the warpath. Without Robertson's careful guidance, some members of the tribe succumbed to their warrior ways and started attacking their white neighbors. The whites in Watauga and nearby settlements were dismayed by the situation and felt compelled to fight back. John Sevier and Evan Shelby answered the call by mobilizing the local militia and subsequently mounting several successful punitive expeditions against the Cherokees.

Sevier's bravery during the Battle of Kings Mountain in 1780 further added to his popularity among his fellow compatriots. Besides being a fearless leader in battle, he was a very charming and hospitable man. After the death of his first wife, he married Kate Sherrill, the pretty young woman he rescued by hoisting her over the wall of Fort Watauga during the Cherokee attack in 1776. By all accounts, they were an attractive couple who frequently entertained friends, neighbors and even complete strangers at their plantation on the Nolichucky River.

When North Carolina briefly ceded its over-mountain lands to the United States in 1784, John Sevier and several other leaders in what is now East Tennessee decided to form a new state. The

Articles of Confederation, despite its many inherent flaws, did contain specific provisions for the establishment of new states in the western region.

In August of 1784, John Sevier and other local leaders held a convention in Johnson City to begin the process of founding a new state. The name Franklin was chosen for the new state to honor the esteemed founding father, Benjamin Franklin. A letter was sent to Franklin requesting permission to use his name and inviting him to relocate to the new state. Franklin replied and graciously gave his consent to use his name for the new state. In his letter he thanked them for their generous offer to relocate there, but declined for reasons of advanced age and pressing business affairs.

By December of 1784, the State of Franklin was formed and John Sevier was elected governor. The State was located in what is now East Tennessee; comprised of settlements near the Holston, Watauga, Tennessee and Nolichucky rivers. The Franklinites, like the Nashville frontiersmen to the west, felt isolated and neglected by North Carolina. Their parent state failed to provide them with the material support and troops needed for protection against Indian attacks.

However, there were several circumstances at play at the time leading to the eventual downfall of the State of Franklin. The commercial states in the northeast were opposed to the State of Franklin because they viewed it as a source of diminution of their control over the weak central government. Besides the prospect of having one more state government petitioning the central government for special considerations, there were also conflicting interests.

After the Revolution, the northern seafaring states wanted closer relations with Britain for commercial trading opportunities. The agrarian southern states sought closer ties with Spain because of her colonial possessions on their southern borders stretching from Florida to the Mississippi River. Navigation along the Mississippi was particularly important to the southwestern frontiersmen who wanted to ship commodities on the river.

At the same time, there was growing discontent in southwest Virginia. Like the Franklinites to their south, many southwest Virginians felt disconnected from their parent state. They too were living along an isolated frontier that was subject to Indian attacks. Many of the settlers complained that Virginia was not providing enough protection.

One prominent southwest Virginian, William Russell, commander of Russell's Rangers before the War, was brevetted to Brigadier General at the end of the Revolution. He fought in the Virginia Line of the Continental Army in several battles, and was captured at Charleston when General Benjamin Lincoln surrendered the city to the British. He was released in a prisoner exchange, and subsequently fought at Yorktown where he witnessed Cornwallis' surrender.

Russell's first wife, Tabitha Adams, died in 1776 shortly after the outbreak of the Revolution. His eldest daughter, Mary, had to care for the younger children while their father was away serving his country. Russell sent Mary and the children to a safer location in Aspendale, Virginia for the duration of the War.

When the War ended, Russell returned to Aspendale where he became acquainted with his neighbor, Elizabeth Henry Campbell, widow of General William Campbell who died in August of 1781. She was also the sister of Patrick Henry, governor of Virginia.

William Russell and Elizabeth Henry Campbell married in 1783, nearly two years after his return from the War. Soon thereafter, they moved to present-day Saltville, Virginia where

Russell started a business producing salt, a very valuable commodity at that time.

By 1783, the secession movement was gaining momentum in southwest Virginia and many of the settlers expressed a desire to join the State of Franklin. One of the leaders of the movement was Arthur Campbell, brother of the deceased General William Campbell and former brother-in-law of Elizabeth Russell.

Ever the patriot and loyal Virginian, William Russell opposed those who wanted to secede from Virginia to join the State of Franklin. At the time, Russell enjoyed a level of prestige among his peers and was representing them in the Virginia Assembly. Russell County, Virginia was named in his honor in recognition of his outstanding service during the Revolution. By using his considerable popularity and influence, Russell eventually succeeded in quashing the secession movement in Virginia. His efforts earned him the lifelong enmity of his Franklinite opponent, Arthur Campbell.

If not for the defeat of the secession movement in Virginia, the State of Franklin would have been geographically larger, more populous, and would have wielded more political clout. Falling two votes short of the requirement for admission to the Confederation under the Articles of Confederation, the fate of Franklin was sealed. By the end of 1788, the State of Franklin ceased to exist and was lost forever.

Benjamin Franklin graciously gave his consent to name the new state in his honor.

Chapter 34

LEGISLATOR AND DIPLOMAT

In 1785, James Robertson made another hazardous journey to North Carolina to confer with William Blount and introduce legislation in the State Legislature. One particularly positive accomplishment was the enactment of legislation for the creation of Davidson Academy in Nashville.

With limited formal education, Robertson was essentially a self-taught man. He picked up what he could with the help of Charlotte and his sister, Ann, and others. He had a thirst for knowledge throughout his lifetime and he envied the educated men with whom he came in contact. There were many educated men like William Blount in the North Carolina Legislature. He witnessed firsthand what a formal education could do for a man, both professionally and socially.

Ever the visionary, he understood that Nashville's potential for growth and prosperity was linked to the establishment of a variety of civic pillars. An institution of higher learning would facilitate commercial and cultural development in the region. Without it, he feared that Nashville might become just another forgotten frontier town.

James Robertson was one of the five trustees of Davidson Academy, a position he continued to hold for many years. The

Academy was located just outside the town of Nashville. One of Robertson's greatest and most enduring legacies was born from the establishment of that institution and its library. From 1785, the Academy grew and changed several times, eventually spawning other institutions of higher learning, including Vanderbilt University. By the mid 1800's, Nashville enjoyed the nickname "Athens of the South" because of its reputation as a center for higher learning and intellectual pursuits.

In 1784, Colonel James Robertson began his informal career as a diplomat. Indian attacks continued against the settlers and he suspected that Spain was the ultimate source of the trouble. In addition to other atrocities, William Overall, a friend of Robertson's who accompanied him on the first journey to the French Lick, had recently been killed by Indians while traveling from Nashville to Kentucky. On behalf of his fellow settlers, Robertson wrote a letter to Spanish Governor Portell with the hope that better relations might induce Spain to abandon its policy of inciting the Indians.

Governor Portell sent a conciliatory reply assuring Robertson that his nation wanted to be a good neighbor, and that he appreciated the Cumberland settler's desire for amicable relations. Colonel Robertson was encouraged by Portell's response and he hoped that his attempt to establish good relations would be successful.

His disappointment was almost immediate because Indian depredations continued, unabated. In one encounter, Philip Trammel and Philip Mason were attacked while skinning a deer. They were assisted by men from Eaton's station; and a pitched skirmish ensued that lasted for some time. Several Indians were killed during the fight, but before it ended, Trammel, Mason and Josiah Hoskins lay dead.

Later in 1784, Thomas Sharpe Spencer, the intrepid longhunter, left the Bluff with three others to go on a hunting expedition. A party of Indians attacked them at Drake's Creek while they were watering their horses. Andrew Lucas was shot through the neck and mouth, but somehow managed to survive, despite losing a lot of blood. The Indians killed and scalped one of the men named Aspie. A musket ball hit Spencer in the thigh, but the bullet split after hitting the bone (due to Spencer's legendary huge stature). He and the other man, named Johnson, continued the fight until the seriously wounded Lucas managed to crawl over to them. Once he was there, the three men managed to elude their attackers and eventually made their way back to the fort where their wounds were treated. All three men ultimately recovered from their wounds.

In another attack that year, Cornelius Riddle was turkey hunting near Buchanan's Station. Hearing his gunshots, a band of Indians set up an ambush and killed him when he returned to retrieve two dead turkeys that he had left hanging on a bush.

In 1785, Moses Brown was killed on Richland Creek. That year Indians also ambushed and killed William Stuart.

At about the same time, Colonel Robertson and two others were surveying land on Piney River when Indians attacked. The warriors killed Edmond Hickman, but Robertson and the other man managed to escape without injury.

In the same year, there was another harrowing incident. A different surveying party consisting of John Peyton, Ephraim Peyton, Thomas Pugh and John Frazier bedded down on a creek on the north side of the Cumberland River. Indians crept up in the darkness and shot at the sleeping men. Three of the four men were wounded, but they all managed to escape into the darkness. The warriors stole their horses, survey equipment and everything else of value that was left behind. Creeks or Chickamaugas were the likely culprits in the attacks because they were under Spanish influence.

That was the first in a series of Spanish diplomatic lessons for Robertson. Spanish officials would make friendly overtures, but their deeds would be decidedly hostile. The diplomatic contacts continued for several years, but Robertson quickly learned one thing for certain; he could not trust the Spaniards.

Chapter 35

TRANSITIONS

There were several events in 1785 that impacted the frontiersmen in Nashville and other settlements in Davidson County. They remained independent from the State of Franklin which encompassed Washington, Sullivan and Greene counties to the east. The reasons why they did not join their eastern neighbors are unclear, but Davidson County was located far to the west, and there were no connecting roads. It should be considered that either the Davidson County settlers had no desire to join them, or that the Franklinites did not invite them to merge with the new state. Either way, evidence is lacking that there was any serious initial consideration of merging the two regions.

However, that year Robertson succeeded in enacting legislation in the North Carolina Assembly to construct a road linking the State of Franklin to Davidson County. That supports the possibility that he wanted to keep his options open regarding Franklin. It took over a year to complete the road and it was not wide enough to accommodate wagons. The "trace" was only wide enough for horses and pack trains, but it was a start.

Of the three ambitious leaders who planned the westward migration to the French Lick, only James Robertson survived long enough to fulfill his dreams. Richard Henderson, the visionary land speculator who orchestrated the Transylvania Purchase, relocated to North Carolina in 1782 and died there on January 30th 1785 at the age of 49.

In 1785, John Donelson was returning from Kentucky to his property in Davidson County. Earlier, he had helped arrange for the treaty with the Chickasaws, and represented the state of Virginia during the treaty negotiations. After successfully completing the treaty, he had good reason to believe that the Indian attacks would subside. His optimism was further buoyed by treaties that were scheduled to be held at Hopewell in late 1785 and early 1786 with the Cherokees, Chickasaws and Choctaws.

Thinking that it was relatively safe for his return, he intended to implement plans for acquiring more land, particularly in the Muscle Shoals area that his flotilla passed thru in late 1779 on the way to the French Lick.

Sadly, the hero and chronicler of that epic river voyage did not live long enough to carry out his plans. John Donelson was killed in January of 1786 while riding along the trail from Kentucky to Nashville. He had finished some business at his property in Davis' Station, Kentucky and was returning to his new home near Nashville. At the time, there was controversy surrounding his death. Most believed that Indians ambushed him, but some suspected that a white traveler killed him during a robbery. Authorities questioned and released one white man who denied any involvement. To this day, no one knows exactly what happened because the authorities never found any witnesses to Donelson's murder.

With the loss of Henderson and Donelson, James Robertson was the only original planner left to insure the survival of the settlements. But it would not be easy. A lot more terror and heartache were yet to come.

Chapter 36

GRIEF AMID CHANGE

The Atrocities continued throughout 1786, with 14 settlers killed that year from Indian attacks. Small bands of warriors terrorized the settlers as they tilled their fields, hunted, traveled between settlements, or as they slept in their cabins.

In response to the attacks, Colonel Robertson carefully selected a group of men who were known for their bravery and tracking skills. Those spies, known as scouts today, were given the responsibility of roaming the area in search of signs of Indians. Two of the most legendary scouts were Captain John Rains and Abe Castleman. They and the other scouts continually patrolled, searching for signs of war parties. Whenever possible, the scouts would ambush and kill hostile Indians. They reported larger war parties to nearby stations where militiamen could be mustered in sufficient numbers to go out and engage the enemy.

The scouting system worked very well due to the courage and skill of the bold frontiersmen who volunteered for the dangerous work. The invading Chickamaugas and Creeks despised the scouts, often torturing and mutilating those they captured. Despite the personal danger, those brave men diligently patrolled day and night, in all kinds of weather.

The scouts' pay was meager because money was scarce in the settlements. Paper money was worthless, and only a few people had Spanish silver coins. Most payments were either in animal pelts from deer, bear, buffalo, beaver, panther, bobcat, fox, or in agricultural commodities such as corn, whiskey or tobacco. The scouts' personal satisfaction, along with the gratitude and admiration of their loved ones and peers, was often as important as the goods they received for their services. But despite their best efforts, they were unable to stop the Indian attacks. In 1787 Colonel Robertson received reliable intelligence that Spanish agents were paying bounties for the scalps of white settlers, just as the British had done during the Revolution.

In May of 1787, there was an Indian attack that profoundly affected Colonel Robertson. His younger brother, Captain Mark Robertson, came to visit James at his newly constructed brick house on Richland Creek. It was the first brick house in the region and was erected with the help of friendly Chickasaw Indians who fired the bricks and carved the wood for the structure. James and Charlotte named their new home "Travelers' Rest" to signify their open door policy of hospitality toward friends and strangers alike. Mark Robertson was attacked and killed by Indians while returning home from Travelers' Rest. It was determined from the number of gunshots and evidence found at the scene that he put up a good fight before he was killed.

The murder of Mark was very painful for James. The two had traveled together through the wilderness to the French Lick, and they had ventured north by canoe to meet with George Rogers Clarke in the Illinois country. They fought alongside one another during various Indian skirmishes, and had pursued warriors into the wilderness. Their brotherly bond of love was strengthened by the numerous harrowing experiences they had endured together. The depth of Colonel Robertson's grief over the loss of his brother cannot be overstated, but his strength of character and even temperament prevented his sorrow from affecting his judgment.

To Colonel Robertson's credit, he resisted the impulse to muster the militia and lead a retaliatory expedition. His response was measured and appropriate for the situation. He waited until the next month before taking any action. Then, he and Colonel Anthony Bledsoe, commander of the newly formed Sumner County Militia, jointly penned a letter to Governor Caswell of North Carolina. They formally asked the Governor to send troops to protect the western settlements. Previous requests of that kind had been denied because of the State's financial problems and a prevailing attitude of indifference toward the plight of the over-mountain settlers.

However, on that occasion Governor Caswell decided to send an officer named Major Evans with a relief party. Earlier, Major Evans had been ordered to begin constructing a wagon road to Nashville, but he and his men had not started the work. Unfortunately, Evans' courtship of an over-mountain woman kept him from promptly following orders.

In the meantime, Robertson started making preparations for a retaliatory raid against the Indians because he doubted that the State would send help. He already had sufficient evidence that Chickamaugas and Creeks from Coldwater were responsible for the recent attacks.

While Colonel Robertson and his officers were organizing the details for an expedition against Coldwater, events of profound historic importance were unfolding in Philadelphia. The Continental Congress was convened from May 25th until September 17th of 1787. The original purpose of the convention was to make substantive changes to the Articles of Confederation. However, largely due to the leadership of James

Madison, Alexander Hamilton and others, the Articles were eventually scrapped in favor of an entirely new framework of governance, the Constitution of the United States.

The U. S. Constitution brought many new changes to the nation. There were provisions for a stronger central government with new executive and judicial branches, as well as other stipulations meant to improve commerce and allow for a centralized foreign policy. One change of particular interest to the frontiersmen was a renewed anticipation of national westward expansion. There were rules and procedures created to establish western territories; as well as specific criteria for admitting new states to the Union.

At about the same time, friction between the State of Franklin and its parent state of North Carolina intensified. That friction, combined with a new United States Constitution and renewed Indian conflicts with the over-mountain settlers, would soon bring about a series of events leading to the downfall of Franklin.

Robertson sent a letter to Governor John Sevier asking for assistance from Franklin at about the same time he sent a similar letter to Governor Caswell of North Carolina. Sevier could not resist his friend's request for help. Without hesitation, Sevier mustered the militia and headed west with over 1,000 men. At the same time, a similar sized force of Indians was heading toward Nashville to attack the settlement. When Indian scouts brought back news of Sevier's advance, the chiefs decided to retreat rather than risk another conflict with their feared adversary.

Even though his men had not fired a single shot, Sevier's decisive response bought additional time for the Cumberland settlers and gave them with a needed respite from all of the bloodshed. It also allowed more time for Colonel Robertson and his officers to properly plan and organize a retaliatory campaign against the Coldwater Indian Village.

Chapter 37

THE COLDWATER EXPEDITION

On June 12th 1787, Colonels Robertson and Bledsoe wrote a final letter to Governor Caswell of North Carolina. They provided a list of persons who had been killed or wounded since the last meeting of the State Assembly in April. There had already been 33 casualties for that year which was only half over. The new list only added to the incredibly high number of recent casualties. They also shared intelligence obtained by friendly Chickasaws that documented the harm caused by Spanish and French traders living among the Chickamaugas and Creeks who were encouraging their attacks against the Cumberland settlements. Robertson and Bledsoe expressed a desire to take action against the offending Indians. In closing, they asked for the Governor's advice on the matter.

From when the letter was sent, it seems clear that they were more interested in documenting their plight than in genuinely seeking his counsel. This conclusion can be made because the expedition began before a response could have been received from such a distant location. By the time the letter was sent to Governor Caswell, elaborate preparations had already begun.

Colonel Robertson arranged for a Chickasaw named Toka and his companion to guide the expedition. Both had been to

Coldwater which was located about eight miles below Muscle Shoals, near what is now Tuscumbia, Alabama. The two Chickasaws provided Robertson with enough intelligence for him to formulate plans for the expedition.

The Colonel chose three subordinate officers for the mission. Lieutenant-Colonels Robert Hays and James Ford assisted with preparations and later served under Colonel Robertson during the land campaign. He selected David Hay to command 50 men for a river expedition consisting of three boats loaded with additional supplies for the army. They were to rendezvous with Robertson's men at a predetermined location on the Tennessee River. In addition to bringing more supplies, another purpose for the river flotilla was to evacuate any wounded men following the attack against Coldwater.

Food rations consisted of jerked venison and corn. Each man received an ample supply of powder and lead. They made floats out of hides that were sewn together and sealed. The land party intended to use them to float men and supplies across the Tennessee River after reaching their place to cross near Muscle Shoals.

By late June of 1787, the preparations were completed; and the militia mustered at Colonel Robertson's plantation on Richland Creek. A lot of fanfare and military discipline were on display during the gathering. Following a short speech from Colonel Robertson, the frontiersmen proudly departed in tight formation as throngs of friends and relatives cheered them on and bade them a hearty farewell. Several onlookers urged them to give the Indians the kind of torment that they had inflicted upon the settlers. About 130 men marched out under the command of Colonel Robertson. Shortly afterward, 50 men under the command of David Hay sailed south with additional supplies for Robertson's men.

Colonel Robertson's younger brother, Captain Elijah Robertson, served as one of his junior officers. Elijah was a capable and experienced frontiersman like their brother Mark, who died in an Indian ambush the month before. Elijah and James previously fought together at the legendary Battle of Point Pleasant in 1774. Both James and Elijah wanted justice for the murder of their brother Mark.

The Chickasaw scouts guided the land expedition for over a week before reaching the place where they were to cross the Tennessee River. When they arrived, they noticed some unoccupied cabins on the other side, as well as a large canoe beached on an island near the opposite shore. Initially there was nobody in sight, but several Indian scouts soon appeared on the other side. However, they did not see the whites on the other side that were hiding in the cane next to the riverbank. The Indians swam out to the canoe, boarded it and started paddling toward the whites on the other side of the river. Suddenly, they turned around and returned the craft to the island. From there, they swam the brief distance to shore and quickly departed in the direction that they had come from.

Colonel Robertson deduced from the Indians' behavior that they might be aware that his army was on the way. Because of the new situation, he decided to gather more intelligence before crossing the river. He ordered Captain Rains and a few others to scout upriver to try to find and capture at least one Indian for interrogation. Unfortunately, Rains' party returned empty-handed just before sundown.

Believing that the Indians might be planning an ambush, Robertson was faced with the choice of either retreating or moving forward. Whenever such life-or-death decisions needed to be made, it was customary to call a meeting of all the men to debate their options. The meeting turned out to be a mere formality because most of the men expressed an eagerness to cross the river and attack, even if they had lost the element of surprise.

The next morning, Colonel Robertson ordered a few men to swim to the island and bring back the canoe. After they returned, several men boarded canoe and started paddling toward the other side. However, it started sinking due to a large leak. Fortunately, everyone made it safely back to shore with the damaged canoe. It turned out to be a large leak that took several hours to properly repair. It was then clear to everyone that the Indians had turned the canoe around the day before because of the leak. Either they were short on time, or they lacked the inclination to do the difficult repair work.

After fixing the leak, the men climbed in once again and pushed off toward other side of the river. The rest of the men either swam across with the horses or used the handmade floats to ferry equipment and supplies to the other side. When all of the men, horses and paraphernalia had finally made it over, it started to rain. By then it was late, so Colonel Robertson ordered his men to take shelter for the night inside the cabins.

By sunrise the next morning, the weather had cleared. Robertson and his officers lead their men out early as they rode along a well-worn trail toward Coldwater. Scouts went ahead to try to prevent a possible ambush along the way. After traveling for several miles, the army eventually caught up with the scouts at a place that overlooked the village. Coldwater was surrounded by corn and other crops; and it was situated near the mouth of a large cave spring that gave the village its name.

Before ordering the attack, Colonel Robertson spoke to his men and warned them against killing innocent women and children. He reminded them that they were obliged to observe the rules of civilized warfare, even if the Indians did not adhere to the same standards.

Afterward, he ordered Captain Rains to take four sharpshooters and deploy them on the riverbank opposite the village. He posted them there to ambush any retreating warriors. After issuing his last-minute orders to Rains and his men, Colonel Robertson led the main body across the river to attack the village.

The battle plan was executed with precision. The whites caught the enemy by surprise and thoroughly routed everyone in the village. Most of the Indians ran to their canoes or jumped into the river as they looked back at their attackers. Many never even noticed Rains and his men firing at them from the opposite bank. Some escaped, but many were shot in their canoes or as they swam downriver.

Among the dead were three French traders, two men and a woman (who was accidently shot). Toka and the other Chickasaw scout pulled 26 dead warriors out of the water, including two chiefs. One of the chiefs was a Creek and the other was a Chickamauga. Few, were killed within the village because nearly everyone fled as soon as the attack began. For his part, Colonel Robertson was very pleased that none of his men were killed or wounded during the engagement.

The raid yielded one surprise. Although they expected to find Spaniards among the Indians, there were only Frenchmen. According to the senior French trader who was taken prisoner, about 35 Chickamaugas and 20 Creeks had recently arrived at the village to gather a large war party to attack the white settlements.

After the battle, a search of the area revealed a large trading post stocked with goods. There were knives, tomahawks, powder, bullets, salt, blankets, cloth, trinkets, paint, coffee, sugar, tafia (French rum) and various other supplies.

Colonel Robertson generously rewarded his Chickasaw scouts for their services. He gave Toka and his companion extra horses, rifles and as many blankets and trade goods as they could pack on their horses. But the scalps they took were more prized than the gifts. After returning to their village, they would display the scalps to confirm their prowess as warriors. And they would tell many new stories about their bravery during the battle.

Colonel Robertson ordered his men to burn the cabins; destroy the crops, food stores and anything of use. Finally, they killed all of the livestock and left the smoldering village in ruin with nothing left to sustain the Indians who managed to escape. Through those actions, Robertson left a clear message to the survivors that they could no longer attack the white settlers with impunity.

The next day, Colonel Robertson distributed of some of the confiscated coffee and sugar to his men. The remainder of the plunder was loaded onto boats, along with the prisoners. Jonathan Denton, Benjamin Drake, and John and Moses Eskridge were put in charge of the prisoners and supplies for the trip downstream to the Tennessee River. They would rendezvous there with the main group who would ride there on horseback.

The two parties successfully rendezvoused at a Chickasaw crossing place on the Tennessee River known as Colbert's Ferry. There, the six French prisoners and one squaw were given their personal belongings, some supplies and a canoe. Appreciating the kindness as well as their freedom, they quickly departed and paddled northward toward their homes near Detroit.

Without delay, the main body continued on toward home by land. The rest transported the remaining plunder in boats. Later while voyaging on the river, they encountered two boats piloted by Frenchmen who were heading in the opposite direction. Thinking that the Americans were their own countrymen, they fired their rifles into the air as a greeting. The Americans managed to board the two vessels before the Frenchmen had realized their mistake. They quickly found themselves staring down the barrels of the Americans' rifles, without having had enough time to reload their own.

While searching the boats, the Americans discovered that they were loaded with a variety of Indian trade goods, including powder and shot. Realizing that the Frenchmen were headed toward the hostiles that they had just defeated, the Americans decided that it would be unwise to allow them to pass.

They confiscated all of the goods and told the Frenchmen that they had the choice of coming with them to Nashville where they would have the opportunity to defend trading with hostile Indians, and ask for the return of their merchandise. Or they could leave their supplies with the Americans and depart unmolested in one of the boats. Fearing for their safety, the Frenchmen chose the second option and quickly departed.

When the boats arrived at Nashville with the two additional vessels and more confiscated merchandise, Colonel Robertson immediately recognized the potential for an international crisis with France, America's ally during the Revolution. Not wanting to alienate a former ally, Robertson immediately penned a remorseful and conciliatory letter to Monsieur Cruzat, French Commandant of St. Louis. Robertson wrote about the hardships endured by the Cumberland settlers, and he explained that frequent raiding parties of hostile Indians had necessitated the Coldwater expedition. He further stated that his men had waylaid the French supply boats on their own initiative since he was not there to guide their actions.

Robertson's letter demonstrated his knowledge of international law, as well as his finesse in handling sensitive diplomatic correspondence. Firearms, powder and lead were rightly considered to be contraband that could be legally confiscated. He acknowledged that the other supplies were not contraband and that his men should not have impounded them. He apologized for the incident and invited the rightful owners to come to Nashville to retrieve their goods. He closed by expressing warm feelings for his French neighbors and a desire to maintain peaceful relations.

The contrite and conciliatory letter succeeded. From then on, Robertson and his fellow frontiersmen were free from any Indians attacks incited by French traders. French authorities were obviously moved by his letter, and they let it be known that their subjects were to refrain from any activities that might be harmful to the Cumberland settlers.

While the attack against Coldwater was a complete success, there was trouble for David Hay's supply flotilla. After navigating along the Cumberland, Ohio and Tennessee Rivers, they had made it as far south as the mouth of the Duck River. When they arrived there, one of the boats turned into the Duck to investigate why a canoe was beached on the embankment.

Earlier, the Indians had seen the boats approaching and had set up an ambush, using their canoe as bait to lure them in. When the boat arrived at the canoe, the Indians opened fire from their hiding places in the cane along the shore. Their initial volley hit four of the men: Josiah Renfroe was killed by a bullet to the head, John Top and Hugh Roquering were badly wounded and Edward Hogan was hit, but not seriously hurt.

With some difficulty and a lot of effort, the survivors were able to maneuver their boat away from the Indians. Using poles and oars to move upstream, they eventually made it back to the safety of the Tennessee River without suffering any more casualties.

Afterward, they held an emergency meeting to discuss the situation. Hay and his men eventually decided to abort their mission and return to Nashville out of concern that the injured men might die if they did not receive proper treatment. They reversed course and headed home along the same route that they came.

When they reached Nashville, they unloaded the injured men at Eaton's Station where they could receive suitable care. Their bullet wounds were nursed over time and all three men eventually recovered.

Chapter 38

THE ARRIVAL OF A FUTURE PRESIDENT

The Coldwater Expedition did not have the desired effect on the hostile Indians. As Cherokee braves matured, some migrated south to the Chickamauga towns. The warrior culture remained strong among the Cherokees and while most of their chiefs counseled for peace, some of the young men opted for the glory of war. Encouraged by the newcomers as well as their Creek allies, the Chickamaugas were bent on revenge against the whites who had killed their warriors at Coldwater.

If Colonel Robertson and his fellow settlers did not yet fully comprehend how deeply ingrained the desire for revenge was in the Indian culture, they soon learned. Small bands of Chickamaugas, Creeks or combined parties continued to ambush settlers. In that way, they could avoid excessive casualties that they would incur during larger assaults. They knew that they could not replace their losses as easily as the whites. Ever increasing numbers of settlers arriving in the western settlements allowed the whites to replace their casualties.

Due to the circumstances, the Indians avoided large-scale attacks and focused on smaller targets of opportunity, such as people traveling between stations or men working in the fields. Because the whites were usually vigilant, they often frustrated their attackers by putting up a good fight or by escaping before incurring too many casualties. Therefore, neither side suffered the level of losses that would have resulted from large-scale Indian attacks.

The Cumberland settlers benefited from the influx of immigrants who arrived in ever increasing numbers. Some came to take advantage of land grants; while others wanted to buy relatively cheap land. In that era, the acquisition of land for farming was the aspiration of many people. Land speculation was a means of becoming wealthy, and many of the western leaders were actively involved in that pursuit. It was considered to be an honorable endeavor for the leading men of that time. Robertson often assisted others by locating land and surveying it in exchange for a quarter of their parcel as payment for his services.

Major Evans eventually followed orders and arrived with a battalion of men to protect Davidson County and the surrounding areas. He and his men were charged with the responsibility for constructing a wagon road from East Tennessee to Nashville. It was also their duty to provide armed escorts for groups of immigrants. His arrival in late 1787 marked the first time that North Carolina responded to any of Robertson's pleas for armed assistance. His first request was in 1781 before the North Carolina Legislature. After that, he made annual requests in person to the Governor and State Legislature, followed by official letters asking for help.

Even with the additional troops and the influx of new settlers, the attacks continued. Scouts patrolled for signs of Indians and attacked them whenever they could. Following an Indian attack, scouts would guide the militia in search of the war party.

In the fall of 1788, a young backwoods lawyer rode toward Nashville during that time of terror and violence. One night after his party and their guards bedded down for the night, he heard what sounded like Indians, and he awakened his companions. He urged them to quietly and quickly depart, which they did. The next day, another group that was traveling behind them was attacked and almost annihilated at nearly the same location. The lawyer's alert and decisive action probably saved his party from a similar fate. Thanks to one of Major Evans' cavalry escorts, he and his fellow travelers arrived safely in Nashville. The young lawyer's name was Andrew Jackson, future President of the United States.

Prior to Jackson's arrival, North Carolina had created a second judicial district. Formerly all judicial matters in the over-mountain region were adjudicated at the Washington District Courthouse in Jonesboro. The newly created Mero District Court was established to handle legal matters in the western Counties of Davidson, Sumner and Tennessee. Tennessee County had just been created out of a portion of Davidson County.

Andrew Jackson was licensed to practice law in North Carolina one year prior to his arrival at Nashville. He came with his Salisbury roommate and fellow attorney, John McNairy, who was appointed to be judge for the new Mero District. He in turn hired Jackson to fill the position of District Solicitor (similar to District Attorney).

Jackson was a self-made man whose early life was defined by poverty and adversity. His widowed mother, Elizabeth, had the task of rearing Andrew and his two brothers in the Waxhaw District of North Carolina. During the Revolution, his oldest brother, Hugh, died while serving in the patriot militia. In 1781, Andrew and his remaining brother, Robert, joined the patriot irregulars in Waxhaw. He and Robert were later captured by British soldiers near their aunt's house. After Andrew refused a British officer's order to clean his muddy boots, the officer retaliated by slashing the boy's head with his saber.

The injured Andrew and his brother Robert were transferred with other prisoners to Camden, South Carolina. At Camden, they were mistreated and imprisoned in wretched conditions where smallpox was rampant. Their mother Elizabeth followed them to Camden and eventually brought them home after their release.

Robert was already gravely ill with smallpox, but he managed to make it home before dying two days later. Andrew was the next to come down with smallpox. However, Elizabeth managed to nurse him back to health.

Once Andrew recovered, Elizabeth traveled 160 miles to Charleston to look after her two nephews who were imprisoned there. She was exhausted by the time she arrived, and she contracted cholera and died several days later. All of his losses, hardships and brutal treatment caused Andrew to despise the British. By most accounts, he hated the British for the rest of his life.

Andrew Jackson was only fourteen years old when he received the news of his mother's death. From then on, he knew that if he had any hope for making it in the world, he would have to do it on his own. And so he did.

After Jackson arrived in Nashville, he quickly settled in and enthusiastically embraced his job as Solicitor. He rented a room from John Donelson's widow. Her daughter, Rachel Robards, was living there at the time because she was having marital problems and was separated from her husband. Rachel would eventually become Jackson's wife.

John Overton was also living there and he and Jackson became roommates. They developed a friendship that lasted for many years.

Like most young men who lived in Nashville during that era, Jackson joined the militia as a private. Colonel Robertson welcomed the newcomer into the community and the two men eventually became good friends, despite the age difference. Both held prominent positions in the community that brought them together professionally and socially. Although their personalities were dissimilar, both enjoyed their friendship and valued each other's loyalty. Jackson was petulant, volatile and rash while Robertson was even-tempered, contemplative and conciliatory. It was truly a case of two opposites who complemented one another.

Jackson was only 21 years old when he arrived in Nashville and Robertson was 46 at the time. Partly because of their differences in age, and also due to their very different personalities, Robertson frequently acted as Jackson's mentor and supporter. Jackson did not always follow Robertson's advice, but he respected his mentor and listened to his wise counsel.

On one particular occasion, Jackson would allow his emotions to override reason. He would reject Robertson's sound advice and it would nearly cost him his life.

Chapter 39

BROWN'S RIVER VOYAGE

In March of 1788, John Sevier's term as Governor of the State of Franklin expired. Later that year, the State faded out of existence. There were several factors that contributed to the downfall. North Carolina demonstrated a renewed interest in keeping that region within its domain. Soon thereafter, an armed confrontation between Sevier's Franklinites and John Tipton's North Carolina loyalists served to punctuate Franklin's demise. The creation of the United States Constitution was the final blow. The Constitution was drafted in 1787 and subsequently submitted to the various states for ratification in 1788. Because the State of Franklin had not been admitted to the Nation under Articles of Confederation, it was neither recognized as a state, nor included in the ratification process.

In May of 1788, John Sevier and the eastern settlers once again went to war against the Cherokees. A settler named Kirk and his family lived on the Little River, about twelve miles south of present-day Knoxville. While he and his son were away from home, a Cherokee named Slim Tom came to the cabin and asked for food. Since Kirk's wife and children knew Tom, they thought nothing of helping him. Mrs. Kirk was unaware that Tom was scouting for a party of warriors who were trying to find out who was at home. After Slim Tom reported that the father and eldest son were away, he and the other Cherokees swept down on the cabin and brutally massacred all eleven members of the Kirk family who were there at the time.

To his horror, when Kirk returned home he discovered the carnage. He sounded the alarm, and the local militia soon formed under the command of John Sevier who continued to be the undisputed local leader, despite the absence of any remaining official title. He and his force of about 700 men attacked several Indian villages in retaliation for the Kirk family massacre. One of the villages was occupied by many peaceful Cherokees, including an affable chief named Abraham. He and another chief, named Tassel, along with four other friendly Indians, were soon rounded up and placed under guard in a cabin. An officer named Hubbard was in charge because John Sevier was elsewhere on militia business.

Shortly afterward, Kirk's son arrived at the cabin. Still grieving from the loss of his mother and siblings, he flew into a rage when he saw the Indian captives. Without hesitation, he removed his tomahawk and buried it into the skull of the nearest Indian, killing him instantly. Hubbard and the guards looked on, without making any effort to intervene, as Kirk successively killed the remaining captives. Witnesses reported that the other Cherokee prisoners seemed to have resigned themselves to their fate. They sat quietly with their eyes downcast and awaited their turn for the full measure of young Kirk's vengeance.

John Sevier arrived at the cabin after the killings and was appalled by what had happened. He was furious that anyone under his command would commit such an atrocity against unarmed prisoners. While he was interrogating Hubbard, Kirk and the guards, his disapproval was obvious to everyone. At some point during the questioning, Kirk interrupted Sevier and asked him what he would have done in his place. The question caused Sevier to pause and contemplate his response. As he thought it over, his anger slowly subsided. Sensing that there was no sympathy for his stance regarding the incident among any of his men, Sevier decided to let the matter drop. He was the unofficial leader of the militia, and he needed to be mindful of the opinions and sympathies of his subordinates. Due the state of affairs, Kirk and Hubbard escaped punishment for their crimes.

In 1788, at least twenty-two immigrant families traveled under armed guard along the narrow road leading to Nashville. Colonel James Brown of North Carolina had served as an officer during the Revolution. He received generous land grants for his service, and that prompted him to relocate his family to Nashville. Brown was a man of some means who owned a lot of possessions, including several slaves. The road had not yet been sufficiently widened to accommodate wagons. Rather than use a pack train, Brown decided that it would be better to transport the people and belongings to Nashville by boat. The timing was bad because war had just broken out between the whites and Cherokees. As a result, it turned out to be a fateful decision.

Brown was a brave man and a careful planner. He oversaw the construction of a large boat on the Holston River. The boat had thick oak gunwales with portholes for protection, and he installed a swivel cannon for additional firepower. Five young men were hired to join his party for added security. J. Bays, John Flood, John and William Gentry and John Griffin served as laborers and riflemen during the voyage.

Colonel Brown sailed down the Holston on May 4, 1788 with his wife, two adult sons, seven children, several slaves and five hired hands. The timing of their departure proved fateful because it was the same month as the Kirk family massacre that ignited warfare throughout the region.

After the boat reached the Tennessee River, they drew near the notorious Chickamauga villages of Running Water and Nickajack. As they came close, they were greeted by four canoes filled with Indians waving a white flag. The canoes came alongside both sides of the boat and the Indians grabbed hold of it. Because there were about 40 Indians, Brown was wary and told them not to come aboard his boat. Among the Indians was a white man who professed friendship and spoke about a recent treaty between the whites and Indians. He said that they only wanted to trade.

Soon they clambered aboard his boat, and started rummaging through the cargo. While Brown was trying to control the situation, more Indians paddled out from where they had been hiding in the reeds along the riverbank. Once they reached the boat, the new arrivals gave the Indians an overwhelming numerical advantage. At that moment, Colonel Brown's fate was sealed.

An Indian with a sword started harassing one of Brown's young sons. Brown came to the boy's aid and reprimanded the warrior. Afterward, when he turned to walk back to another section of the boat, the Indian attacked him from behind. The Indian's sword slashed Brown's neck so deeply that it nearly cut off his head. The warrior shoved his lifeless body overboard and watched it slowly sink beneath the surface.

There was some initial uncertainty among the whites about what had just occurred. Amid all of the confusion, no one actually saw the attack. Meanwhile, most of the Indians were busy moving the cargo and supplies from the boat into their canoes.

Incredibly, after the murder of Colonel Brown, the Indians continued their expressions of friendship. They offered the survivors their hospitality for the night. Everything had happened so fast that the whites were in a state of shock and confusion. The

Indians quickly separated the youngsters, women and slaves from the white men and put them in their canoes to take them ashore. They told the five young hired hands to steer the boat downstream to a calm spot where they could tie it up before coming to the village.

As the boatmen were heading downriver, Indians who had concealed themselves along high points on the riverbank fired down at the unprotected men. The hail of gunfire killed some of the men and wounded others. Afterward, several warriors retrieved the boat and brought the wounded survivors to their village. Once there, the Indians amused themselves by torturing their prisoners before slowly burning them alive at the stake.

Once the canoes containing the captive women, children and slaves had landed on shore, the Indians divided them up amongst themselves to use as slaves. Joseph Brown was twelve years old at the time and he later provided a written narrative of his time in bondage. He revealed that his captors initially wanted to kill him out of concern that he might escape and lead the whites back to attack the village. Although he narrowly survived execution, he soon found himself working as a slave for his Indian master. Over time, his treatment gradually improved as he became more familiar with his Indian captors.

Joseph and the other Brown family survivors eventually regained their freedom in a prisoner exchange arranged by John Sevier after he heard the news about their captivity from a friendly white trader.

The Indians' initial concern that Joseph Brown might later return and guide the way for whites to attack the villages was well-founded. A few years later, he would do just that.

Chapter 40

BLOODSHED AND DIPLOMACY

The Chickamaugas and Creeks continued their retaliatory attacks against the Cumberland settlements throughout 1788. Bloodshed and terror reigned throughout the region as roving bands of warriors exacted their cruel revenge in response to the Coldwater Expedition.

The Indians used spies to obtain useful information before planning their attacks. Their spies provided information about the locations of the settlements and the strength of their defenses. They also found out where the whites' leading men lived and passed the information on to their chiefs who devised plans for the attacks.

In March of 1788, a war party was searching for targets of opportunity near Colonel Robertson's plantation on Richland Creek. His son Peyton and boy named John Johnston were working at a nearby sugar camp where they were busy bringing in buckets of maple sap to boil down to make molasses and sugar. They were so consumed by their chores that they failed to see Indians closing in.

The warriors captured the boys and subsequently murdered twelve-year-old Peyton as revenge for his father's attack against

Coldwater. They took the Johnston boy back to their village and held him captive for several years.

James and Charlotte were heartbroken over the loss of their son. He died before reaching manhood, but in many ways he had already matured beyond his age. Youths on the frontier had numerous responsibilities such as hunting, farm chores and self-defense that forced them to mature earlier than their peers living in the towns and cities to the east.

While still grieving over the loss of his son, Robertson quickly turned his attention to securing the release of Peyton's friend, John. Soon afterward, he wrote a letter to the Chief of the Creeks on behalf of the Johnston family. Although Robertson's effort was unsuccessful, he rose above his own grief to try to help the other family.

Colonels James Robertson and Anthony Bledsoe were the two prominent leaders at that time. Robertson enjoyed preeminence throughout the region. Bledsoe was in command of the Sumner County militia and served in the State Assembly. Robertson represented Davidson County, and both men worked closely together to pass legislation and enhance the security for their fellow settlers.

The Indians knew where Robertson and Bledsoe lived and targeted them both, as well as their families, for death. The Indians' ultimate goal was to kill the leaders and demoralize the rest of the settlers to the point that they would flee the region.

Whenever the Indians went on the warpath, additional white scouts would patrol the area to defend against their attacks. Some of the scouts used specially trained bear hounds to hunt for warriors. The dogs were very good at picking up the smell of Indians. A few exceptional hounds were even known to abandon a bear chase to pursue the scent of Indians.

One such dog that showed a preference for hunting Indians was owned by the Castleman family. His name was Red-gill, and he was a legendary Indian hunter. Either alone or at the head of a pack, Red-gill would lead the way. The Indians dreaded dog pursuits because they were difficult to elude. The hounds were fast, and they presented difficult targets for the warriors' muskets. Whenever Indians shot at the pursuing dogs, they often missed their mark. That would give the hounds an opening to attack the warriors before they had time to reload.

Robertson and Bledsoe sent letters to successive Governors Caswell and Martin of North Carolina asking for protection against the Indians. They also penned letters to their friend, John Sevier, asking for his assistance. They even wrote a conciliatory letter to Alexander McGillivray, the mixed-breed Chief of the Creeks. McGillivray replied in a friendly manner and wrote that sufficient blood had been spilled to even the score for the Coldwater Expedition. He ended by stating that he and his people wanted peace.

Unfortunately, McGillivray was an intelligent and crafty character who was not to be trusted. The Spaniards had recently granted him an officer's commission and a generous annual stipend for his services. Like the Spanish officials who were his mentors, McGillivray was proficient in the arts of deception and treachery. Therefore, the atrocities committed by the Creeks and their Chickamauga allies continued, unabated.

Desperate to find help, Robertson and Bledsoe traveled to Kentucky in mid-1788 to consult with Boone and other leaders. Robertson and Bledsoe were worried because the Coldwater Expedition had not discouraged the Indians from attacking. In fact, the Indians' desire for revenge had only motivated them to increase their raids. Although the Kentuckians were sympathetic to the plight of their southern neighbors, they were unable to promise reinforcements until after they had completed their fall corn harvest.

On July 20th 1788, the Indians were successful in assassinating another leading man. Due to increasing number of Indian attacks, Colonel Anthony Bledsoe had evacuated his station and relocated his family to his brother's fort at Bledsoe's Lick. The night they arrived there, Colonel Bledsoe awakened to the sound of stampeding livestock and barking dogs. When he and his Irish servant, Campbell, stepped outside to investigate the cause of the commotion, both men were ambushed by Indians. Campbell was shot dead and Colonel Bledsoe was mortally wounded. He died from his wounds the next day.

Colonel Robertson was shaken by the news. He had already endured the deaths of so many friends and loved ones. This one hurt more than most because Bledsoe was a close friend and advisor whose leadership skills, intelligence and strength of character would be sorely missed. The leadership void brought back sad memories for Robertson. It reminded him that the Indians had already killed or driven off most of his original friends and neighbors.

It seemed as though the carnage would never end. But as always, Robertson kept his grief and his fears to himself. No matter how worried or desperate he was, as the settlers' leader, he knew that he had to maintain his composure. A display of steadfast resolve was imperative in order to avoid a widespread panic among his fellow settlers.

James Robertson mentions the death of his son in this letter.

Chapter 41

THE UNITED STATES OF AMERICA

Despite the number of Indian atrocities, the frontier population continued to grow. Many immigrants were veterans of the Revolution who were eager to claim their land grants, regardless of the danger. The veterans were brave men who survived the perils of war. The lure of a better life, made possible by land grants, for many was stronger than any fear of Indians.

Because of a weak National Government and the mostly unsupportive parent state of North Carolina, James Robertson felt compelled to make diplomatic overtures toward his enemies. He named the Mero District after Esteban Miro (despite the misspelling of his name), a Spanish army officer serving as governor of the Spanish colonies of Florida and Louisiana. Robertson wanted to hold the Spaniards and Indians at bay to help his people survive. Despite his diplomatic overtures toward Miro and Chief Alexander McGillivray, he knew that neither the Spaniards nor the Indians could be trusted. The settlers' population, while continuing to grow, was still too low to insure their survival. By resorting to diplomacy, Robertson believed that he could buy more time to prevent a full-scale war that could result in the destruction of the frontier settlements.

Robertson understood the intentions of Spanish officials and carefully controlled the negotiations. He knew that they were corrupt, and he used their greed to get what he wanted. Spain controlled navigation on the Mississippi River and one of Robertson's objectives was to gain permission to ship goods along the river to market. He eventually persuaded Miro to open up the Mississippi River after showing him the means by which he and other Spanish officials could profit from the settlers' commercial transactions along the river.

A prominent Kentucky leader named James Wilkinson was also negotiating with Miro at the time, but his motives were different from Robertson's. Wilkinson was an intelligent and ambitious man. There is ample evidence to suggest that he conspired with Miro to transform Kentucky either into a fiefdom or a Spanish colony. Wilkinson wanted to do it for his personal wealth and power; and Miro encouraged his conspiracy because it would create a barrier against the westward expansion of the United States.

Miro tried to accomplish the same goal in Tennessee, but Robertson and Sevier understood his motives and bought more time and concessions by playing along. There is no evidence to suggest that either man was interested creating a new country or becoming a province of Spain. Robertson and Sevier communicated regularly with each other and they jointly outmaneuvered Miro during the course of negotiations. Both men were patriotic Americans who really wanted no part in such schemes.

While Robertson's settlers continued to struggle for their very survival, the newly created United States Constitution was sent to each state for ratification. For various reasons, especially concern about a central government that was too powerful, ratification seemed to be uncertain in North Carolina and other states. Having recently freed themselves from British tyranny, many Americans were wary of a strong central government that could potentially overburden the states and oppress the people. They had earned their freedom by winning the Revolution and they were determined to keep it. Despite a lot of controversy and rancor, all of the states eventually ratified the Constitution after reaching an agreement that Congress would enact a Bill of Rights to preserve individual freedoms and States' rights. In 1789, Congress passed the first ten amendments to the Constitution, known as the Bill of Rights, and sent them to each state for ratification. In that same session, Congress elected George Washington as the first President of the United States under the new Constitution.

Those momentous events boded well for the settlers living in the regions that are now the states of Kentucky and Tennessee. Through prior agreements with the federal government, Virginia and North Carolina ceded their western territories to the United States. Congress subsequently established the Territory Southwest of the Ohio River. The United States did so in anticipation of carving new states out of the region.

President Washington appointed John Sevier as Brigadier General of the Washington District and James Robertson as Brigadier General of the Mero District. William Blount was appointed Governor of the new Territory. The arrangement worked well because Robertson, Sevier and Blount were mutual friends who had previously worked well together. The three men were concerned about the safety of the people and wanted to encourage new settlers. A population increase would bring in more riflemen to provide greater security. It would also move the region closer to the number of residents required to apply for statehood.

All three men were involved in land speculation, but Blount was the most aggressive and probably the least altruistic in his motives for acquiring property. He was also wealthier, worldlier and more educated than Robertson or Sevier. However, each of the three men was a natural leader and highly intelligent. Blount and Sevier were more gregarious than Robertson who tended to be rather serious and more reserved. Robertson and Sevier enjoyed immense popularity among their fellow frontiersmen who respected them for their leadership, courage and deeds.

Chapter 42

PRESIDENT WASHINGTON

George Washington entered the office of President of the United States with a wealth of military experience. In addition to his service during the Revolution, he fought in the French and Indian War as an officer in the colonial militia.

In 1754, twenty-two-year-old George Washington led a body of militia who ambushed a French and Indian contingent on the Maryland frontier. It was the first armed conflict in a struggle between Britain and France over control of the western frontier. Shortly afterward, on July 4, 1754 Washington was forced to surrender Fort Necessity to the French and Indians who had besieged the fort.

The following year, on July 9th 1755 Washington served with heroic distinction during General Braddock's disastrous defeat ten miles from Fort Duquesne on the Monongahela River. Braddock was mortally wounded and most of the other officers were either killed or wounded by French and Indian forces before Washington assumed command and organized an orderly retreat. His decisive action ultimately saved the remainder of Braddock's army from annihilation.

Through those and other experiences on the frontier, Washington gained a firsthand understanding of the unique cruelties associated with Indian warfare. Robertson and other frontier leaders knew about Washington's fighting experience and expected him to be sympathetic toward their plight. They anticipated that Washington would provide military assistance to help them survive the frequent Indian attacks.

Although Washington understood the dangerous state of affairs on the frontier, the daunting circumstances he faced after becoming President kept him from providing aid. The Nation continued to experience financial problems from the Revolution and lacked sufficient revenue to pay off old war debts and run the government. Therefore, Washington was financially unable provide any material assistance to the settlers.

Besides the potential financial drain that frontier settlers posed for Washington and Congress, there were commercial and diplomatic considerations that were at odds with providing any real help.

Congressmen from the northeastern states were hostile toward the western settlers because they viewed them as possible competitors against their own commercial shipping and trading interests. Permanent free navigation along the Mississippi River would provide a new route for the import and export of merchandise and agricultural commodities. They also feared that the eventual admission of new states to the Union would dilute their own power in Congress and with government officials.

Probably the most important concerns for Washington were diplomatic. The Nation's finances were unsound and he knew that the United States lacked the resources to prevail in another war with any of the European powers. Britain, France and Spain each had respective colonial holdings in adjacent northern, western and southern lands that bordered the United States. Washington understood that American expansion posed a potential threat to their colonial interests.

Washington and his Secretary of War, Henry Knox, believed that avoiding war with any of those three nations was essential for the survival of the United States. It was clear to them that Europe's history of nearly constant warfare between various competing nations showed their propensity for going to war over the slightest rivalry or provocation.

Washington and Knox also understood that Indian wars could be costly and have unintended consequences. Therefore, they tried to avoid getting involved in such conflicts, if at all possible.

Robertson and the Cumberland settlers were concerned about Spanish incitement of the Cherokees, Chickamaugas and Creeks. Spain supplied the Indians with guns, ammunition and other supplies that enabled them to sustain their war of attrition against the whites. At the same time, the American settlers to the north were being tormented by the Shawnees and their Indian allies who were being instigated by the British and French.

The aforementioned considerations made Washington wary of becoming involved in the Cumberland Indian conflict. For several years, Washington and Knox maintained correspondence with Robertson about the Indian attacks. His letters usually contained appeals for troops, arms or other specific types of assistance; and the responses from either Washington or Knox nearly always denied his requests.

Therefore, Robertson and his fellow settlers were left to fend for themselves.

George Washington sat for this portrait. This is probably a good likeness of him at the time he was corresponding with James Robertson.

Chapter 43

MEANWHILE ON THE FRONTIER

Washington's inauguration at the Federal Building in New York (seat of the U.S. government in 1789) brought no immediate or gradual changes to the harsh existence endured by Americans living on the western frontier. Colonel Robertson and his fellow settlers gradually realized that their circumstances might not improve anytime soon. What changed for them was the source of their frustrations which shifted from politicians in North Carolina, who had failed to adequately protect them, to the new federal government led by President Washington.

Thirteen Cumberland settlers were killed by Indians in 1789. Thirty-one were slaughtered the year before and 54 had died from Indian attacks in 1787. The decline in deaths over that three-year period was likely due to the increased preparedness and organization of the militia, rather than a decrease in the Indians' determination to drive them out. Increasing numbers of new settlers also provided more men to help defend the settlements.

In June of 1789, Indians attempted to kill Colonel Robertson while he and several others were working in the field adjacent to his home. Before he was able to get back to the safety of the stockade surrounding his house, he was shot in the foot. He and the others were able to get inside and close the gate with the

Indians in close pursuit. The attack ended once the Indians realized that they could not press the assault without sustaining casualties.

While Robertson and his wife Charlotte were dressing his wounded foot, he ordered his brother Elijah to muster a group of militiamen to pursue the Indians. Andrew Jackson was one of over sixty men chosen to take part in the chase. Once the men were assembled, Colonel Robertson selected Captain Samson Williams to lead the group.

The men followed the Indian's trail for some time before Capt. Williams selected twenty men, including Andrew Jackson, to quickly move forward on a forced march to catch up with the fleeing Indians. They eventually found the Indians encamped on the far side of the Duck River. To avoid detection, the whites traveled about a mile up the river before crossing. While moving back down toward the Indians' camp, they became disoriented in the darkness while moving through the thick cane. Capt. Williams ordered his men to halt and sleep there until morning.

At sunrise, the men cautiously moved forward until they saw the camp. The Indians were just preparing to eat when Williams and his men rushed toward them and began firing. The Indians were caught off guard and fled across the river, leaving most of their belongings behind. The whites killed five warriors and wounded several others during the assault.

In the camp they recovered sixteen guns, powder horns, shot pouches, blankets and other articles that the Indians had left behind during their hasty escape. Since they were caught off guard by the ambush, the Indians apparently believed they had eluded their pursuers. Convinced that the warriors could do no further harm without their weapons, Colonel Williams did not try to follow the fleeing survivors.

Although the Indians killed thirteen settlers that year, the whites inflicted even higher casualties upon them. With each passing year, the settler population grew and their preparedness improved. Despite their dogged determination to exterminate the whites, the Indians' position grew progressively untenable because their own population remained static. They could ill afford warrior losses sustained during skirmishes. However, neither the warring chiefs nor their Spanish benefactors had yet realized that they could not win a war of attrition against the ever-growing population of settlers.

John Sevier was a heroic man and first governor of Tennessee.

Chapter 44

SOUTHWEST TERRITORY

On May 26, 1790, President George Washington signed into law a bill passed by Congress that established the United States Territory South of the River Ohio. The new Territory was commonly known as the Southwest Territory and it encompassed the lands that comprise present-day Kentucky and Tennessee.

The Tennessee portion of the Territory was divided into two districts. The western district was named the Washington District. It comprised Washington, Sullivan, Green and Hawkins Counties. The Mero District in the eastern part of the Territory included Davidson, Sumner and Tennessee Counties. As stated earlier, President Washington appointed John Sevier as Brigadier General of the Washington District and James Robertson as Brigadier General of the Mero District. Both men were experienced militia officers and seasoned Indian fighters who were highly qualified to serve as Brigadier Generals in the United States Army.

President Washington attempted to pacify the Creek Indians who had been wreaking havoc among the settlers in the newly created Southwest Territory. He authorized his Secretary of War, Henry Knox, to convene treaty negotiations for that purpose in New York. Alexander McGillivray and several other Creek chiefs were invited to attend. In his usual fashion, the wily McGillivray was duplicitous in his discussions with Knox. His empty proclamations of a sincere desire for peace brought significant rewards for himself and the other Creek chiefs. He left New York with a United States officer's commission, a $1,555 annual stipend and several gifts for himself and the other chiefs.

Unfortunately, Knox was unaware that McGillivray had already received a Spanish officer's commission with an annual stipend from the Spanish Crown. While he and the other chiefs made a few small concessions, they received a lot more than they gave up. Before the ink was dry on the 1790 Treaty of New York, the Creek attacks against the settlers resumed, while McGillivray denied any responsibility for the renewed violence. Although Washington and Knox had made a sincere effort to help the beleaguered settlers, they were clearly duped by the clever McGillivray.

In addition to his considerable responsibilities as Brigadier General for the Mero District, Robertson accepted a temporary appointment as Chickasaw Indian Agent. His reputation as a treaty negotiator, as well as his prior experience as Cherokee Indian Agent, made him an excellent choice to maintain the peace with the Chickasaws. Earlier, Robertson had prevented the likely annihilation of the settlers by making peace with the powerful Chickasaw tribe, and he had developed friendships with Piomingo and the other Chickasaw chiefs. He skillfully managed his relationships with them through honesty and straightforwardness. He also provided them with suitable gifts and hospitality which were greatly appreciated. It was always difficult to obtain gifts and supplies for the tribe, but he always managed to acquire them because he understood the absolute necessity of carefully managing relations with the Chickasaws who were fearsome warriors. They had the means to wipe out the white settlers, but Robertson's keen understanding of Indians helped him pacify them. In time, his careful management transformed them into reliable allies.

By the time the Southwest Territory was created, Nashville had acquired some of the trappings of a civilized town. Much of the progress was due to the selfless efforts of James Robertson. He made an astounding 14 trips back and forth through the wilderness from Nashville to North Carolina between 1781 and 1790 to represent the Cumberland settlers in the State Legislature. The mere fact that he was not killed by hostile Indians or felled by bad weather and harsh wilderness conditions gives testament to the survival skills that he acquired since his early days.

As mentioned earlier, in 1769 he had nearly starved to death while re-crossing the mountains alone to retrieve his family and fellow settlers in North Carolina who were waiting there for him to guide them to Watauga. On his way back to get the others, the young greenhorn became lost for fourteen days and nearly starved to death before he was rescued by two hunters. Afterward, he recovered and guided the awaiting immigrants back over the mountains to settle in Watauga.

As a North Carolina Legislator, Robertson secured the passage of several bills that benefited his constituents. In the Assembly, he became closely associated with the seasoned politician, William Blount, who helped him craft and pass a lot of his legislation. In return, Robertson assisted Blount with frontier land speculation. Blount purchased Revolutionary land grants from veterans and Robertson located, surveyed and recorded his parcels in exchange for a percentage of the land.

By 1790, Nashville had become a well-established town. It had a tavern named The Red Heifer, a Methodist Church and an iron foundry. James Robertson built Cumberland Iron Works on a fork of Barton's Creek to meet the growing demand for farm implements, pots, kettles and other manufactured items that were needed by the growing population in Nashville and the other settlements in the Cumberland region.

Earlier, Robertson crafted legislation to establish the town of Nashville out of the Nashborough settlement. He established Davidson Academy through legislation that set the foundation for a good educational environment in the town. Although he had a limited education himself, he was a visionary who understood the benefits of a formal education. Through his efforts and those of others who followed, Nashville eventually evolved into a center for higher learning. By the nineteenth century, Nashville became known as the "Athens of the South" because of its solid academic reputation.

Chapter 45

NORTHWEST TERRITORY

In 1787, the Confederation Congress established the Territory Northwest of the River Ohio, commonly known as the Northwest Territory, in anticipation of the nation's westward expansion. It was subsequently reconfirmed by the United States Congress under the new Constitution. The Territory encompassed a huge swath of land covering what are now the states of Ohio, Indiana, Illinois, Michigan, Wisconsin and the northeastern part of Minnesota.

Although Great Britain officially ceded that region to the United States in the 1787 Treaty of Paris, the British continued to maintain a presence there to exploit the lucrative fur trade. In much the same way that Spain was inciting violence among the Indians in the south, Britain continued to covet the northern lands. It used the northern tribes as pawns in a strategy to annex the region into British colonial territory.

To further their aims, the British armed the Indians and encouraged them to attack every white settlement as far south as Kentucky. Due to the circumstances, the northern frontiersmen endured atrocities similar to those that were heaped upon settlers in Tennessee. While there was some overlap, such as small bands of Indians venturing north to raid and vice versa, Britain largely manipulated the northern tribes while Spain incited the southern Indians.

In an effort to drive the white settlers out of the Northwest Territory, ten northern tribes formed a confederation. The Shawnees and Miamis provided the largest number of warriors among the tribes who were armed and instigated by their British benefactors. The Indians attacked and slaughtered innocent settlers wherever they could be found.

Due to the extent of the northern atrocities, President Washington felt compelled to protect the settlers and reassert American sovereignty in the Territory. In 1790, he authorized Secretary of War Henry Knox to send a military expedition against the northern tribes. In October of that year, an army of over 1,400 men led by General Josiah Harmar went to quell the violence. Confederation Indians led by Little Turtle and Blue Jacket later ambushed Harmar's army in the Indiana region and killed 129 of his men. The stunning defeat forced him to retreat and abandon his campaign.

Washington reacted to the news of Harmar's defeat by ordering a second expedition to be led by the governor of the Northwest Territory, Major General Arthur St. Clair. When General Robertson heard the news, he persuaded Chief Piomingo to take 50 Chickasaw warriors and ride north to join St. Clair's army. Piomingo and his warriors met up with St. Clair's army, but they left the campaign the day before it was attacked. Piomingo had sensed that St. Clair was a weak leader with poorly trained soldiers who were headed toward disaster.

At dawn the next day on November 4, 1791, Indians led by Little Turtle, Blue Jacket and Tecumseh attacked. Nearly 2,000 warriors assaulted St. Clair's weakly defended camp and completely routed the defenders as the army officers tried unsuccessfully to restore order and mount a defense. The stunning defeat resulted in the largest number of army casualties in any Indian battle in United States history. Of the 920 soldiers and officers, 632 were killed and 264 were wounded. In addition to the army casualties, 200 civilian camp followers were also slaughtered and scalped.

President Washington was stunned and chagrined by St. Clair's unexpected defeat. Following news of the disaster, he became overly cautious before authorizing any more campaigns against the hostile Indians. It would take two more years before Washington would authorize a third expedition against the northern tribes.

The defeats of Harmar and St. Clair resulted in more heartache for the Tennessee settlers. Generals Robertson and Sevier had to depend on their respective local militias. President Washington made it clear in letters to both men that he would not authorize any offensive expeditions against the southern Indians who were attacking innocent settlers. The President was preoccupied with Indian hostilities in the Northwest Territory and he wanted to avoid any escalation of violence in the Southwest Territory. Washington worried that if the northern and southern tribes ever united, a larger Indian war could break out along the entire western frontier. And he knew that he lacked the financial resources to fight a full-scale Indian war.

In the meantime, Governor Blount tried unsuccessfully to persuade the Cherokees to meet and negotiate a new peace treaty. They did not trust Blount and were afraid of an ambush; so they rejected his offer. Blount then turned to General Robertson and asked for his help. The Cherokees knew that Robertson was a man of his word and they trusted him. After he met with them at Chota and calmed their fears about an ambush, they agreed to parley with Blount at White's Fort. White's Fort was located at the site that Blount had chosen for the capitol of the Southwest Territory. He named the town Knoxville to garner favor with Secretary of War Henry Knox.

On July 12, 1791 the Treaty of Holston, also known as Blount's Treaty, was finalized between the United States government and the Cherokees. However, hostilities quickly resumed because some of the Cherokees had no intention of peace; while others did not even participate in the negotiations. Blount was sincere in his attempt to follow President Washington's order to pacify the Indians along the southwestern frontier, but renegade warriors had not yet come to realize the futility of their attacks against the settlers.

General Arthur St. Clair led his army into the worst defeat in the history of the American Indian wars.

Chapter 46

A SON SAVES HIS FATHER

During the winter of 1791-92, Governor Blount had the streets surveyed for the Territorial capitol at Knoxville. He also began construction of a large log house that was to serve as his executive mansion. Knoxville grew rapidly and assumed some of the trappings of civilization. The Territory's first newspaper, the Knoxville Gazette, was founded by George Roulstone and began printing on November 5, 1791.

Blount was an energetic and ambitious governor who was determined to see the Southwest Territory grow and prosper under his leadership. He established a new county, Knox County, with Knoxville as the county seat. From there, Blount continued making important administrative appointments for the benefit of the Territory. He appointed officers in each county (Washington, Sullivan, Greene, Knox, Davidson, Sumner, Hawkins and Tennessee). Blount selected prominent men from each of those counties to fill positions as magistrates, sheriffs, deputy sheriffs, constables, registrars, coroners, court clerks, county attorneys and militia officers.

The two military districts, Washington and Mero, were also the two judicial districts. Governor Blount appointed Robertson's friend, William Cocke, as Attorney General for the Washington

District and his other friend and protégé, Andrew Jackson, as Attorney General for the Mero District. Blount also appointed Jackson to be the Judge-Advocate for the Davidson County militia regiment. It was the first official military appointment for Jackson and marked the beginning of what would become an outstanding career that would eventually elevate him to the White House. Aside from his brief teenage stint in the militia during the Revolution, Jackson earned his all of early military experience and training while serving under General Robertson in the Davidson County militia.

In spite of Governor Blount's Treaty of Holston in July of 1791, Indian attacks were on the rise. While most of the Cherokees remained peaceful, the troublesome Chickamaugas increased their raids under the leadership of John Watts, their new mixed-breed chief. In 1792, Watts replaced the notorious Dragging Canoe who died at age 60 of an apparent heart attack following an all-night scalp dance. Assisting Watts were other mixed-breed warriors who had lived among the whites and provided him with valuable intelligence that led to deadlier attacks. The Indian raids became widespread throughout the Territory. In response, General Sevier posted troops between the Five Lower Towns of the Chickamaugas and the settlers in the Washington District to block incursions into the settlements. His decisive action was somewhat effective in reducing casualties in the eastern part of the Territory. The Indians' fear of Sevier, combined with his militia blockade of the routes to the eastern settlements, caused the warriors to shift their attention to the scattered Cumberland stations in the Mero District.

The vast Mero District was sparsely populated and more difficult to defend. General Robertson sent out scouts and mounted militia to search for war parties. Although Governor Blount refused to authorize offensive campaigns against the

Chickamaugas' Five Lower Towns that launched most of the raids, Robertson adopted aggressive offensive measures within his district. Under Blount's restrictions, it was his best strategy since it reduced the likelihood of surprise attacks, and it made the Indians worry about being ambushed while they roamed the area looking for targets of opportunity.

Robertson and Sevier corresponded regularly to coordinate their defenses. The Indians feared and loathed Sevier because of his numerous campaigns against them, causing death and destruction wherever he went. Some of the Cherokees believed that he had supernatural powers because he had not been injured or killed in over 35 skirmishes. His daring and bravery made him a hero among the settlers, and a feared enemy of the Indians.

Chief John Watts was a crafty, intelligent leader who usually made good strategic decisions. His force was a motley band of renegade Cherokees, Creeks, Shawnees, Delawares, half-breeds and former slaves. His warriors were unified by a desire to kill and plunder. Watts was their Chief and Bloody Fellow, The Breath, The Glass, Double Head, Man Killer, Pumpkin Boy and Bob Benge were some of his trusted subordinates. He and his warriors were indeed the worst of the worst.

By 1792, President Washington's worst fears had materialized. Hostile Indians were attacking white settlers all along the western frontier, from the Northwest Territory to the Southwest Territory. Governor Blount and Generals Robertson and Sevier had done everything they could to keep the peace with the Indians, but they were unsuccessful.

In January of 1792, two of Valentine Sevier's sons, Robert and William, were ambushed and killed while canoeing down the Cumberland River to reinforce a group of besieged settlers. A third son, Valentine Sevier junior, and a companion named John Rice also died that month in a separate ambush. Valentine Sevier,

General John Sevier's brother, lost three sons and he was heartbroken. Valentine wrote a grief-stricken letter to his brother informing him of the deaths of his three sons. In his heartbreaking letter, Valentine asked his brother to send out one of his older surviving sons so that he might have some comfort during his time of grief.

On May 24, 1792, General Robertson and his son, Jonathan, were ambushed near his station. The General was shot through both arms, knocking him off his horse. Jonathan was shot in the hip, but remained on his horse until he saw the Indians rushing in to finish off his wounded his father. Though wounded himself, Jonathan dismounted next to his father and fired at the approaching warriors. Jonathan's shot caused the Indians to halt for a moment. The brief pause allowed just enough time for Jonathan to help his father on his horse and they rode double toward the station amid a hail of gunfire.

After arriving safely at the station, Charlotte treated their wounds. One of General Robertson's arms was so seriously damaged by a bullet that it never completely healed. It was later said by someone who knew him well that he endured pain and occasional oozing from the wound for the rest of his life. Jonathan eventually made a full recovery from the bullet wound in his hip.

Despite his injuries, General Robertson stayed in command and ordered his brother, Colonel Elijah Robertson, to mobilize the militia to pursue the offending warriors and to attack any other war parties they could find. Elijah and his men followed the Indians' trail, but they were unable to catch up. Afterward, they searched for signs of other war parties, but failed to find any. Having no success, they later returned to Nashville and disbanded.

While still convalescing from his wounds, General Robertson acted on Governor Blount's orders to make arrangements for a formal treaty with the Chickasaws and Choctaws. Anthony Foster secured the attendance of the Choctaws who were previously under the influence the Spain, and Robertson brought in the Chickasaws. He knew from experience that the Indians would appreciate good food, whiskey, supplies, arms, jewelry, paint and other items. Despite the difficulty in obtaining the goods and making all of the necessary arrangements, Robertson saw to it that everything was ready when the Indians arrived in Nashville on August 2, 1792.

Governor Blount and General Pickens came to the treaty grounds as representatives of the United States. Many of the Chickasaw and Choctaw chiefs brought their extended families to the gathering. The negotiations progressed well and the Indians from both tribes were impressed by the cordial atmosphere, hospitality and gifts. The talks and entertainment continued for several days before the formal treaty was signed on August 10th, 1792. From then on, the Chickasaws and Choctaws remained loyal to the United States.

For the United States, the treaty was both necessary and timely because it created an alliance with two powerful tribes at a time when the other western tribes were at war with American settlers. At the treaty grounds, the Choctaws had an opportunity to get to know Robertson after hearing good things about him from their Chickasaw allies. Many of the Choctaws were so impressed with Robertson's character and personality that they became his friends. Most of those friendships lasted for the rest of his life. Robertson knew that the very survival of the Cumberland settlements depended on his friendships with members of both tribes. The new treaty with the Chickasaws and Choctaws meant that the two tribes would protect their flanks and the settlers could continue to, "stay and fight it out", as Robertson was fond of saying.

Robertson sent out four scouts to patrol for Indians a month after the treaty was signed. Rains and Kennedy went in one direction while Clayton and Gee went another. On the trail, Clayton and Gee encountered an invading force of about 700 Cherokees, Chickamaugas, Creeks and Shawnees led by John Watts. The unfortunate scouts tried to get away, but they died in a hail of gunfire.

Meanwhile, Rains and Kennedy returned without sighting any Indians along their route. Despite their favorable report, Abe Castleman remained skeptical because there had been two separate credible reports that the Indians were about to attack in mass. On a hunch, the veteran scout decided to ride to Buchanan's Station about four miles east of Nashville to warn them about the danger and to check things out for himself. When he arrived, Castleman discovered that there were only twenty-one riflemen, including himself, to protect the fort.

Meanwhile, John Watts got into a dispute over strategy with a Shawnee chief named Tom Tunbridge. Watts wanted to attack Nashville first and then destroy the weaker outlying stations. Tunbridge wanted to attack Buchanan's Station before going to Nashville. For the sake of maintaining unity and keeping his large army intact, Watts relented and the Indians headed toward Buchanan's Station.

They arrived at dusk on September 30th. Eager for a fight, the Indians left their horses about a mile from the fort. They could see the lights from inside the fort as they advanced on foot. The warriors anticipated that their surprise attack would overwhelm the fort's defenders.

Fortunately for the settlers, Abe Castleman had told everyone at the fort that a friendly half-breed named Fiddleston had arrived at Nashville to warn the settlers about Watts' plans to attack the Cumberland settlements. His warning came on the heels of another similar warning that General Robertson had received from Chief Piomingo of the Chickasaws. Castleman's disturbing news caused Major John Buchanan to post extra sentries with orders to remain vigilant.

Fortunately, there was a full moon and the guards saw the large body of warriors advancing toward the fort. As soon as the sentries were able to make out the shadowy figures, shots rang out and two of the Indians fell dead. The gunshots served as an alarm for everyone in the fort. The Indians had lost the element of surprise when the battle commenced. All of the station's defenders scrambled to their assigned posts and began firing at the enemy. The moonlight illuminated the shadowy figures that were easy targets for the fort's experienced riflemen as they remained protected from the Indians' gunfire by the fort's walls or the blockhouse portholes.

The heated battle lasted throughout the night and gun smoke filled the night air as the Indians repeatedly tried to scale the walls. Mrs. Buchanan bravely joined the fray by ordering the women and children to reload the men's rifles and to put out fires started by the Indians. The warriors repeatedly tried to set the walls and block houses on fire, but the women and children bravely exposed themselves to gunfire and arrows as they poured buckets of water down on the fires. Some of them even took over the positions of fallen riflemen.

Chief Tom Tunbridge was shot dead while placing a torch at the base of one of the blockhouses. Chief John Watts was wounded during the battle. By sunrise, the Indians had sustained many casualties and their leadership was disrupted. Seriously wounded himself, Chief Watts abandoned the siege and ordered a retreat.

Chapter 47

ALL-OUT WAR ON THE FRONTIER

The bloodiest year for the Cumberland settlers was in 1780 when Indians killed 63 of the original frontiersmen. The second largest number of casualties occurred in 1793 when the Chickamaugas, Creeks and their Indian allies waged total war against the settlers in a final, desperate attempt to drive them out. That year, 55 settlers died and countless others were wounded. Several more were kidnapped and held for ransom.

Indian war parties blocked the roads to Nashville and randomly attacked settlers travelling between stations. The warriors laid a bloody siege against all of the settlements as they stole horses, burned crops and drove off livestock in a frenetic attempt to exterminate the white settlers.

As those events were taking place, government officials seemed to be out of touch. Governor Blount wrote to Robertson and ordered him to dismiss troops that had been sent for their defense. In the letter he stated, "You must keep down the expenses. This is a constant injunction from Philadelphia."

Secretary of War Henry Knox wrote to Robertson and revealed how out of touch he was with life on the frontier by inquiring, "Cannot the Indians be appeased by gifts? Have not most of their acts been provoked and done in retaliation?"

Even worse, some of the settlers were angry with Robertson for refusing to lead another offensive campaign like the Coldwater Expedition. Either they were ignorant of the restraints that President Washington and his Secretary of War had placed upon him, or they knew about it and did not care. On one occasion, a disgruntled settler placed an anonymous letter on Robertson's doorstep. The letter had an accusatory tone and blamed Robertson for being too weak to lead. The letter had a sting to it because the charges could not have been more false.

Although Generals Robertson and Sevier admired President Washington and genuinely wanted to carry out his orders, the situation had become intolerable. In their correspondence to each other, they made indirect comments about going after the Indians. They used ambiguous language that each could understand, but not clear enough to put either man in jeopardy of insubordination in case their letters were intercepted and forwarded to the President. Clearly, both men wanted to launch offensive attacks against the Chickamaugas' Five Lower Towns, but their orders prevented them from following their military instincts.

Meanwhile, President Washington's attention was focused on the Indian attacks in the vast Northwest Territory. He believed that the circumstances there were more serious because the Indians were firmly under the control of the nation's former enemy, the British. He considered them to be a bigger threat than the Spanish who were inciting Indian attacks in the Southwest Territory. Therefore, Washington held back Robertson and Sevier while he concentrated on the northwestern Indian uprising.

Still stinging from the successive defeats of Generals Harmar and St. Clair, Washington selected General Anthony Wayne to organize a third campaign against the Northwest Indian

Confederation. Wayne knew that training and discipline were essential for victory. Because of those concerns, he saw to it that his men had sufficient training, armaments and supplies for a successful campaign.

By 1793 General Wayne's well-trained and well-provisioned army was ready for departure. He led the force of over 3,000 men north from present-day Cincinnati to engage the enemy. Along the way, he built a series of forts to safeguard his supply lines and protect his army against attacks from the rear. He was a general who clearly understood the difficulties that lay ahead. Wayne's meticulous planning and preparations would lead to victory in the following year.

Meanwhile, the Cumberland settlers could not go to sleep at night, plow their fields or travel the roads without fearing an Indian attack. One of the first attacks occurred on January 18th 1793 when Major Evan Shelby and two others were killed while returning by canoe from Kentucky with a load of salt. At least 6 more were slaughtered in three other raids that month, including Anthony Bledsoe, son of Colonel Anthony Bledsoe who was mortally wounded during Chief Watts' unsuccessful attack against Bledsoe's Station.

On March 28th of that year, Governor Blount sent a letter to General Robertson informing him about rumors that the Chickamaugas and Creeks were planning an attack during the full moon in April. Robertson hardly needed the warning since the settlements were already under attack. Notably, Blount reversed his earlier admonition to dismiss the troops to cut costs. However, the Governor's intelligence was correct and the attacks did indeed intensify in April.

One of the first April casualties was another Bledsoe. Colonel Isaac Bledsoe was working in the field near his house when warriors attacked and killed him. The Indians murdered nine or ten others in scattered ambushes throughout the far-flung region prior to a large-scale attack near the end of the month.

On April 27th a large war party of over 200 Indians attacked Greenfield Station. They had arrived the night before to set up an ambush along the road leading from the fort to the fields. After a group of slaves left the fort in the morning to go to work, the Indians started shooting at them. Several white men, who were preparing to leave the station, immediately ran outside and started returning fire. They made it to a fence that they were able to use for cover while they continued to shoot at the enemy.

Their aggressive bluff succeeded; the Indians quickly retreated with a few stolen horses. Five white marksmen had managed to successfully defend the station because the Indians were unaware that there were no other riflemen left inside to protect the fort. Incredibly, only one slave and one white defender died during the attack.

On April 27th 1793, the Secretary of War did something that would give hope to General Robertson. Pursuant to the recently signed treaty at Nashville, the Secretary authorized a large shipment of arms and supplies for the Chickasaws. The shipment included: 500 muskets, 2,000 pounds of powder, 4,000 flints, 100 gallons of whiskey and a gunsmith with tools to service the weapons. It was a sign that the government was able to provide at least some material support, if it wanted to. While the Secretary provided nothing for the settlers themselves, at least the United States was helping its new ally. The shipment demonstrated the government's goodwill toward the Chickasaws and it helped to maintain their loyalty.

On July 1st of that year, Indians attacked Hay's Station. They killed Jacob and Joseph Castleman and wounded Hans Castleman. The loss of his family members enraged the venerable scout, Abe Castleman, and he was bent on revenge. General

Robertson authorized Castleman to organize a company of volunteers to search for the Indians under strict orders not to go beyond the Tennessee River.

Abe Castleman and his volunteers eventually arrived at the Tennessee River before they were able to catch up with the Indians. Ten of the men followed Robertson's orders and turned back after reaching the river. But Castleman and five others decided to cross the Tennessee and move downriver in search of Indians. Disguised as Indians, Castleman and his men were able to get close enough to ambush a large group of warriors. They managed to kill several Indians and scatter the rest. After their successful surprise attack, Castleman and his men re-crossed the Tennessee and returned to Nashville.

There is no record of General Robertson's reaction to Castleman's disregard for his orders, but he was likely pleased that his trusted scout was able to get his revenge against the Indians. It was something Robertson himself wanted to do, but orders from above prevented it.

By October of that year, General Sevier had had enough of Indian attacks in his district and he launched a retaliatory campaign against the Cherokees, Chickamaugas and Creeks. His campaign followed two significant events.

The first occurred when Sevier authorized a raid against a group of Indians who had gathered to discuss peace with federal negotiators. Afterward, John Watts led a large war party to get revenge by attacking settlements near Knoxville. They laid siege to Calvert's Station and the fighting ended after Watts promised safe passage for the fort's inhabitants in exchange for their surrender. A renegade chief named Doublehead and several Creeks disobeyed his orders and slaughtered their prisoners.

After the massacre of the innocent civilians at Calvert's Station, General Sevier mobilized a large body of militia to chastise the Indians. He led his volunteers on a successful campaign that culminated in the defeat of the Cherokee village at Etowah and the killing of their leader, Chief Kingfisher. That was Sevier's last military campaign, and his victory was a blow to the Indians' morale.

On December 1st, 1793 General Robertson's son, twenty-one-year-old James Randal Robertson, and another young man named John Grimes went to trap beaver on Cany Fork, east of Nashville. While they were setting their trap lines, a band of Chickamaugas and Creeks ambushed and killed both men. Recognizing that James Randal was General Robertson's son, the warriors cut off the young man's head and carried it back to the Lower Towns as a war trophy.

News of the loss of another son in an Indian attack was devastating for James, Charlotte and the entire Robertson family. Through the long, cold winter they grieved and General Robertson's sorrow slowly turned into anger. His forbearance had cost the life of another loved one. That was his breaking point. Neither President Washington nor Governor Blount would be able to hold him back any longer. They had forced him to disregard his own best instincts for far too long. He was ready to make an offensive strike against his Indian tormentors, regardless of the consequences.

Chapter 48

THE BATTLE OF FALLEN TIMBERS

If there was ever a white man who understood Indians, it was James Robertson. He not only knew them well, but he liked them and viewed them as fellow human beings, rather than mysterious incomprehensible savages. Many of his contemporaries saw Indians in a substantially different light. During that era, whites often viewed them as sub-human savages.

General Robertson had witnessed Indians committing unspeakable atrocities. They had mercilessly slaughtered many of his close friends and family. Beginning in his early years at Watauga, Robertson understood that if he and his family and friends were going to survive on the frontier, they would have to reach out to the Indians. That is exactly what he did, first with the Cherokees and later with the Chickasaws, Choctaws, Chickamaugas and Creeks.

Robertson devoted the time and effort to learn tribal languages and customs. He was willing to visit their villages and meet with them on their own terms. Whenever they accepted an invitation to visit him, he always treated them like honored guests who were worthy of the best frontier hospitality and entertainment that he could provide. Over time, Indians and whites alike learned to appreciate his remarkable diplomatic and linguistic abilities.

When General Robertson received news about a third campaign against the Northwestern Indian Confederacy to be led by General Anthony Wayne, he knew that the Chickasaws would want to participate. The Chickasaws were among the most fearsome warriors on the frontier and the warrior spirit was as deeply ingrained in their culture as it was in any other western tribe.

After the most recent treaty at Nashville, General Robertson saw to it that the arms and supplies delivered in Nashville for the Chickasaws were promptly transported to them. He chose his eldest son, Jonathan, to personally escort the shipment to Chickasaw Bluffs and to make sure that everything arrived in good condition. Jonathan fulfilled his mission and the Indians were very satisfied with their gifts from the United States government. They were particularly pleased with the small swivel cannon which they found to be very powerful and impressive after Jonathan gave them a firing demonstration.

In late July of 1794, General Robertson arranged for Piomingo and several chiefs to depart from the Chickasaw Nation with over 60 of their best warriors and travel north to join General Wayne's campaign against the northwest Indians. By pre-arrangement, Piomingo and a few chiefs separated from the main group along the way to visit Philadelphia and meet with President Washington. While there, Piomingo and the other chiefs enjoyed the warm hospitality, uniforms, medals and gifts that they received from President Washington, the Secretary of War and other government officials.

In the meantime, the main body of Chickasaw warriors caught up with General Wayne and joined his army. They were a welcome addition because the Chickasaws had a reputation as brave warriors who were always eager for a good fight. General

Wayne immediately put the Indians to work as scouts for the expedition.

August 20th 1794 was the day of the battle. Blue Jacket, leader of the Confederacy Indians, selected a spot to intercept Wayne's advancing army of over 3,000 soldiers and warriors. Blue Jacket positioned his warriors directly in their path behind a field of felled trees near the British-held Fort Miami. When the Chickasaw scouts reported the location of Blue Jacket's warriors to General Wayne, he halted the advance and convened a council of his officers. They promptly formulated a battle plan before cautiously resuming their advance toward the enemy's position. As soon as his army arrived in front of Blue Jacket's warriors, General Wayne gave the order to attack.

Blue Jacket's warriors were outnumbered by 2 to 1, and they were soon overwhelmed by General Wayne's well-trained soldiers and cavalry. A rout quickly ensued after the cavalry circled behind the Indians' position and sent them fleeing toward nearby Fort Miami. When the retreating warriors arrived at the fort, they found themselves locked out. The fort's British commander did not want to risk starting a war with the United States, so he ordered his men to bar the gates and prevent the fleeing Indians from entering the fort.

Unable to find refuge inside the fort, Blue Jacket's Indians suffered additional losses that punctuated their already humiliating defeat. Wayne's men subsequently laid waste to the surrounding villages, crops and livestock.

General Wayne had managed to succeed where his two predecessors had failed. The Battle of Fallen Timbers, as it became known, crushed the Indian rebellion in the Northwest Territory and established peace in the region that lasted until Tecumseh's War in 1811.

Following their great victory while serving with General Wayne, the Chickasaw warriors returned to their villages located along the Mississippi River. They brought home many scalps taken from their Indian enemies as proof of their heroism in battle; which they proudly recounted in countless stories around their campfires.

Piomingo and the other chiefs who met with President Washington came home at about the same time as the warriors who fought in the Battle of Fallen Timbers. The chiefs were wearing their new uniforms and showing off their medals and gifts. They had many impressive stories to tell about meeting "The Great White Father" as well as other important events that occurred during their visit to Philadelphia. The Chickasaws had proven themselves to be faithful allies of the United States.

General Anthony Wayne defeated the Northwest Indian Confederation at the Battle of Fallen Timbers.

Chapter 49

THE NICKAJACK EXPEDITION

Small bands of Chickamauga and Creek warriors roamed throughout the Mero District in 1794, wreaking havoc throughout the region. As was customary at the time, people usually abandoned the smaller stations and sought refuge in the larger forts. In doing so, they risked losing their crops and homes that they had worked so hard to build and maintain. The Indians routinely burned the houses and destroyed the crops wherever they went. A few settlers chose to stay put, regardless of the consequences. Such choices often had fatal outcomes when war parties came across those isolated, lightly-defended stations.

Sometimes Indians showed mercy toward innocent women and children by kidnapping them and taking them back to their villages to hold for ransom. Other times, the scalped and mutilated bodies of women and children were found lying alongside the men. The behavior of Indians was unpredictable. If they won a skirmish without suffering many casualties, they were less inclined to slaughter women and children. But even under the best scenario, the warriors' deeds were often capricious and cruel.

Two well-known early settlers died in 1794. The first was Thomas Sharpe Spencer, a man of enormous stature. The Indians nicknamed him "Bigfoot" because his footprints were so large.

Spencer had survived many frontier skirmishes, but in 1794 his luck ran out when he was killed in an Indian ambush. Spencer was one of the original long-hunters who came to hunt in the French Lick region before the arrival of Robertson and the first settlers. Legend has it that Spencer once spent the winter living in a hollow tree trunk following the departure of his fellow hunters. He was best known for his selfless generosity after he broke his own knife in two to give half to a fellow hunter who needed a knife for the journey back to civilization.

The second early settler to die that year was David Hood. He passed away from natural causes, a rarity during those violent, turbulent times. Hood was a bit of a local celebrity for having survived a particularly brutal Indian attack in the early days of the settlement. In the winter of 1782, while he and two other men were walking to Fort Nashborough, they were ambushed by Indians. The other men managed to escape, but Hood was shot, scalped and left for dead. After "playing possum" for a short time, Hood got up and walked toward the fort, only to encounter the same Indians again. They mocked him and laughed at his pitiful condition before assaulting him again and leaving him for dead a second time. Later that day, his two companions came searching for him. They found Hood's body and brought it back to the fort where they left it outside in the snow for burial the next day.

The following morning, some women went outside to prepare Hood's body for a proper burial. To their surprise, they noticed that he was still breathing. They brought him inside to attend to his wounds. James Robertson, known as a frontier surgeon, treated his scalp and gunshot wounds. Charlotte and the other women subsequently nursed him back to a full recovery. A jovial man by nature, Hood later enjoyed telling stories to the children and he often joked about how he had hoodwinked the Indians by "playing possum".

Between 1793 and 1794, General Robertson, General Sevier and Governor Blount were secretly communicating amongst themselves about the need to go after the Lower Towns of the Chickamaugas since most of the war parties came from there. In 1793, Congress debated the issue of authorizing an offensive campaign against the Indians who were attacking settlers in the Southwest Territory, but it adjourned before passing any legislation to provide relief for the beleaguered people. Although President Washington sympathized with the settlers' plight, he believed that he lacked the constitutional authority to authorize military action without Congressional approval.

Governor Blount's subsequent involvement in planning an expedition against the offending Indians is unclear, but General Robertson's involvement is certain. For some time, he and his fellow frontiersmen had wanted to attack the Lower Towns. Congress' failure to take action, combined with the killing of another son, James Randal Robertson, cemented the General's decision to act.

In 1794 Indian raids against the inhabitants of the Mero District resumed, unabated. In August, General Robertson received reliable information from a Chickasaw chief named William Colbert and a white physician who lived among the Chickasaws that the Creeks and Chickamaugas were planning to send a large war party to attack the settlements. For that reason, Robertson decided that it was the right time to attack the Lower Towns.

General Robertson took Joseph Brown, the Bosley brothers and a few others to scout for a suitable horseback route to Nickajack and the other Lower Towns. Joseph Brown, by then already a young man, was the boy who was captured by Indians 1788 after they killed his father during their river voyage to Nashville. While in captivity, young Brown lived in the Lower Towns and became acquainted with his surroundings. Ever since his release in a prisoner exchange arranged by John Sevier, Joseph Brown had been eager to avenge his father's death. When the scouting party returned to Nashville, General Robertson was pleased to announce that young Brown had helped them locate a suitable route for an expedition.

Because the offending Indians had also raided settlements in Southeast Kentucky, General Robertson was able to arrange for Kentucky volunteers under the command of their senior officer, Colonel Whitley. Colonel Ford brought militiamen mustered from the area between Nashville and Clarkesville. Colonel Montgomery, who had recently lost his relative, Major Montgomery, to the Indians, led militiamen from Clarkesville. And General Robertson gathered volunteers from Nashville and the surrounding area.

Governor Blount dispatched troops under the command of Major Ore to patrol for signs of Indian war parties. Major Ore arrived in Nashville at the same time Robertson's men were preparing for the expedition. General Robertson gave Major Ore written orders authorizing the expedition and gave him the authority to cross the Tennessee River and attack the Lower Towns if he found tracks showing that war parties had crossed the river. Ore's arrival in time to join the expedition, and his willingness to participate, implies that Governor Blount was involved in planning the attack.

At the agreed upon time, all of the militiamen, including Ore's men, rendezvoused at a location near Buchanan's station. General Robertson authorized the expedition from Nashville, but did not go with his men. The General's absence left Colonel Montgomery as the senior officer to assume command of the expedition. On September 7th, 1794 over 1,000 men departed from Buchanan's Station heading toward the Tennessee River; Joseph Brown and the Bosley brothers led the way as scouts.

Five days later, the army arrived at the pre-selected site for crossing the Tennessee River, about four miles below the Indian town of Nickajack. Early the next morning, the men crossed the river, proceeded to the town and surrounded it before starting the attack. When the battle began, the Indians were caught off guard and most tried to flee. Some of the warriors managed to escape, but many were killed inside the town or in the river as they tried to swim to safety. When the skirmish ended, the army took nineteen Indian women and children as prisoners.

Afterward, the army rode toward the larger village of Running Water, located about four miles upriver from Nickajack. By then, the Indians at Running Water knew that the whites were coming, and they tried to mount a defense. Warriors were posted at the narrows leading to the town, but they were soon routed by the advancing militia. Afterward, the men quickly advanced through the narrows and entered the town where they killed any remaining warriors. When the fighting ended, the whites burned the town and either seized or destroyed or anything of value that could be used by the Indians who managed to escape. The army confiscated horses, livestock, arms and ammunition and other items to bring home.

The number of Indian casualties was estimated to be over seventy, but the exact number was unknown because many of the Indians were shot in the river as they tried to flee and their bodies floated downriver. For their part, the whites suffered only three wounded; a lieutenant and two privates.

Before leaving, the militiamen retrieved several pieces of evidence linking the Spaniards to the Indians. A chief known as "The Breath of Nickajack" died in the attack, and the men found a Spanish officer's commission among his possessions. They also found and confiscated a large cache of Spanish weapons and munitions among his belongings.

The militiamen became infuriated when they found several fresh scalps and personal property that belonged to the Indians' white victims. Then, everyone knew why their expedition was sent.

Chapter 50

THE AFTERMATH

General Wayne's victory at the Battle of Fallen Timbers broke the Indian Confederation in the Northwest Territory. General Sevier's successful Etowah Campaign subjugated the hostile Cherokees in the eastern part of the Southwest Territory. And the Nickajack Expedition, ordered by General Robertson, caused a pause in the raids by the Chickamaugas and Creeks.

Soon after the destruction of Nickajack and Coldwater, General Robertson sent a letter to Chief John Watts of the Chickamaugas. General Robertson used his customary cordial diplomatic language to once again express a sincere desire for peace. However, Robertson's correspondence to the influential chief ended with a clear and unmistakable warning: if the attacks against the settlers did not cease, he would order more offensive attacks against the Indians.

After contemplating the carefully phrased contents of General Robertson's letter, Watts eventually decided to seek peace. The earlier victories of Generals Wayne and Sevier undoubtedly influenced his decision. Unfortunately, it took some time for Robertson's letter to reach Watts and war parties had already gone out to avenge the destruction of Nickajack and Running Water.

About forty Indians attacked Valentine Sevier's station at Clarkesville on November 11th, 1794. Their surprise attack resulted in the deaths of two more of his sons, Joseph and John, and the scalping of his daughter, Rebecca. Several members of the Snider and King families also perished in the attack.

On November 27th, 1794 Indians killed and scalped Colonel John Montgomery, leader of the Nickajack Expedition, and wounded Julius Sanders and Charles Beatty. There were numerous other scattered Indian attacks throughout the Mero District following the Nickajack Expedition. Various Indian parties waged war throughout the District until April of 1795 when the attacks finally ceased.

A new affront to Generals Robertson and Sevier occurred when the new Secretary of War, Timothy Pickering, refused to allocate funds to pay the troops for Sevier's Etowah Campaign and Robertson's Nickojack Expedition. Like his predecessor, Pickering seemed to believe that the settlers were to blame for the violence on the frontier.

It should be noted that Robertson and Sevier were eventually vindicated by the United States Congress during the 1798 session. That year, a resolution was passed that commended each man for his respective successful campaign against the hostile Indians. That same act of Congress allocated full pay and reimbursement for expenses to the officers and men who participated in the Etowah and Nickajack expeditions.

For his part, General Robertson had had enough of irrational directives and orders from afar. Neither Pickering nor his predecessor, Knox, seemed to understand or sympathize with the plight of the settlers in the Southwest Territory. On October 23rd, 1794 General Robertson sent a letter of resignation to President Washington. Robertson was fifty-two years old at the time, and he had many business and civic responsibilities in Nashville that were more than enough to occupy a man of his age. Out of respect for General Robertson's many patriotic contributions during and after the Revolution, President Washington left Robertson's letter of resignation on his desk for over a year without taking any action. It took a second letter from Robertson in which he set a date certain for his resignation before it was finally accepted.

Although he no longer retained his commission as Brigadier General in the United States Army, James Robertson's peers continued to address him as "General Robertson" for the remainder of his life. It was their way of showing their respect for him and his service to the frontier settlements.

Chapter 51

STATEHOOD

Governor Blount ordered a census of the Southwest Territory in 1795. It was a congressionally mandated preliminary qualification to apply for statehood. Despite the dangerous and harsh conditions on the frontier, new settlers continued to migrate over the mountains in search of a new life. The Southwest Territory offered relatively cheap land and an abundance of wild game where a man could carve out a new life for himself and his family. A little money and a lot of hard work and dogged determination were all that were required to achieve a modest level of prosperity. Even the ever-present threat of Indian attacks failed to stem the flow of newcomers to the region.

The census was completed and certified by Governor Blount on November 28, 1795. The population of the Southwest Territory was 77,262. It was more than enough to meet the statutory requirement of 60,000 or more residents for the Territory to qualify to apply for statehood.

Pursuant to that goal, Governor Blount scheduled a Statehood Convention to be held in Knoxville on January 11th, 1796. Following protocol, five representatives from each of the eleven counties in the Territory were selected to represent their constituents. Davidson county residents selected James

Robertson, Andrew Jackson, John McNairy, Thomas Hardeman and Joel Lewis to represent them at the Convention.

James Robertson played an active role throughout the Convention chaired by William Blount. A State Constitution and Bill of Rights were drafted and office holders were elected. James Robertson was influential in passing a clause in the Bill of Rights guaranteeing the free navigation of the Mississippi River. Westerners had long sought free navigation as a reliable means for exporting agricultural commodities and importing manufactured goods. John Sevier was elected Governor, William Blount and William Cocke were elected Senators, and Andrew Jackson was elected to the House of Representatives.

Among the various matters of business conducted during the Convention was the choice of a name for the new State. They settled on the name "Tennessee", a Cherokee word meaning "Big River". That choice necessitated renaming Tennessee County which had previously used that name. Members of the Convention voted to split the County in two. Tennessee County ceased to exist and became Montgomery County (named in honor of the fallen Colonel John Montgomery who was killed by Indians after the Nickajack Expedition) and Robertson County (named in honor of General James Robertson).

Although James Robertson took an active role throughout the Convention, he was no longer interested in holding public office. He had already served several terms in the North Carolina Assembly alongside William Blount. After resigning his military commission, Robertson was looking forward to having more free time to devote to his family, his farm and his business interests. Even if he had wanted to be the State's first governor, he would not have been able to win an election against his friend, John Sevier. Like Robertson, Sevier was a living legend. He was one of the heroes of the Battle of King's Mountain; and he was a natural leader and an exceptional Indian fighter who had given his people a good measure of security during tumultuous times. The eastern part of the Territory had a larger population and the people there were fiercely loyal to the charismatic Sevier. The westerners were equally loyal to Robertson, but there were fewer of them.

More importantly, James Robertson neither sought nor desired to hold elective office again. He was content to provide leadership during the Convention and to promote and assist his friends in winning their respective elections. John Sevier, William Blount, Andrew Jackson and William Cocke were all good friends and he was pleased to assist them in securing election to their respective influential positions.

After the Statehood Convention was adjourned, the United States Congress voted to admit Tennessee to the Union on June 1st, 1796.

William Blount's service in the United States Senate came to an abrupt end soon after his term began. He became involved in a British conspiracy to incite the Cherokees and Creeks against the Spanish in West Florida. Blount wrote a letter detailing the plot to aid the British in their plan to take control of the Spanish colony. His letter was intercepted and eventually turned over to the new President, John Adams, who in turn passed the letter on to the Senate on July 3rd, 1797. Many of Blount's colleagues considered the correspondence to be treasonous, and five days later the Senate voted 25 to 1 to expel him.

Despite the scandal, for which he was never prosecuted due to a lack of supporting evidence, Blount remained popular in Tennessee. Following his return to Knoxville, he was elected to the Tennessee State Senate in 1798. He soon rose to become speaker of the Senate before his untimely death from natural causes on March 21st, 1800 at age 50.

This is a map of the United States before the Louisiana Purchase.

Chapter 52

CALL TO SERVE AGAIN

George Rutledge was appointed to replace John Sevier as Brigadier General in eastern Tennessee and James Winchester became Brigadier General in the west after James Robertson resigned. On November 13th, 1797, Andrew Jackson was appointed to fill William Blount's United States Senate seat after Blount's expulsion. Jackson's military career also advanced when he was commissioned Major-General of the Tennessee militia. Robertson recognized Jackson's intelligence, leadership ability and ambition by enthusiastically supporting the young lawyer's political and military promotions.

Robertson's desire to spend more time attending to family, business and civic responsibilities was curtailed when a state assemblyman from Davidson County resigned. The people of Davidson County elected Robertson to finish his term. He represented the County in the Tennessee State Assembly from 1798 to 1800. When his term ended, it was the last time he held an elected position. However, it was not the end of his remarkable career in public service.

Indian attacks in Tennessee ended by 1795, but treaty negotiations were drawn out for a long period, primarily because mistakes were made in earlier treaties with the Cherokees. In the

1792 Holston Treaty, Blount erred by granting the Cherokees rights to land they did not own. The land in question belonged to the Chickasaws. Although none of the tribes held deeds to their land, title was claimed either by conquest or occupation. Decades earlier, the Chickasaws gained title to the land by conquest after defeating the Cherokees and Shawnees in a war over the disputed territory. Warfare was the means by which Indian territories either expanded or contracted for countless centuries prior to the arrival of white settlers.

In his eagerness to make an agreement with the Cherokees and their notorious brethren, the Chickamaugas, Blount granted the Cherokees land that they claimed was theirs. When the boundaries were drawn, Blount acceded to their demands by formally acknowledging their illegitimate claim to land west of the Tennessee River that actually belonged to the Chickasaws.

The land dispute made subsequent negotiations with the Cherokees at Tellico more complicated because earlier mistakes had to be corrected. First Blount, and later Governor Sevier, sought help from James Robertson with the treaty negotiations. He was helpful because he understood the legitimate Chickasaw claim to the disputed territory, as well as the false claim of the Cherokees.

Robertson was personally acquainted with many of the Cherokee chiefs from his time in Watauga, and from his stint as Indian Agent. The chiefs believed that Robertson was a trustworthy white man who spoke the truth. He understood their language and customs and served as a fair minded intermediary. He supported the concerns of one side or the other based on what he deemed to be fair. That was why the Cherokees always insisted that he be included in treaty negotiations.

The government's representatives invited Robertson to participate because he spoke Cherokee and served as a bridge between the two cultures. Robertson's mediation at the Tellico negotiations was difficult because the wily Cherokee chiefs had previously hoodwinked Blount at Holston. The Chickasaw land granted to the Cherokees in the prior treaty had to be taken back for two compelling reasons. First, the land belonged to the Chickasaws by conquest. Second, white settlers were flooding into the region and would resist eviction.

The First Treaty of Tellico was signed on October 2nd, 1798. In the agreement, the Cherokees ceded land between the Clinch River and the Cumberland Plateau, as well as land between the Tennessee and Little Tennessee Rivers. The Second Treaty of Tellico required no land concessions. The Third Treaty of Tellico was completed in 1805. In that treaty, the Cherokees ceded all land north of the Duck River and all land south and east of that point to the Tennessee River, including the remainder of the Cumberland Plateau.

The Creeks also decided to choose peace. Their leader, Alexander McGillivray, died in 1793. His two nephews, William Weatherford and William McIntosh became important Creek chiefs. Sensing the futility of further warfare, they signed a peace treaty on June 29th, 1796.

Previously, the Creeks had suffered a humiliating defeat after they attacked the Chickasaw settlement at Logtown in 1795. When they received word that a large Creek war party was coming, the Chickasaws sent an urgent letter to Robertson requesting corn, supplies and armaments to defend themselves. Without hesitation, he satisfied their request and added to it a group of white volunteers under the command of Kasper Mansker. With the help of Mansker's volunteers, the Chickasaws dealt a decisive defeat to the Creek invaders. In a brief battle at Logtown the Creeks suffered a shameful defeat when they panicked and fled, leaving behind all of their wagons and baggage for the victorious Chickasaws to claim as trophies of war.

After Tennessee became a state, James Robertson continued working as a trustee for Davidson Academy. Both he and Charlotte recognized the need for formal educational opportunities in Nashville. Their own children benefited from that worthy educational institution. The legacy of Davidson Academy is Nashville's exemplary educational and cultural atmosphere that continues to this day.

James Robertson sold Cumberland Iron Works to one of his workers in 1804. Afterward, he began contracting to build roads. In 1804, he constructed a road from his plantation westward to the town of Charlotte (named in his wife's honor) in Dickinson County. The next year, he widened and improved the road from Nashville to Natchez in what is now Mississippi. In addition to road contracts, he continued farming on his plantation. He also continued to survey lands for new arrivals. Overall, it was a busy time of peace and prosperity for Robertson and his family.

James Robertson's older brother, Charles, moved to Nashville sometime around the turn of the century. Charles' arrival was indeed welcome because their brother, Elijah, had died of "yellow Jaundice" on April 4th, 1797. James was saddened by Elijah's death because they were nearly inseparable ever since their time together at Watauga. Both were at the Battle of Point Pleasant, and they subsequently fought alongside each other during several Indian skirmishes. Charles' arrival helped to fill the void left by the deaths of two brothers who came with James to settle in Nashville.

This is an early French portrait of a Chickasaw Warrior.

Chapter 53

AARON BURR AND ANDREW JACKSON

John Adams served only one term as president of the United States. His bid for a second term failed after losing to Thomas Jefferson and his running mate, Aaron Burr. Under the flawed rules at the time, Congress had the responsibility of selecting Adams' successor because there was a technical electoral tie between Jefferson and his own running mate, Burr (the rules were later changed). Even though Burr was the Vice-Presidential candidate, his ambitions got the best of him and he refused to step aside in favor of Jefferson. Congress eventually elected Jefferson President, leaving Burr with the largely ceremonial office of Vice President.

By most accounts, Burr did well in his role as President of the Senate during his four years as Vice President. Nevertheless, because he attempted to bypass Jefferson in the 1800 election and elevate himself to the office of President, Jefferson's party abandoned Burr. They nominated a different running mate for Jefferson in his successful 1804 campaign for a second term.

The most significant accomplishment during Jefferson's first administration was the Louisiana Purchase in 1803. Napoleon Bonaparte had recently acquired the territory from Spain in order to expand France's colonial holdings in North America. However, a subsequent successful slave rebellion on the French island colony of Haiti drained the French treasury and resulted in unacceptably high casualties.

Due to the unexpected loss of money and military manpower in Haiti, Napoleon was forced to abandon his colonial aspirations in favor of acquiring additional funds to pay for his costly, and eventually unsuccessful, war with Britain. To obtain more funds to continue the war, Napoleon's emissaries approached Jefferson about buying the Louisiana colony. President Jefferson was a visionary who recognized that Napoleon's offer was a good opportunity for the United States to expand its borders and impede the colonial aspirations of Britain and Spain. Those circumstances set the stage for what would become the most beneficial land acquisition in United States history.

Jefferson negotiated the Louisiana Purchase for fifteen million dollars, but the acquisition was not universally popular among American citizens. It was opposed by most federalists, especially in the commercial northeast, who favored closer trading ties with Britain. Republicans, and especially those who were western farmers like James Robertson, favored the purchase because it opened the entire Mississippi River region to commerce and international trade through the Port of New Orleans.

After he was dropped from the 1804 republican ticket, Aaron Burr suddenly found himself without a suitable official position. In 1804 he ran an unsuccessful campaign for governor of New York. Burr's loss in that race was partly due to opposition mounted by his federalist arch-rival, Alexander Hamilton. Blaming Hamilton for his loss, the long-simmering political feud between the two men finally came to a boil when Burr challenged Hamilton to a duel.

Hamilton accepted, and the two antagonists eventually squared off for a duel in New Jersey (because dueling was illegal in New York). After meeting at the chosen location with their seconds, they agreed upon the rules governing the duel. Afterward, the adversaries took ten paces, turned and fired. Burr hit Hamilton with a fatal shot that caused his death the next day.

Although Burr won the duel, his reputation was destroyed after he killed Hamilton. Burr was despised by Hamilton's federalist friends, and even many of Burr's embarrassed republican friends turned their backs on him. With his reputation in tatters, Burr was desperate to rehabilitate himself in the eyes of his peers. In his quest to satisfy his enormous ego and restore his reputation, he eventually involved himself in a conspiracy to seize the Spanish colonies in Florida and Texas.

To gain support for the venture, Burr travelled throughout the western region meeting with receptive local leaders. After a trip to New Orleans, he visited Nashville to build support for his plan to seize the Spanish colonies. Burr could not have chosen a more receptive audience for his enterprise. Spain was despised for Instigating a bloody 15-year Indian war of attrition against the white settlers from 1780 to 1795. Memories of the Indian atrocities and Spanish duplicity still infuriated the survivors.

When Aaron Burr arrived in Nashville in early 1806, he received a warm welcome from James Robertson and other community leaders. The former vice president was probably the most noteworthy person who had ever come to visit. As patriarch of the growing town, Robertson hosted a welcoming dinner at his home. Most of the prominent local leaders, including Andrew Jackson, came to the event.

Those who attended were amply entertained by the celebrated guest who displayed his charming and witty gift for storytelling. His receptive audience listened with rapt attention to what their worldly guest had to say about the nation and international affairs. James Robertson and Andrew Jackson were particularly interested in Burr's attitude toward Spain.

Burr correctly observed that the Spanish empire was in a state of gradual decline after a series of costly wars and other affairs that drained the royal coffers. He asserted that the United States was an infant nation that needed room to expand. Burr's declaration that it was time to relieve Spain of Florida and Texas made sense to the citizens of Nashville.

Robertson and Jackson despised the Spaniards. They were witnesses of the destruction wrought by Spanish deceit. Spanish officials armed and supported hostile Indians while falsely expressing friendship toward the white settlers. Robertson's extensive experience with Spanish diplomats made him loathe their mendacious ways.

Burr made it a point to curry favor with Andrew Jackson because he was a Major General of the Tennessee militia. He subsequently spent several days as a guest at the home of Rachel and Andrew Jackson, where Burr and Jackson had plenty of time to discuss plans for seizing Spanish territory.

Afterward, Burr left Nashville and headed north to visit leaders in Kentucky and Ohio to garner their support for his grand scheme.

While Burr was away, people in Nashville started hearing news about how his plan was viewed by President Jefferson and the political establishment in Washington, D.C. (the nation's new capital). Robertson and Jackson were surprised to learn that Burr's plan was viewed as a treasonous conspiracy by the establishment politicians. Robertson, Jackson and other Nashville leaders were troubled by the news that forced them to rethink their support for their charismatic new friend.

When Aaron Burr returned to Nashville several months later, his reception was much different than the first time. His arrival brought a cool greeting from prominent members of the community. There is no record of Robertson meeting with Burr during that visit. However, Andrew Jackson did confer extensively with Burr. During their time together, Jackson had many pointed questions arising from what he had read and heard about political opposition in Washington. There was even talk of treason.

Burr left Nashville in late December of 1806 after failing to convince Jackson of the righteousness of his plans. The mood among Nashville's leading citizens had completely changed as well. After Burr left town, rumors swirled that he was a traitor to the United States. The word was that Burr wanted to set himself up as the leader of a separate nation, rather than seizing the Spanish colonies for the United States. President Jefferson went so far as to send a letter to western leaders asking them to steer clear of Burr's conspiracy.

Burr's seemingly treasonous conspiracy was intolerable for the patriotic citizens of Nashville who burned him in effigy. The people felt that they had been duped by a treasonous scoundrel. Whether it was true or not (Burr's actual motives and intentions remain unclear to this day), he was viewed as a traitor. Each new bit of information that came in about Burr confirmed the suspicions of Robertson and Jackson. They came to believe that it was time to call for volunteers to come to the aid of the United States and block the alleged conspiracy.

To help Major General Jackson raise volunteers, James Robertson and a group of elderly local veterans of the Revolution and Indian wars banded together. Calling themselves the "Invincibles" or "Silver Grays", they published an open letter signed by former General Robertson and his men pledging to serve under Jackson to protect and defend the United States. The Silver Grays started drilling and began making preparations to go to war to protect their nation. James Robertson was 62 years old at the time and some of his men were even older.

Before an expedition could be mounted against Burr, news arrived in Nashville that Burr had been arrested near Spanish Florida. When General Jackson received the news, he disbanded his regular volunteers. He sent a very complimentary letter to James Robertson and his Silver Grays in which he commended them for their readiness to defend their state and the nation. He thanked them for volunteering and ordered them to stand down.

The charges against Aaron Burr were eventually dropped due to insufficient evidence. When he was released from confinement, his political career was over and his reputation was destroyed. Left without any career prospects, Burr soon fled to Europe where he lived for several years while trying in vain to get support for his various grandiose international schemes. In 1812 he returned to the United States as a broken man.

James Robertson's protégé, Andrew Jackson, became a military hero and was later elected President of the United States.

Chapter 54
OTHER EVENTS

On October 25th, 1803, a new county was formed from portions of Robertson and Montgomery Counties. It was named Dickinson County and Charlotte (previously named in honor of Charlotte Robertson) was the county seat. The creation of the new county reflected the growing population in Middle Tennessee.

The post-statehood era was a busy time for the Robertson family. Charlotte continued to care for her husband and children. In addition to her substantial domestic chores, Charlotte was continually entertaining visitors. Some of the guests were new settlers or unexpected Indian guests, many of whom arrived at her door unexpectedly without an invitation.

James and Charlotte were devout Presbyterians who displayed Christian virtues as a matter of course in their daily lives. No stranger was ever turned away, and requests for food and shelter were always granted at Travelers' Rest. Half-naked Indians received the same warm reception as white visitors.

There were countless times when Indians came to Travelers' Rest to see James Robertson about some grievance involving their interactions with whites. Chickasaws and other friendly Indians often passed through Nashville to trade. Sometimes they would be mistreated by bad whites or others who simply hated Indians. Robertson was a former judge and Governor John Sevier appointed him justice of the peace. Therefore, any complaints brought to him were thoroughly investigated.

One example of Robertson's judicial fairness toward everyone, including Indians, occurred around the turn of the century. One day, an Indian hunter came to him with a complaint that some bad whites had accosted him, forcing him to flee without his pelts and personal belongings. Robertson questioned the man at length, and then went to investigate.

Robertson visited the place where the incident occurred and was able to verify the Indian's story. He followed up, and was able to return the Indian's pelts and other property that were left behind when he fled. Later on, a squaw showed up at the Robertson's door with a gift of prime venison roast. She explained that she was the hunter's mother and that she wanted to show her gratitude for the assistance her son received.

There are other recorded instances of James Robertson helping Indians and mediating grievances and undoubtedly many more that are long-forgotten.

Robertson continued to be the go-to person for Indian treaties. In 1804, he helped with the Tellico Treaty between the Cherokees and the United States. In 1805, he answered the War Department's call to serve as Indian Agent to the Chickasaws and the Choctaws. He negotiated with the Chickasaws first. It took him about 6 months to negotiate the sale of a portion of their land for $22,000 in cash, $10,000 worth of merchandise and a $2,000 annual allowance.

Immediately after finishing the treaty with the Chickasaws, Robertson headed south to negotiate with the Choctaws. He successfully completed an agreement with the Choctaws to sell a portion of their land along the Homochitto River. Later, the tribe agreed to sell additional lands along the Alabama and Tombigbee Rivers. It was the first time that Robertson lived among the

Choctaws. While there, he developed lasting friendships with many of the chiefs and warriors. As with the Cherokees and Chickasaws before them, the Choctaws were quickly impressed by Robertson's "winning ways".

Robertson's friendly relations with the Chickasaws and Choctaws would later be put to good use in defending the nation against Indian allies of the British during the War of 1812.

In January of 1806, a dispute arose between Andrew Jackson and a prominent Nashville resident named Charles Dickinson. Horseracing was a popular recreational pastime and many of the men in town liked to place bets. Jackson owned one of the best racehorses in the region named Truxton. Joseph Erwin believed that his horse, named Ploughboy, could beat Truxton.

When the challenge was announced, Nashville citizens were eager to bet on the race. Erwin agreed to pay an $800 bond if his horse failed to appear on the day of the race. As race day approached, Erwin became nervous about Ploughboy's ability to beat Truxton, and he pulled his horse from the race. It was easier to pay for the no show than to lose the $2,000 that he had wagered for his horse to win.

When Erwin tried to change the terms of payment for the bond after pulling his horse from the race, Jackson became enraged and accused Erwin of reneging on his promise. Eventually, Erwin's son-in-law, Charles Dickinson, injected himself into the dispute. Word reached Jackson that Dickinson had insinuated that Rachel Jackson was a bigamist because she married Jackson before the divorce from her first husband was finalized. Although it was technically true, Jackson was overly sensitive to such accusations.

The feud was fueled by rumors and innuendos, and by February of 1806 Jackson and Dickinson seemed to be headed for a duel. Dickinson had dueled before and was reputed to be an excellent marksman. James Robertson became concerned for both men as the vitriol and heated rhetoric escalated. They were his friends and he was concerned about their welfare. He was particularly worried about Jackson out of concern that Dickinson would likely kill him in a duel.

Robertson wrote a letter to Jackson on February 1st, 1806 in which he listed the various reasons why he should not duel with Dickinson. Portions of his letter are included here: "No honor can be attached either to the conquered or the conqueror, and certainly the consequences ought to be taken in view. Should you fall, your talents are lost to your country, besides the irreparable loss your family and friends must sustain... Will you pardon me, my friend, when I tell you I have been longer in the world than you have..." (Robertson was 64 years old at the time and Jackson was 49). He went on to assure Jackson that no one in Nashville would question his bravery, and that most of the citizens would approve if he decided not to participate in a duel.

In March of that year, Erwin changed his mind and the horserace was on again. It was scheduled to take place on April 3rd, 1806. All of the rumors, insults and accusations over the preceding months only served to heighten interest in the race and increase the betting.

Race day brought a record crowd of onlookers, as well as additional gambling on the outcome. The race consisted of two heats of two miles each. Truxton beat Ploughboy in both heats; despite the fact that he had not fully recovered from a thigh injury that he had incurred earlier while in training. Jackson won over $10,000, and later said that he probably would have won twice that amount if his horse had shown no signs of injury prior to the race (Truxton's thigh was visibly swollen before the race).

Soon after the event had taken place, Charles Dickinson returned to Nashville from a business trip to New Orleans. Evidently, he was still fuming over earlier insults that were traded between Jackson and himself because he published a new set of insults against Jackson in the local newspaper. He called Jackson, "... a worthless scoundrel, a poltroon and a coward." Those words alone showed that Dickinson was still spoiling for a fight.

The new round of insults was sufficient to agitate Jackson, causing him to publish an equally insulting response in which he challenged Dickinson to a duel. Neither reason nor the wise counsel of James Robertson could restrain Jackson from taking the bait. It was clear that Dickinson intended to kill Jackson. In fact, Dickinson was so confident about his own marksmanship that he thought there was no reason to fear Jackson. Therefore, he published a response in which he accepted Jackson's challenge to a duel.

Each man had a second who negotiated the time, date and place for the duel. They selected a location in Kentucky because dueling was still legal there. The two antagonists and their seconds agreed to meet on the field of honor just before sunrise on May 30th, 1806.

Witnesses on the day of the duel reported that Dickinson seemed to be in high spirits, and even cocky, just before the face-off. Jackson was reportedly somber, grim and resolute. While he was only an average shot with a pistol, Dickinson was such a good marksman that he once reportedly shot three holes in a silver dollar at a distance of 24 feet. Jackson knew that he was at a disadvantage, but he refused to back down.

The two men met just before sunrise with their seconds and other witnesses (James Robertson was adamantly opposed to dueling and refused to attend). Both men received their instructions to stand and face each other at a distance of 24 feet. When they were both ready and standing at their assigned places, the second shouted, "fire!" Dickinson fired the first shot. Everyone thought that he had missed because Jackson just stood there in his long overcoat seeming unfazed, with a grim expression on his face. Dickinson's face turned pale, and he seemed to be visibly shaken as he stood there waiting for Jackson to fire. Jackson remained poised as he carefully took aim and squeezed the trigger, but nothing happened. He examined the pistol and quickly realized that he had only half-cocked the unfamiliar dueling pistol.

Jackson pulled the hammer all the way back and took careful aim once again. He gently squeezed the trigger and the pistol fired, hitting Dickinson in the liver. The mortally wounded Dickinson fell to the ground writhing in pain. His wound was treated, but he died the next day.

Neither Dickinson nor any of the witnesses knew that his shot had actually hit Jackson. The well-placed shot hit Jackson in the chest and the ball had stopped about one inch from his heart. Only Jackson's determination and composure kept him from showing any sign of his injury before he took aim and fired the deadly shot.

The critically wounded Jackson was initially treated at the scene before he was returned to Nashville for more treatment and convalescence. The wound was nearly fatal, but his health gradually improved after being bedridden for several months. It was too risky to try to remove the ball that was lodged next to his heart, so it stayed embedded there for the rest of his life.

Jackson's reputation did not seem to suffer very much; probably because he nearly died, and by the time he recovered, the incident was a distant memory. Although Nashville had grown, it was still in the process of changing from a rough and tumble frontier outpost to a more enlightened city. Most of the citizens who had witnessed the dispute unfolding had already decided that each man deserved what he got.

For Andrew Jackson, the duel was a matter of honor. Whether right or wrong, he defended his honor with an exceptional display of grim determination and extraordinary poise under fire.

Chapter 55

ROBERTSON SERVES IN THE WAR OF 1812

James Robertson's service to his fellow man and his nation continued until the end. In his later years, he slowed down a bit, but the desire to serve his country remained strong.

There were two important developments that convinced him that his country needed his services once again. The British were boarding American vessels on the high seas and impressing (kidnapping) American seamen who were forced to serve on British ships. Despite protests from American diplomats, the practice continued as the two nations inched closer to war. Many in Britain failed to take American independence seriously. They believed that it was just a matter of time before their nation would reclaim its lost American colony.

At about the same time, the northern Indian tribes under the leadership of Shawnee Chief Tecumseh and his brother, Prophet, had become restless. Their movement, centered in Prophet Town, advocated a return to the traditional Indian way of life as practiced by their ancestors. Tecumseh and Prophet actively sought to bring back the Northwest Indian Confederation and form an alliance with the southern tribes.

From prior experience, Robertson knew that the British were adept at inciting their Indian allies against the Americans. He also recalled the northern tribes' prior attempt to unite with the southern Indians. If they succeed in doing so, it would likely result in another bloody Indian war against the whites living along the western frontier.

With those developments weighing heavily on his mind, the retired general wrote the War Department to request reappointment as agent to the Chickasaws. As soon as they granted his application, he immediately went to live at the Chickasaw Agency. Soon after his arrival, he learned that Shawnee emissaries had already visited the tribe. They brought a war belt with them and tried to persuade the Chickasaws to join them in an all-out war against the Americans. They might have succeeded if not for Piomingo, Colbert and other influential chiefs who were friendly toward the Americans. The prominent chiefs eventually convinced the others to remain as allies of the United States. After the decision was made, the Chickasaws rejected the war belt.

Once Robertson began living among the Chickasaws, they never again waivered in their allegiance to the United States. However, a crisis soon arose that could have changed the situation. A group of white rangers under the command of Captain Mason were patrolling along the southern Tennessee frontier to block the passage of hostile northern Indians. One day while on patrol, the rangers mistook a friendly Choctaw for a northern Indian and killed him by mistake. The unfortunate blunder caused uproar among the Choctaws and their Chickasaw allies.

Leaders from both tribes came to Robertson to plead their case. They told him that because they were allies of the United States, they should be given the responsibility of patrolling for enemy Indians. They told him that they were eager to fight against America's enemies. Their idea made good sense to

Robertson because it would give the Chickasaws and Choctaws an outlet to channel their warrior impulses in ways that would be helpful for the United States. Robertson arranged for the white rangers to disband, and Indians assumed their duties. The grateful Chickasaw and Choctaw warriors took their responsibilities seriously, and they did an excellent job of protecting travelers and blocking the passage of northern Indian emissaries.

Despite Robertson's efforts, the British did succeed in turning one sub-tribe of Creek Indians against the United States. By then, the War of 1812 between Britain and the United States had already commenced. On August 30th, 1813, the Red Stick Creeks, led by the mixed-breed Chief William Weatherford, made a deadly attack against Fort Mims in present-day Alabama.

In one of the worst Indian massacres in American history, Weatherford's Red Sticks gained entrance to the fort through an unsecured gate and unleashed a merciless attack against everyone in the fort. They slaughtered all of the defenders as well as innocent men, women and children who had sought refuge inside the fort. The merciless Creek warriors killed over 500 people within the walls of Fort Mims. Fortunately, a few managed to escape and news of the massacre quickly spread throughout the region.

When word of the massacre reached Nashville, General Andrew Jackson took immediate action by activating the militia and preparing to launch a campaign against the Red Stick Creeks (the other Creek tribes remained at peace with the United States).

As soon as the news reached the Chickasaws and Choctaws, they wanted to join the fight. James Robertson agreed to escort a select group of the best warriors from each tribe to rendezvous with General Jackson's army. They needed a white escort to prevent terrified settlers from mistaking them for hostile warriors.

According to Joseph Brown, survivor of the Tennessee River massacre and scout for the Nickajack Expedition, James Robertson and his Chickasaw and Choctaw warriors joined General Jackson's army near Talladega in present-day Alabama. Nearby, a band of friendly Creeks were trapped inside a fort surrounded by Weatherford's Red Sticks. A camouflaged friendly Creek managed to sneak out and deliver a message for General Jackson. The note explained their desperate situation and ended with an urgent plea for him to come to their aid.

General Jackson immediately ordered a 30-mile forced march toward the besieged fort. His army arrived nearby and camped for the night on November 8th, 1813. That night, Jackson conferred with his officers and devised a battle plan for his arm of nearly 1,200 infantrymen and 800 cavalrymen.

Just before sunrise, his officers deployed their men to their assigned positions. They encircled the Red Sticks, as well as the besieged fort. Once the surprise attack commenced, the outcome was never in doubt. The Red Sticks were outnumbered by over three to one, and they suffered nearly fifty percent casualties during the battle. Their losses would have been larger, but some of them broke through the American lines and fled to some nearby hills where they were able to elude their pursuers.

After leading his warriors in battle, James Robertson needed to visit the Choctaw Agency before returning to his post at the Chickasaw Agency. The purpose of his visit is not known, but he likely escorted some wounded warriors back to their villages. The return was treacherous and dangerous because the creeks and streams were swollen from heavy rainfall. The 71-year-old Robertson and his companions were forced to swim across the cold, fast-moving water. The long, arduous journey took a severe toll on the old man's body.

Robertson was back at the Chickasaw Agency by December 9th, 1813. On that date, he wrote a letter to Tennessee Governor Willie Blount (half-brother of deceased former Governor William Blount) about matters pertaining to the Choctaws.

On April 4th, 1814 he wrote another letter to Governor Blount. In the correspondence he mentioned that he had recently returned from Nashville where he had gone to settle a legal case. He also wrote that he had been bedridden with rheumatism for two weeks while in town. He concluded by stating that his return trip to the Chickasaw Agency was very painful and difficult because of his illness.

Robertson's aged body was simply worn out after years of arduous physical activity. Thereafter, his painful condition grew worse. He sensed that the end was near when he wrote to his wife asking her to come to the Agency and bring a feather bed. He was suffering from excruciating pain, and he hoped that the bed would provide some relief.

After Charlotte arrived, his condition rapidly deteriorated and he slipped in and out of delirium caused by inflammation of the brain.

On September 1st, 1814 James Robertson died. The following day, he was buried at the Chickasaw Agency, near the school that he built to educate the Chickasaw children.

Robertson's Indians patrolled the southern region to prevent Prophet and other Shawnees from uniting the northern and southern tribes with Britain against the United States.

Chapter 56

HONOR AND RE-INTERNMENT

James Robertson died before witnessing the United States victory over Britain in the War of 1812. He would have been very proud of the subsequent battles won by his friend and protégé, General Andrew Jackson. Jackson and his fellow Tennesseans fought bravely while subduing the Red Stick Creeks; and they subsequently won a stunning victory against the British army at the Battle of New Orleans.

James Robertson rendered his services to his people, the state of Tennessee and his nation longer than any of his contemporaries. His close friend, John Sevier, was the only one who rivaled his level of service. Sevier, who died a year after Robertson in 1815, served almost as long as Robertson. Sevier had an extraordinary military and political career. After serving as Governor of Franklin before its dissolution, Sevier became the first elected Governor of Tennessee and subsequently served several two-year terms. Later, he served in the United States Senate.

William Russell of Virginia fought alongside Robertson at the Battle of Point Pleasant in 1774. He subsequently fought in numerous battles during the Revolution as a colonel in Washington's army. At the end of the war, he was brevetted to brigadier general in recognition of his extraordinary service. Russell died unexpectedly from an illness in 1793 while in route to serve in the Virginia Legislature.

Robertson's friend, Daniel Boone, guided him over the mountains in 1769. While the Robertson's lived in Watauga, Boone was a regular guest in their home, and he and Rebecca were baptized there by an itinerant Methodist preacher. Later, Boone founded Boonesborough and Robertson founded Nashborough. A few years after the Battle of Blue Licks, considered by some to be the last battle of the Revolution, Boone moved west and eventually settled in present-day Missouri. Like Robertson, Boone liked and respected Indians. It is said that when he died in 1820, his best friends were his Indian neighbors.

Another acquaintance of Robertson was George Rogers Clarke. Clarke rendered extraordinary military service along the western frontier during the Revolution. Following an aborted planned campaign against Spanish colonies in 1794, he retired from public service. He was financially ruined because he had spent nearly all of his own money to help finance his various military campaigns during the Revolution. Later, he struggled with bouts of alcoholism while living in relative obscurity. Clarke suffered a stroke that left him disabled until a second stroke caused his death in 1818.

In 1825, the State of Tennessee passed legislation honoring James Robertson's enormous contributions to the state. The bill included a provision to exhume his remains from the Chickasaw Agency and return them to Nashville for re-internment in the Nashville Cemetery.

On the day that his remains were returned to the city that he had founded, most of the citizens of Nashville turned out to witness the event and pay their respects. Both sides of the main thoroughfare were lined with people. Their eyes were fixed on the top of the hill to the west, awaiting his return. Without notice, the solemn funeral procession suddenly appeared at the top of the road. It was accompanied by the sound of a drum beat that was matched by the slow, deliberate cadence of the military honor guard accompanying his remains. The horse drawn wagon carrying his flag draped coffin slowly progressed down the hill toward the awaiting crowd.

When the honor guard and carriage finally arrived and then slowly passed by, men removed their hats out of respect and tears streamed down the cheeks of a few old veterans of the Indian wars. Charlotte Robertson was there, along with her surviving adult offspring, among the crowd who came to pay their respects.

The procession halted in front of the stately stone church where the ceremony was to be held as people filed inside to hear the tribute. Judge Haywood, a friend of James Robertson, delivered a thorough and moving eulogy to the assemblage. Many of those in attendance were brought to tears during Judge Haywood's thorough and deliberate recitation incidents relating to James Robertson's character and lifetime achievements.

Following the ceremony, the funeral cortege reformed and slowly proceeded to the newly established Nashville Cemetery. As the crowd moved outside, they walked behind the wagon for the short distance to the cemetery.

At the Nashville Cemetery, the attending pastor made a few brief remarks followed by a prayer. Afterward, James Robertson's remains were carefully reinterred in a modest above-ground crypt.

The Father of Tennessee and Founder of Nashville finally came home to rest for eternity.

BIBLIOGRAPHY

Author's Name	Book Title	Published by	Year
Thomas Perkins Abernethy	From Frontier to Plantation in Tennessee: A Study in Frontier Democracy	Chapel Hill The University of North Carolina Press	1932
Pat Alderman	Nancy Ward, Cherokee Chieftainess	The Overmountain Press Johnson City, TN	1990
Pat Alderman	The Over Mountain Men	The Overmountain Press Johnson City, TN	1986
Harriette Simpson Arnow	Seedtime on the Cumberland	University of Nebraska Press	1995
Ted Franklin Belue	The Hunters of Kentucky	Stackpole Books 5067 Ritter Road Mechanicsburg, PA	2003
Ted Franklin Belue	The Long Hunt: Death of the Buffalo East of the Mississippi	Stackpole Books 5067 Ritter Road Mechanicsburg, PA	1996
Carole Stanford Bucy	The Nashville City Cemetery	The Nashville City Cemetery Assoc., Inc	2000
Carol Farrar Kaplan	History Carved in Stone	The Nashville City Cemetery Assoc., Inc	2000
H.W. Brands	Andrew Jackson: His Life & Times	Double Day Random House	2005

Author	Title	Publisher	Year
Andrew Burnstein	The Passions of Andrew Jackson	First Vintage Books	2004
Brenda C. Calloway	Americans First Western Frontier: East Tennessee	Overmountain Press Johnson City, TN	1989
Jerry E. Clark	The Shawnee	The University Press of Kentucky	1993
Ann Crabb	And The Battle Began Like Claps of Thunder: The Siege of Boonesboro	Ann Crabb 2071 Greentree Dr. 1778 Richmond, KY	1998
Louise Littleton Davis	Frontier Tales of Tennessee	Pelican Publishing Company - Gretna	1981
Louise Littleton Davis	More Tales of Tennessee	Pelican Publishing Company - Gretna	1983
Max Dixon	The Wataugans First Free & Independent Community on the Continent	The Overmountain Press Johnson City, TN	1989
Doug Drake, Jack Masters & Bill Puryear	Founding of the Cumberland Settlements -The First Atlas Showing Who Came, How They Came & Where They Put Down Roots	Warioto Press 1512 Cherokee Rd. Gallatin, TN	2009 1779-1804

276

Lyman C. Draper	The Life of Daniel Boone	Stackpole Books 5067 Ritter Road Mechanicsburg, PA	1998
Walker T. Durham	Before Tennessee: The Southwest Territory	Rocky Mount Historical Wakestone Book Society -Rocky Mount Parkway Piney Flats, TN	2003
Wilma Dykeman	Tennessee Woman: An Infinite Variety	Wakeston Books Newport, TN	1993
	With Fire & Sword 1780, The Battle of Kings Mountain	National Park Service U.S. Department of Washington, D.C.	
	A History of Tennessee	Wakeston Books Newport, TN	
Joseph J. Ellis	His Excellency: George Washington	Alfred A. Borzoi Books	2004
John Mack Faragher	Daniel Boone	Owl Books Henry & Holt & Company, NY	1993 1992
Harold U. Faulkner	American Political & Social History	Appleton-Century-Croft, Inc., NY	1952
Lawrence J. Fleenor, Jr. & Dale Carter	The Forts of the Holston Militia	Big Stone Gap, VA	2004
William Robertson Garrett; Albert Virgil Goodpasture	History of Tennessee, its People and its Institutions	Brandon Printing Comp. Nashville, TN	1990

Author	Title	Publisher	Year
Noel B. Gerson	Franklin America's Lost State	Crowell-Collier Press, NY	1968
James R. Gilmore (aka Edmund Kirke)	The Advance-Guard of Western Civilization	D. Appleton & Comp. New York, NY	1888
	The Rear Guard of the Revolution		1886
Anita Shafer Goodstein	Nashville, 1780-1860: From Frontier to City	University of Florida Press Gainesville, FL	1989
George Grant & Stephen Mansfield	Faithful Volunteers: The History of Religion in Tennessee	Cumberland House Nashville, TN	1997
Will T. Hale & Dixon Merritt	A History of Tennessee and Tennesseans I, II, III	The Lewis Publishing Chicago & New York	1913
Neal O. Hammon & Richard Taylor	Virginia's Western War, 1775 – 1786	Stackpole Books 5067 Ritter Road Mechanicsburg, PA	2002
John Haywood	The Civil and Political of the State of Tennessee	The Overmountain Press Johnson City, TN	1999
Craig L. Heath	The Virginia Papers: Vol. 5ZZ	Heritage Books Arcata Graphics Kingsport, TN	2006
Robert Kincaid	The Wilderness Road	Arcata Graphics Kingsport, TN	1992

Author	Title	Publisher	Year
Paul Kelley	Historic Fort Loudin	Fort Loudin Assoc. Vonore, TN	1958
Billy Kennedy	Women of the Frontier	Ambassador Publishing Greenville, SC	2004
	In the Hills of Tennessee, The Scots-Irish	Causeway	1995
	Heroes of the Scots-Irish in America	Ambassador Publishing Greenville, SC	
Anne Klebenow	200 Years Through 200 Stories: A Tennessee Bicentennial Collection	University of Tennessee Knoxville, TN	1997
Bruce Lancaster	The American Revolution	Mariner Books	2001
Phillip Langdon	Tennessee: A Political History	Providence House Publishers – Hillsboro Press Franklin, TN	2000
Virgil A. Lewis	History of the Battle of Point Pleasant: Fought Between White Men and Indians, 1774	The Tribune Printing West Virginia (1990)	1909
Michael A. Lofaro	Daniel Boone: An American Life	The University Press of Kentucky	2003
Thomas Edwin Matthews	General James Robertson: The Father of Tennessee	The Parthenon Press Nashville, TN	1984
John Bach McMaster	McMaster's Primary History	American Book Comp.	1901

	of the United States		
Lynn Montross	Rag, Tag, and Bobtail: The Story of the Continental Army, 1775-1783	Harper & Brothers Publishers, NY	1952
Daniel L. Morrill	The Southern Campaigns of the American Revolution	The Nautical & Aviation Publishing Corp. of America Mount Pleasant, SC	1993
Gary B. Nash	The Unknown American Revolution	The Overmountain Press Johnson City, TN	2005
Patrick O'Kelley	Nothing but Blood and Slaughter: Vol. One 1771-1779	Patrick O'Kelley Booklocker, Inc.	
Dale Payne	Narratives of Pioneer Life and Border Warfare: Personal Recollections, Memoirs and Reminiscences of Indian Campaigns, Captivities and Pioneer Life on the Eastern Frontier	Communication 110 West 12th Avenue North Kansas City, MO	2004
Catherine M. Petrini	The Cherokee	Kid Haven Press 27500 Drake Road Farmington Hills, MI	

Author	Title	Publisher	Year
A.W. Putnam	History of Tennessee: Or Life and Times of General James Robertson	Nashville, TN	1859
J.G.M. Ramsey	Annals of Tennessee	The Overmountain Press Johnson City, TN	1999
Teodore Roosevelt	The Winning of the West, Vol. 1	The Current Literature Publishing Comp., NY	1905
Frank B. Sarles, Jr. & Charles E. Shedd	Colonial and Patriots VI	U.S. Department of Interior Washington, D.C. Stackpole Books 5067 Ritter Road Mechanicsburg, PA	1964
Michael C. Scoggins	The Day It Rained Militia: Huck's Defeat and the Revolution in the South Carolina Backcountry	History Press 18 Percy Street Charleston, SC	2005
J. Ed Sharpe	The Cherokees, Past & Present	Cherokee Publications Cherokee, NC	
E.D. Thompson	Nashville Nostalgia	Western Publishing Inc. Nashville, Tennessee	2003
Francis Marion Turner	Life of General John Sevier	The Overmountain Press Johnson City, TN	1997

Tom B. Underwood	The Story of the Cherokee People	Cherokee Publications	1961
Stewart Edward White	Daniel Boone, Wilderness Scout	Doubleday Page & Co. Garden City, NY	1923
Esmond Wright	Fabric of Freedom 1763-1800	Hill & Wang, NY	1990
State Historical Society of Wisconsin	Frontier Defense on The Upper Ohio, 1777-1778: Compiled from the Draper Manuscripts in the Library of Wisconsin Historical Society and Pub. at the Charge of the Wisconsin Society of the Sons of the American Revolution	Wisconsin Historical Madison, Wisconsin	1912

INDEX

A

Abraham, Cherokee Chief 64, 69, 71-72, 190
Adam, a slave 29-31, 34
Adamson, James 13
Adams, Tabitha 162
Agent Cameron 77
Alamance River 21
American Revolution vii, 14, 21, 54, 60-61, 85, 153, 275, 281-282, 284
Anaconda Plan 60-61, 77, 81, 86, 97
Appalachian 1, 11, 23, 60, 275
Appalachian Mountains 1
Articles of Confederation 159, 161, 163, 173, 189
Asher's Station 125, 129
Aspie, George, killed 150
Attakullakulla 12-14, 17, 52

B

Barton, Samuel, Colonel 145, 157
Battle of Alamance 22, 58
Battle of Fallen Timbers 233-234, 241
Battle of Fort Watauga 68, 95
Battle of Freeland's Station 141, 144
Battle of Kings Mountain 135, 141, 160
Battle of Long Island Flats 70, 74
Battle of Point Pleasant 48, 67, 75, 81, 85, 95, 177, 251, 272, 281
Battle of Taliwa 16
Battle of the Bluff 144
Battles of Lexington and Concord 54, 60
Bays, J. 191
Bean, Lydia 7, 65
Bean, William 7, 24, 65
Beloved Woman 17, 65-66
Benge, Bob 220
Bernard, old man killed 126
Big Bend 100
Big Jim 30-31
Big Lick 54
Bill of Rights 201, 245
Black Drink 17
Blackmore, John 112
Bledsoe, Anthony, Colonel 173, 195, 197, 227
Bledsoe, Anthony, son of Colonel Anthony Bledsoe, mortally wounded 227
Bledsoe, Isaac, Colonel, killed 227
Bledsoe's Station 125
Bloody Fellow 220
Blount, William vii, 158, 165, 201, 212, 245-246, 248, 270
Blount, Willie, half-brother of William Blount viii, 270
Blue Jacket 215, 233
Blue Ridge 136
Blue Ridge Mountains 136
Bonaparte, Napoleon 253-254
Boone, Daniel vii, 1-2, 7, 28, 31-33, 41-42, 45, 51-53, 56, 65, 75, 86-87, 89, 93, 98-99, 102-103, 130-131, 134, 273, 279, 281, 284
Boone, Jemima 86-87
Boone, Rebecca 28, 38, 273
Boonesborough 54, 86-88, 90,

130-132, 134-135, 141, 273
Boone, Squire 2, 28, 31-32, 86, 131
Bosley brothers 237-238
Boston Massacre 58
Boston Tea Party 59
Bradley, Edward 131
Brown, Jacob 23-24, 50, 95
Brown, James, Colonel 191
Brown, Joseph 193, 237-238, 269
Brown, Moses, killed 167
Buchanan, Alexander, killed 146
Buchanan, John 147, 224
Buchanan, John, Major 224
Buchanan, William 131
Burr, Aaron 253-255, 257-258

C

Caffrey, John 114
Callaway, Flanders 131
Callaway, Richard 131
Calloway, Betsy 86
Calloway, Fanny 86
Calvert, Frederick 91
Calvert's Station 229
Cameron, Alexander 61, 64
Campbell, Anthony, Colonel 91
Campbell, Arthur 163
Campbell, Elizabeth Henry 162
Campbell, servant named killed 197
Campbell, William, Colonel 138
Campbell, William, General, deceased 162-163
Caney Fork 127
Captain Arbuckle 82
Captain Leiper 128, 146
Captain Leiper, killed 146
Captain Rains 177, 179
Captain Thompson 69-70

Carter, John 22-24
Carter's Valley 22, 41
Cartwright, Robert 116
Carver, Ned, killed 126
Castleman, Abe 171, 223, 228-229
Castleman, Hans wounded 228
Castleman, Jacob and Joseph killed 168, 228
Castleman, Jacob, killed 150
Castleman, Joseph, killed 150, 228
Castlewood 26-29, 31-32, 34, 38-39, 42, 56
Caswell, Richard, Governor 92
Cave Creek 13
Charles, a slave 29-32, 34
Cherokee 11-18, 22, 27, 30, 34-37, 43, 52-55, 57, 61, 64-66, 69, 71, 73-81, 91-92, 94-99, 105, 154-155, 160, 170, 184, 189-191, 205, 211, 216-217, 219-220, 223, 229-231, 241, 245-246, 248-250, 260-261, 277-278, 282-284
Cherokee Billy 34-37, 96
Chickamauga 11, 79-81, 91-92, 94, 126, 145, 155, 159, 167, 171, 173, 175, 179, 184, 194, 196, 205, 219-220, 223, 225-227, 229-231, 235, 237, 241, 249
Chickamauga Creek 79, 81
Chickamaugas 11, 80, 92, 94, 126, 145, 155, 159, 167, 171, 173, 175, 179, 184, 194, 205, 219-220, 223, 255-227, 229-231, 237, 241, 249
Chickasaw 12, 53, 64, 99-100, 127, 129, 133, 142-143, 154-156, 159, 170, 172, 175-177, 179-180, 211, 215, 222, 224, 228, 231-234, 237, 249-252, 259-261, 267-270, 273
Chief Blackfish 88, 130
Chief Cornstalk 44, 46-47, 81-83, 88

Chief Dragging Canoe, or Dragging-Canoe 64, 69, 81, 91, 94
Chief Kingfisher, killed 230
Chief Logan 41, 43-44
Chief Old Abraham 64, 71
Chillicothe 130, 132
Chillicothe, Shawnee Capital 130, 132
Choctaw 64, 99, 127, 154-156, 159, 170, 222, 231, 260-261, 267-270
Chota 11, 13, 16-17, 36, 61, 64, 66, 77, 79, 92, 96, 216
Christian, William, Colonel 77, 95
Civil, George 128
Civil, Jack 128
Clark, George Rogers vii, 55-56, 85-86, 98, 107, 127, 132, 172, 273
Cleveland, Benjamin 137-138
Clinch River 39-41, 45, 57, 61, 65, 74-76, 112, 114, 250
Clinch River valley 39-40, 45, 57, 61, 65, 74-76
Clover Bottom Massacre 128
Cocke, William 44, 69, 218, 245-246
Colbert, William 237
Coldwater 173-176, 178, 181-182, 184, 194-196, 226, 241
Coldwater Expedition 181, 184, 194, 196, 226
Colonel Whitley 238
Committees of Safety 63, 90
Constitution 174, 189, 200-201, 214, 237, 245
Coody, Archy 114
Cooper, James 72
Cooper, Tucker 72
Cornwallis, Lord, General 136-137, 151, 153, 162
Cotton, John 116
Crabtree, Isaac 29, 34, 131

Creek 7, 12-13, 16, 29, 41, 64, 79, 81, 95, 99, 106, 112, 119, 126, 155, 159, 167, 171-173, 175-176, 179, 184, 194-196, 205, 210-212, 220, 223, 225, 227, 229-231, 235, 237, 241, 246, 250, 268-269, 272
Cumberland Compact 123-124, 149, 157
Cumberland Gap 53, 106, 109
Cumberland Iron Works 212, 251
Cumberland Region 123, 125, 128, 213
Cumberland River 5, 57, 99-100, 107, 110, 112, 118, 126, 167, 220

D

David, Robert Lieutenant 70
Davidson Academy 165, 213, 251
Davidson County 157-158, 169-170, 185-186, 195, 219, 244, 248
Deckard rifle 3, 106, 137
Declaration of Independence 23, 61, 63
Delaware 27, 30, 41, 43, 46, 53, 126, 220
Denton, Jonathan 180
De Peyster, Captain 138
Dickinson, Charles 261-262
Divine Guidance 4, 51, 101
Donelson, John 98, 102, 110-112, 124, 127-128, 144, 154, 170, 187
Double Head, or Doublehead 220, 229
Drake, a man named 29-30
Drake, Benjamin 180
Dr. Vance 145
Duck River 182, 208, 250
Dunmore's War 85

E

East India Company 59
Eaton's Station 121, 144-145, 148, 166, 183
Elinipsico 83
Erwin, Joseph 261
Eskridge, John 180
Eskridge, Moses 180
Etari 11
Etowah 230, 241-242

F

Father Gibault 86
Faulin, William 36
Ferguson, Patrick, Colonel 135
Fincastle County, Virginia 66
Five Lower Towns 219-220
Flood, John 191
Ford, James, Lieutenant Colonel 176
Fort Blair 75
Fort Cahokia 86
Fort Chiswell 62, 65
Fort Jefferson 127, 133, 143
Fort Kaskaskia 86
Fort Lee 64, 66, 69
Fort Loudin 12-13, 280
Fort Miami 233
Fort Nashborough 128, 134, 141-142, 145, 150, 236
Fort Patrick Henry 76, 78-79, 91, 96, 98, 112
Fort Pitt 84-86
Fort Prince George 13-14
Fort Randolph 81-82
Fort Union 125
Fort Vincennes 86
Fort Watauga 64, 66, 68-69, 71, 76, 95, 136, 140, 160
Foster, Anthony 222
Franklin, Benjamin 161, 164
Franklinites 161-162, 169, 189
Frazier, John 167
Freeland, George 105
Freeland, Jacob, killed 150
Freeland's Station 125-126, 141, 144, 149
Free Will 101
French and Indian War 12, 14, 26, 43, 58, 81, 203
French Broad River 78, 113
French Lick 57, 98-100, 102-105, 107-112, 160, 166, 169-170, 172, 236

G

Gage, Thomas, General 60
General Hand 82
Gentry, John 191
Gentry, William 191
Gill, Peter, killed 146
Gilmore, a young man 82
Girty, George 86
Girty, James 86
Girty, Simon 86
Goin, David, killed 145
Goodman, Daniel 88
Governor Caswell, North Carolina Governor 173-175
Governor Spotswood 26
Gower, Abel Jr., killed 128
Gower, Abel, killed 128
Greathouse, Daniel 41, 44
Great Island Town 79
Griffin, John 191
Grimes, John 230

H

Hamilton, Alexander 174, 256
Hamilton, a young man 82
Hamilton, Henry 61, 130
Hanly, James 105
Harmar, Josiah, General 251
Harrison, Reuben 113
Harrod, James 54
Harrodsburg 54-56, 86, 88
Hay, Joseph, killed 126
Hays, Robert, Lieutenant Colonel 176
Hay's Station 228
Henderson, Richard 51-52, 54-55, 57, 85, 98, 102, 120, 123, 128, 144, 169
Henderson's Cherokee Treaty 57
Henry, Patrick 57, 76, 78-79, 85, 91, 96, 98, 112, 162
Hickman, Edmond, killed 167
Hogan, Edward, wounded 182
Holston Treaty 249
Honeycutt 5-8
Hood, David, scalped and left for dead died of natural causes (1794) 236
Hood, William, killed 150
Hoskins, Josiah, killed 150, 166
Hubbard, an officer named 190-191
Husband, Herman 21

I

Intolerable Acts 59-60
Invincibles or Silver Grays 257
Iroquois 26-27
Isbell, Zach 24

J

Jackson, Andrew, future President vii-viii, 186-187, 208, 219, 245-246, 248, 284, 253, 255-258, 261, 265, 268, 272, 277-278
Jackson, Elizabeth, Andrew Jackson's mother 186-187
Jackson, Hugh, died 186
Jackson, Rachel 256, 261
Jackson, Robert, Andrew Jackson's remaining brother 186
Jefferson, Thomas 51-52, 133, 253
Jennings, Jonathan, killed 116, 126
Jennings, Mr. 116, 126
Jennings, Mrs. 117
Jim, a slave named, killed 128
Johns, old man named killed 127
Johnston, John 194
Jonesboro 95, 186
Jones, John 24
Jones, John Gabriel 56
Josiah Hoskins, dead 150, 166
Journal of a Voyage, by John Donelson 112
Judge Haywood 274

K

Kanawha River 45, 82
Kennedy, George, killed 146
King family, several members killed 242
Kingsport, Tennessee 69
King's Proclamation Line of (1763) 23, 26, 55
Kirk family, Mr., Mrs., son 189-191
Knights of the Golden Horseshoe 26
Knox, Henry, Secretary of War

205, 210, 215, 217, 225
Knoxville 11, 92, 189, 217-218, 229, 244, 246, 281
Knoxville Gazette 218

L

Lewis, Andrew 44
Lewis, Charles 46
Lieutenant Moore 70
Little Turtle 215
Logan's Station 86
Logtown 250
Lord Dunmore 44-45, 48, 85
Louisiana Purchase 247, 253-254
Lower Blue Licks 88
Lower Towns 219-220, 226, 230, 237-239
Loyalists 63, 189
Lucas, Andrew, shot 167
Lucas, Isaac 147
Lucas, Robert 24

M

Madison, James 173-174
Major Evans 173, 185-186
Major Lucas, mortally wounded 142
Major Montgomery, killed 238
Major Ore 238
Manifee, James, wounded 129, 146
Manifest Destiny 51, 101, 109, 151, 275
Mansker, Kasper 110, 250
Mansker's Station 145
Martin, Joseph 154
Martin's Station 132
Mason, a man named, killed 150

Mason, Philip, killed 166
McClelland, John, Captain 88
McDowell, Joseph, Major 136-137
McGary, Hugh 88
McGillivray, Alexander, Creek Indian Chief 159, 196, 199, 210-211, 250
McIntosh, William, Creek Chief 250
McKee, Alexander 86
McMurray, William, killed 150
McNairy, John 186, 245
Mendenhall, John 29-30, 32, 35
Mendenhall, Richard 29-30, 32, 35
Mero District 186, 199, 201, 210-211, 219, 235, 237, 242
Miami 27, 215, 233
Milliken and Keywood, killed 126
Mingo 27, 41, 43, 46, 53, 65, 87
Miro, Esteban, Spanish Governor of Florida and Louisiana 199
Mississippi River 85-86, 127, 133, 153, 162, 200, 204, 234, 245, 254
Monsieur Cruzat, French Commandant of St. Louis 181
Montgomery, John, Colonel 238, 242, 245, 259
Montgomery, John, Colonel, Killed 242
Moonshaw, Joseph, wounded 146
Moore, a boy named 72
Mrs. Jones, survivor 127

N

Nashborough 125-128, 132-134, 141-142, 144-145, 150, 154-155, 157, 213, 236, 273
Nash, Francis, a general killed

during the Revolution 125
Natchez 119, 251
Neely, William 105, 126
Neely, William, killed 126
Neowee 79
Nickajack 192, 235, 237, 239, 241-242, 245, 269
Nickajack Expedition 241-242, 245, 269
Nolichucky 23, 41, 50, 95, 160-161
Nolichucky Jack 95
Northwest Indian Confederation 234, 266

O

Oconostota 13-14, 52, 96
Ohio 12, 26-27, 45-47, 86, 112, 119-121, 127, 182, 201, 210, 214, 256, 284
Old Hop 12
Otari 11
Overall, William 105, 166
Overall, William, killed 166
Overton, John 187

P

Parker, William 22
Patriots vii, 63-64, 77, 84, 97, 135-139, 283
Peyton, Ephraim 114, 167
Peyton, John 167
Peyton, Mrs. 117
Pickering, Timothy, Secretary of War 242
Piomingo, Chickasaw Chief 154, 211, 215, 224, 232, 234, 267
Ploughboy 261-262

Pluggy 87-88
Pocahontas of the West 17
Powell's valley 29, 34, 38, 41, 56, 75, 84
Preston, William Colonel 39, 65, 75
Prophet, Shawnee Chief 266, 271
Pugh, Thomas 167
Pumpkin Boy 220

Q

Quigley, Parick, killed 145

R

Rains, John, Captain 171
Ramsey, Henry 127
Red Chimneys 139
Red Hawk 82-83
Red Stick Creeks 268, 272
Red Sticks 268-269
Reeves, Charlotte 2
Regulator Rebellion 22
Regulators 21-22, 52, 59
Renfroe, Joseph, killed 127
Renfroe, Josiah, killed 182
Renfroe, Moses 121
Renfroe, Peter, killed 150
Renfroe's Station 127
Rice, John, killed 220
Richland Creek 126, 167, 172, 176, 194
Riddle, Cornelius, killed 167
Robards, Rachel 187
Robert, a slave named 105, 107, 134, 141-143
Robertson, Anne 72

Robertson, Charles 24, 64, 77, 95, 135
Robertson, Charles, James Robertson's older brother 24, 251
Robertson, Charlotte 2, 38, 95, 147-148, 151, 165, 172, 195, 208, 221, 230, 236, 251, 259, 270, 274
Robertson, Delilah, daughter of James Robertson 95
Robertson, Elijah 177, 221
Robertson, Elijah, died of "yellow jaundice" 251
Robertson, Felix, Robertson's son 141
Robertson, James vii-viii, 2, 4, 6, 9, 17, 24, 36, 38, 44-46, 48, 50, 52, 62-67, 71, 77-78, 90-92, 95, 101, 109, 111, 118, 134, 145, 149, 154, 159-160, 165-166, 169-170, 195, 198-199, 201, 210, 212, 245-246, 248-249, 251, 255-257, 259-261, 263, 268-270, 272, 275
Robertson, James Randal, killed 230, 237
Robertson, James Randolph, killed 128
Robertson, James, son of James Robertson 128
Robertson, Jonathan, son of James Robertson 95, 109, 221, 232
Robertson, Mark 105, 172
Robertson, Peyton, murdered 194
Roquering, Hugh, wounded 182
Ruddle's Station 132
Running Water, village 192, 239, 241
Russell, George 24
Russell, Henry 30
Russell's Rangers 39, 62, 74-75, 162
Russell, William Captain, Colonel, Brigadier General 26-29, 39, 41, 45-46, 56, 61, 63, 65-66, 69, 78, 81, 84, 162-163, 272

S

Sevier, John vii, 24, 50, 62, 64, 66, 68, 71-72, 78, 90-91, 94-95, 135, 137, 154, 160-161, 174, 189-190, 193, 196, 201, 209-210, 221, 238, 245-246, 248, 259, 272. 283
Sevier, Joseph, killed 242
Sevier, Rebecca, scalped 242
Sevier, Robert, killed 220
Sevier, Valentine 24, 45-46, 48-50, 67, 220-221, 242
Sevier, Valentine junior, killed 220
Sevier, William, killed 220
Shawnee 27, 30, 41, 43-44, 46-47, 53, 65, 74-75, 81-86, 88-90, 96, 99, 120, 130, 132, 205, 215, 220, 223, 249, 266-267, 271, 278
Shelby, Evan 45, 154, 160, 227
Shelby, Evan, Major, killed 227
Shelby, Isaac 47, 69, 91, 136-137
Sherill, Kate 68
Slim Tom, a Cherokee 189-190
Smith, James 24
Smith, William 131
Snider family, several members killed 242
South, John 131
Spanish Governor Portell 166
Spencer, Thomas Sharpe 128, 149, 167, 235
Spencer, Thomas Sharpe, killed 235
Starr, a white Indian trader 78
State of Franklin 161, 163, 169, 174, 189

St. Clair, Arthur, Major General 215, 217
Stoner, Michael 2, 28-29, 38-39, 42, 45, 75, 86, 89
Stone's River Station 125
Stuart, John 13, 43, 61, 77
Stuart, William, killed 167
Swanson, Edward 105, 147
Sycamore Shoals 54, 62, 98

T

Tamotlee 79
Tassel, a Cherokee Chief 190
Tea Act 59
Tecumseh 215, 233, 266
Tecumseh's War 233
Tellico River 13

W

Whigs 63, 137, 139
White, Zachariah 105, 146
White, Zachariah, killed 146
Wild Rose 16-17
Williams, Jarot 66
Williams, Samson, Captain 208
Winchester, James 248
Wolf Hills 34-35, 37
Womack, Jacob 24

Y

Yellow Creek 41

ABOUT THE AUTHOR

The Bays Family has deep roots in Southwest Virginia dating back to Colonial Times. What is now Russell County is the region where most settled. The author's father, grandfather and great-grandfather all resided in Lebanon, Virginia. Others before them lived in Elk Garden and Corn Valley. And Peter Bays served as a soldier in the American Revolution.

Because of this lineage, Bill Bays researched his family history and became fascinated with historical events of that early American era. He decided to document one man's extraordinary contributions toward the early western expansion of the Nation. James Robertson's belief in Manifest Destiny and his contributions to making that philosophy a reality has earned his recognition.

Bays and his wife Nancy, who served diligently as his research assistant, traveled throughout the first western frontier where they visited important sites and conducted research along the way. These experiences helped the author to accurately chronicle the life of James Robertson and his over mountain contemporaries' contributions in winning the American Revolution. Afterward, they helped establish new U.S. territories, which later became states, west of the of the vast Appalachian Mountains.

Bill and Nancy Bays now live on a small ranch in Ventura, California and enjoy the company of their sons and grandchildren. This book is dedicated to his ancestors and the entire Bays family.

Bill Bays earned his B.A. from Claremont Men's College, now Claremont McKenna College, and an M.A. from California State University at Fresno. This was followed by a Community College Counselling Credential and an academic Doctorate in Clinical Hypnotherapy from the American Institute of Hypnotherapy. He worked as a counselor for 11 years and as a private therapist for over 12. A man of many interests, he owned several businesses along the way. He is retired, but his love of history has kept him busy researching and writing. Two other American history projects are currently in process.

www.ingramcontent.com/pod-product-compliance
Lightning Source LLC
LaVergne TN
LVHW091548070526
838199LV00029B/606/J